Frederick Hancock

The Parish of Selworthy in the County of Somerset

Some notes on its history

Frederick Hancock

The Parish of Selworthy in the County of Somerset
Some notes on its history

ISBN/EAN: 9783337429355

Printed in Europe, USA, Canada, Australia, Japan

Cover: Foto ©ninafisch / pixelio.de

More available books at **www.hansebooks.com**

THE PARISH OF SELWORTHY.

Two hundred copies only printed.

SOUTH AISLE OF CHURCH OF ALL SAINTS, SELWORTHY.

THE PARISH OF SELWORTHY

IN THE

COUNTY OF SOMERSET

Some Notes on its History

BY

FREDERICK HANCOCK, M.A., S.C.L., F.S.A.

RECTOR OF THE PARISH.

Taunton:

BARNICOTT AND PEARCE, FORE STREET

1897

BARNICOTT AND PEARCE
PRINTERS

TO

THE RIGHT HONOURABLE

SIR T. D. ACLAND, BART., P.C., D.C.L., ETC.,

IN SLIGHT RECOGNITION OF MANY KINDNESSES,

THESE FEW NOTES ON A PARISH, THE BEST INTERESTS

OF WHICH HE AND HIS FOREBEARS HAVE ALWAYS

MADE THEIR ANXIOUS STUDY,

ARE RESPECTFULLY INSCRIBED BY THE

WRITER.

ERRATA.

Page 20, line 22, for "Luccombe," read "de Luccombe."

Page 41, line 1, for "The Church of St. John the Baptist," read "The Church of All Saints."

Page 64, line 9, for "Recorce," read "Recorie."

Page 48, for "Alicia," read "Johanna or Joan."

Page 57, line 1, etc., for "the elder William Blackford," read "the elder William Blackford's father."

Page 168, line 9, for "1689," read "1690."

Page 210, line 28, for "Jane," read "Joane."

Page 246, last line and last but one, for "largely royalist," read "much disturbed."

Page 256, last line but one, for "*Sonicera Periclymenum*," read "*Lonicera Periclymenum*."

Page 258, last line but five, for "*Campanula hederacea* or *Wahlenbergia*," read "*Campanula* or *Wahlenbergia hederacea*."

Page 259, line 9, for "*Sarothanus scoparius*," read "*Cytisus scopiarius*."

CONTENTS.

ILLUSTRATIONS.

INTRODUCTION.

THE writer primarily intended to include some account of the parish of Luccombe and of the hamlet of Bossington in the following notes, but he is glad to think that the history of these districts is now in abler hands than his.

He lays claim to little original research as far as the more general subjects treated of in these pages are concerned; and for much that may be of original interest in them he is indebted to the contributions of kind friends. His thanks are due to Mr. ACLAND, SIR A. W. FRANKS, K.C.B., F.R.S., Pres. S.A., Col. BRAMBLE, F.S.A., Mr. BIDGOOD, Mr. F. T. ELWORTHY, Mr. L. WEBBER-INCLEDON, Mr. F. J. ROWBOTHAM, Mr. C. BIRMINGHAM, and Mr. C. KILLE for valuable assistance. And he is especially indebted to the Rev. Prebendary HOOK for the correction of proof sheets; to the late Mr. WINSLOW JONES and his courteous executor, Mr. W. S. BATTISHILL, for much of the history of the manor of Selworthy, and of some of

the families connected with it; to the Rev. F. W. WEAVER for a good deal of valuable information, and for the correction of proof sheets; to Mr. C. E. H. CHADWYCK-HEALEY, Q.C., for extracts from the Subsidy Rolls; and to Miss ALICE MAY for the notes on the Flora of Selworthy, and the accompanying illustration.

Put together during a series of some years, in odd minutes stolen from more serious work, and at first with no definite intention of publication, a number of references have been lost in the earlier part of the book, which unfortunately cannot now be replaced.

For local names, the principal authorities consulted have been EDMUNDS'S *Names of Places*, I. TAYLOR'S *Words and Places*, LEO'S *Local Nomenclature of the Anglo-Saxons*, and F. FERGUSON'S *River Names.* The general histories principally used have been LINGARD'S, GREEN'S, HALLAM'S, and E. THOMSON'S. From Mr. CHESTER MASTER'S admirable little book much information has been gained on the subject of Parochial Registers. And a multitude of other books have been read, bearing generally on the difficult subject of parish history, too many in number to specify.

A HISTORY OF SELWORTHY.

CHAPTER I.

Etymology and Prehistoric Remains.

THE parish of Selworthy, until the recent act of parliament amending the parochial divisions for purposes of taxation, was bounded on the north and east by Minehead and a portion of Timberscombe, on the southeast by Wootton Courtenay, and on the south and west by Luccombe. By the act referred to, however, the hamlet of Bossington, and East Lynch, an outlying portion of Timberscombe, were made part of Selworthy parish, so far as lay purposes are concerned. As anciently defined, the parish consisted of 2,219 acres, of which about 804 acres were arable, 670 pasture and meadow, and 358 common land. There are 308 acres of woodland, exempt from tithe by prescription, and 54½ acres of glebe; 22½ acres of river bed, roads, wastes, etc., are also exempt.

The parish is divided into two tithings—Allerford and Blackford—and comprises the following hamlets: Bossington, West Lynch, Allerford, Brandy Street, Holnicote or Budleigh Hill, Blackford, Tivington, and

Tivington Knoll. There are, besides, several detached farms, with cottages attached to them.

It has been well said that much of the history of a parish is written in its place names; but it is with the greatest diffidence that the writer approaches this difficult subject, which is yet in its infancy. As, however, Old English names, like Greek and Hebrew names, always had meanings attached to them, he ventures, in writing down some of the older place names found in Selworthy, to make a few suggestions as to their possible derivations.

The names of the various hamlets and of the fields, although we find here and there a trace of earlier settlers, appear to show us that the Anglo-Saxons were the first to regularly colonise and allot the land of our valley, and many of the names have survived the long series of centuries with scarcely a change. When our Old English ancestors first invaded England they came in tribes and families, headed by their patriarchal leaders. Each tribe was called by its leader's name, with the termination "ing" (signifying "family") appended; and where they settled they gave their patriarchal name to the "mark" or central point round which they clustered. The Old English names were generally of one syllable, and it was not until later Saxon times that compound names came into use.

Beginning with Bossington, the derivation of the name at once suggests itself; to "Boss," the name of the original settler, add the patronymic termination "ing," and again "tun," the homestead or settlement, and we have our word "Bossington"=the homestead of the family or tribe of the Bossingas. The name

Boss is derived probably from one of the Old German words for "a bear," a root to which many of our every-day names are to be traced.

Adjoining Bossington, as we ascend the valley, is the hamlet of Lynch. This word, which has an old Norse sound, seems to point to some settlement of the Norsemen here, or perhaps to some fortified post which the Wyckings held for a while, in touch with their ships in Porlock or Bossington Bay, as a convenient centre for harrowing the neighbouring district. This name is not an uncommon one in the district, and is generally met with near the coast. Further up the valley we have other Norse words in the two Holts (N. a "wood"), and Robin How (N. a "hill").

Next we come to the largest of our hamlets, that of Allerford. Aldheri was the name of the steward of Queen Edith, who held the manor of Selworthy at the time of the Conquest; and it has also been suggested that the name may be connected with the famous Œligar. But the hamlet must have had a name before the time of Edward the Confessor, or before earl Œllgar ruled over our seaboard, and the name seems to explain itself as Alderford, *i.e.*, "the ford by the alders." In Domesday it is Alresforda. The vernacular "Aller," Mr. F. T. Elworthy tells us, is the correct name of the Alnus; and literary English corrupted it so late as the eighteenth century. It was *alr*, *aler*, and *olr* in the Old English, and so it remains in the mouths of the people. There are several Allerfords in Somersetshire (two are mentioned in Domesday), besides more than one place called *Aller*. Alresford, in Hampshire, retains its old plural form.

Adjoining Allerford is the hamlet of Brandy Street, a picturesque cluster of houses nestling cosily beside the Aller Water, amidst green meadows and sunny orchards. The name seems to mark the place where the Roman road along the coast passed on to Porlock. And this suggestion is corroborated by the fact that a little further on a few Roman coins were recently found during some excavations. Brandy looks like another Norse name. Brandi is the name of a Northman in the Landnamabok. It means "the sword-bearer," and is a common name in Iceland still. Thus, then, the name of the hamlet may point to another Norse settlement in connection with the one at Lynch.

Next we reach Holnicote, which in Domesday is written Hunecot. The Saxons were fond of borrowing the names of neighbouring nations, and thus we find "Hun" no uncommon name among them. Hun is found in various German dialects, and signifies a "giant," and to this word Grimm traces the name of the Huns. To Hun add "cot," (A.S. a cottage), and we have the cottage of Hun, or Huna, a name which is found in an Anglo-Saxon charter of manumission. Hun, too, was the name of the Ealdorman of the Somersoetas, who was killed at the great battle of Ællandun, which united England under king Egbert.

In the adjoining parish of Wootton Courtenay we find Huntsgate and Hunsham, and it seems to the writer very probable that Holnicote may have formed part of the possessions of the same person from whom Huntspill and Hunstile are named. The late Mr. F. H. Dickinson raised on this point the interesting question as to whether the Roman road from Minehead to Porlock crossed Holnicote, or turned off to Bossington. "The submarine forest," he writes, "marked in the map along Porlock Bay, makes it possible that, in Roman times, there was land—possibly much land—where there is now sea; and Bossington may have been much more important than Porlock. There are right angles in the roads towards Bossington at Brandy Street, which makes me think of Roman mensuration."

As we pass on towards Minehead we reach two detached cottages called Stratford, which suggest again the Roman road which must at one time have run along this valley. A little further on is the hamlet of Blackford, where an ancient manor house once stood, and which gives its name to the tithing. The name is probably an exact description, either of the blackness of the stones in the river bed, or the deep shadow of overhanging trees, although we are tempted to seek its derivation in the O. E. personal name "Blaca," a name found in the *Liber Vitæ*, and also in Domesday.

The derivation of the name of the hamlet of Tivington, which now forms the principal portion of this tithing, does not at first seem quite so obvious. But here, evidently, are the patronymic ending "ing," and the O. E. *tun*, "the garth" or "enclosed place." But what was the name of the leader who established his colony where this hamlet from under the shelter of its wooded hills looks down over Holnicote to the sea? Possibly he possessed a name akin to our familiar names Tye, Tighe, Tyson, Tuson, etc., which are derived from the name of the Teutonic god of war—the god from whom we have our word Tuesday—Ty, or Tyr, according to the Scandinavian or Frisian form, the Anglo-Saxon of which is Tiw or Tye. The followers of Tye would call themselves Tivingas, and their residence would be the "tun," or enclosure. Perhaps, also, the name of the hamlet which gives its name to the parish, Selworthy, may be thus derived. The O. E. "worth," an estate, farm, etc., is sometimes found alone, as in Worth, and very often in compounds, as Wordsworth, Charlesworth, etc. (I. Taylor, *Place Names.*) Sel was a common name amongst our Old English ancestors. Here then, perhaps, came Sel with the early settlers, and, where beneath the coombe the hillside spreads out fair and fertile to the southern sun, took up his abode; and the hamlet where he lived was called after him, Selworthy. The name, however, may be Sealworthe, "the willow field." In Domesday it is written Seleurda.

Subjoined is a list of some other place names in the parish.

Farms.

Lower Lynch.	Selworthy Farm.	Vickerys.
Higher Lynch.	Adams.	Cockerhill.
East Lynch.	Double Tenement.	Home's.
Hoopers.		Baker's.
Farthings.	Zeal's.	Staddon's.
Troytes.	[Here again, perhaps, is the name Sel, or Seala. The farm lies at the bottom of Selworthy Coombe.]	Barley Ground.
[Perhaps from common Celtic root, "tre," a "dwelling," *cp.* Treves, Trieste, etc.]		Higher Lynch.
		Gribble's.
		Mene.

There are two Menes lying contiguous to one

another, one in Selworthy parish the other in Minehead parish. These two farms are situated on top of the precipitous cliffs behind Selworthy Beacon. The name has a British sound, and it suggests that some of the earlier inhabitants of the valley, driven from their ancient homes, perhaps, when that great soldier king Ine (688—725) crossed the marshes of the Parret, hitherto the boundary of west Wales, and planted the fortress of Taunton on the banks of the Tone to protect his conquest of what is now Somerset, still held their own amidst the fastnesses of the North Hill.

It is a question, however, whether our own inaccessible borderland did not remain in the hands of its ancient owners until the battle of Burford, in 758, had settled the division of Britain between the three equal powers of Northumbria, Mercia, and Wessex. Then Offa of Mercia turned his arms against his Welsh neighbours, and drove their king, Powys, from his capital, Shrewsbury; and the West Saxons, following his example, made themselves masters of the Welsh territory of Dyvnaint (which still retains its name of Devon), and thus advanced their boundary to the Tamar.

Hills.

Bossington Beacon, 800 feet. Selworthy Beacon, 1,014 feet. Bury Castle; an ancient camp.

Valleys.

The parish consists mainly of a wide valley, which starts from beneath Grabhurst Hill and runs down to the sea. The following coombes in the North Hill range belong to Selworthy parish, and run south and south-west into the valley :—Lynch Coombe, Allerford Coombe, Holnicote Coombe ; while, running north-west and north, down to the sea, are Hurlestone Coombe, East Coombe, Henner Coombe, Grixy Coombe.

Streams.

Allerford Water. Horner Water. This stream, which bounds for some distance the parish on the west, seems to possess a very ancient name. It is an undisputed fact, we believe, that no words have resisted time so firmly as river names. New comers change the names of places, but those of rivers, "coming they knew not whence, and speeding on they knew not whither," remained unaltered, save that sometimes we find two names given to one water, the later nation adding its own name to the river, in addition to its older one.

This was notoriously the case with hills and mountain strongholds, *e.g.* Dunkery, in which case the O. E. "Dun" is prefixed to the British "curig." In Horner we seem to trace the Sanscrit root "var," to "bedew," *cp.* the Greek ἔρση, and the Gaelic "uaran." The endings "en," "er," "is," appear often to be phonetic.

Fords.

Venniford.	Allerford.	Stratford.
Blackford.	New Bridge.	[The ford where the Roman road passes.]
Brandy Street.	Green Bridge.	

Roads and Lanes.

Eight Acre Lane.	Luccombe Lane.
Tivington Lane.	Dean's Lane, pronounced "Danes."
Long Lane.	

Dane's Lane leads down from the cliffs and the moor to East Lynch, and marks, perhaps, the route of some Danish incursion. The cross-way above East Lynch is called "Danes Cross," and the fields about the cross-way, "Danes Fields."

At Cross Roads.

Tivington Cross. Danes Cross. Allerford Cross.
Venniford Cross. Long Lane Cross. Pylles Cross.

Mills.

Lynch Mill. Pylle's Mill. Pill means a "tidal ditch," and the derivation raises the interesting query as to whether the Allerford Water was at one time tidal.

Commons and Moors.

North Hill.
Tivington Common.
Heddon (High Down) Common.

Woods.

Tivington Plantations.
Hanger Wood.
[O. E. "Hanger," a wood.]
Venn Plantation.
Whitemans Moor.
[Witmans, *cp.* Wistmans wood on Dartmoor.]
Road Wood.
Brakeley Wood.
Great Wood.
Cockers Hills.
Selworthy Plantations.
Holnicote Plantation.
North Hill Plantation.
Allerford Plantation.
Brakeley.
Stratford Wood.
The Paddocks.
Ebbs Hill Wood.
cp. O.E. "Ebba," a personal name.

Some older Field-names.

Great How (*cp.* O. N. "haughr," a mound or burial place) a field on Lynch.

Ham Meadow. There were two "Hams" in O. E.; one has become the modern *home*, but the other remains in the very common west country name for a flat, alluvial piece of meadow land, usually bordering a river.

Rydery, *cp.* O. E. "rud," or O. N. "raudr," red, whence, perhaps, the common local surname, Ridd. The stone from the quarry of this name is of a red colour.

Dove Cot, the site of the ancient manorial dove-cot on Blackford, still standing.

Witch. Witch is the M. E. name for an Elm, now surviving in Witch Elm, Witch Halse, etc.

Long Hale and Broad Hale. Hale probably means "hollow," indicating the concave shape of these fields; or it may be derived from "helan," to cover, hence Long Hale may be "long furrow," but "long hollow" is more probable.

Wrex Park, *i.e.* Rushy Paddock.

Dippit. Minners. Stoopers. These names refer, perhaps, to old mining operations.

Burrow Landshare.

Cockershill, perhaps from O. E. personal name, "Cuccwin"; *cp.* Cockerington, Lincolnshire, and Cockington, Devonshire.

Horridge, O. E. "hor," grey.

Rexham=Rushy Meadow.

Hangermead. The mead by the wood, O. E. "hanger," a wood.

Holbridge. O. E. "hol," a low place or hollow.

Higher Walls. Higher Walls is a field on Mene Farm (see above). Does the name mean Higher

Welsh, and indicate a possession held by the earlier inhabitants after the O. E. settlement?

Sanctuary, part of the glebe.

Conygarth, on Troytes Farm, appears to mark the site of an ancient rabbit warren; *cp.* "Conygar," at Dunster. This warren, which is not far above Blackford, probably formed a portion of that manor.

Hanger.	Lamb Park.	Hamstile.
Needle.	Oxenledge.	Kenibeere.
Rylands.	Boobies.	No Man's Land.
Pritty.	Bloomham.	

Existing Roads.

The high road from Minehead to Porlock enters the parish of Selworthy at the bottom of Venniford hill, and continues through the hamlets of Budleigh Hill, Holnicote, and Brandy Street, across the Allerford Water, and continues its course to the west, skirting the hamlet of Allerford. It was, perhaps, a Roman road, carried across what must have been in earlier days an extensive marsh occupying the greater portion of the valley, as the names of Venniford, Blackford, and Stratford appear to show.

At Venniford is a three-cross-way, from which a road branches to the left, and winds through Tivington into the parish of Wootton Courtenay, whilst the lane on the right runs up the hill, and, dividing after a few hundred yards, sends a branch to the right, back towards Minehead, from which another branch ascends the hill and issues on Hindon Down. The branch to the left passes the ancient homestead of East Lynch, and, turning to the right, also ascends the hill, and ere long meets the narrow road which leads through Hindon along the hillside to Selworthy Church. This cross-way is called Danes Gate, and records, perhaps, the descent by some body of Danes who had left their ships anchored in one of the little bays which indent the North Hill on the sea side.

The narrow and ancient road, which from this point passes on to Selworthy Church, is paved in places, and commands fine views of land and sea. Below are the green meadows and waving woods of Holnicote, across the valley the dark moor slopes up to distant Dunkery, and ahead are the grey waters of Porlock Bay. This road passes by the rectory and its ancient tithe barn, leaving Selworthy Green on the right hand, and soon reaches a cross-way. On the right the road winds along the hill side, paved here and there, while the remaining branch, arched over with ancient trees, runs steeply down to join the main road at Holnicote. Another road branches off the highway at Allerford, and pursues its course to Bossington. A foot-path crosses from this road to the Porlock road.

Other lanes are :—

Eight Acre Lane.	Cross Lane.
Long Lane.	Watery Lane.
Clay Hill Lane.	Highway to Porlock.
Selworthy Lane.	Highway to Bossington.

From the ancient farm house, now divided into cottages, just above Tivington farm house, a lane, the course of which can still be traced under the orchard hedge, ran up to meet the lane which, branching off to the left from the top of Venniford, drops down to Troytes farm just below the chapel of St. Leonard, and passes on to Tivington Square. It then turns to the right and meandering on past Blackford meets the road from Porlock highway to Luccombe.

Besides these public roads, there are the many miles of walks which wind over the moor and through the woods down to the sea, and, reaching the shore, pass on from cliff to cliff and bay to bay. These walks, forty miles of which it is said open from the little wicket gate on Selworthy Green, have been made almost entirely by the late Sir Thomas Acland and his son, the present baronet. The late Sir Thomas, with the artistic taste which he possessed in so eminent a degree, planted the many acres of moor and common between Selworthy and the sea, and then began the vast network of walks which now intersect these woods, and traverse the moor and cliffs. Sunday after Sunday, as the villagers like to relate, he used to climb the coombe from Selworthy Church with his children and grandchildren, training them, as the touching memorial to him at the head of the coombe records, "in all things pure and true."

A bridle path starts by the church and runs up Selworthy Coombe, meeting the lane ascending from East Lynch. These two form a rough road which runs towards East Meyne, and then turns to the right across the moor, to Minehead.

A well-defined camp, which looks as if it had been a stronghold of an earlier race, adapted by the Romans for the purpose of commanding the road along the valley, crowns the steep hill above Selworthy Church. Its area is nearly two acres. It is strongly fortified by a rampart of stone and earth, and protected by a ditch on every side except on the north, where the ground falls very precipitously. On the moor side is another large rampart, which must have formed an outwork for the principal fortification. On the north-east side of this camp, Savage relates, "a part of the rampart has been thrown into the fosse, which it has more than filled, and it now forms a small mound of barrow-like form. It may be supposed that the principal work had been taken by storm by an enemy, the slain being thrown into the fosse, and a part of the rampart heaped upon them."

But the mound in question is more likely to be the result of some unsuccessful investigations conducted here, under the auspices of Captain Fortescue, in November, 1807. "We failed," says one of those present at the time, "to find anything beside a little charcoal, generally an infallible criterion to induce us to think the mounds sepulchral; though, probably, we might not have fallen on the exact spot where the urns or the interment, of whatever kind it might be, were deposited, being ignorant of the science of barrow opening."[1] It is a curious fact that an encampment should have been mistaken for a series of barrows!

1. *Tour in Quest of Genealogy*, p. 131.

CHAPTER II.

Manors.

THE origin of parishes has been for long a vexed question. Some have traced back our parochial system to Alfred, but it is more probable that the division of dioceses into parishes did not take place simultaneously. The rural churches which were erected successively as the needs of a congregation arose, or the piety of a landlord dictated, were, in fact, a sort of chapels dependent on the cathedral, and served by itinerant ministers at the bishop's discretion, or by dependants of the lord of the manor, appointed by the bishop or at the lord's nomination.[1]

"The bishop himself received the tithes, and apportioned them as he thought fit. But a capitulary of Charles the Great, founded on an ancient canon apparently, regulates their division into three parts, one for the bishop and his clergy, a second for the poor, a third for the support of the fabric of the church. Some of the rural churches obtained by episcopal concessions the privileges of baptism and burial, which were accompanied by a fixed share of tithes, and seemed to imply the residence of a minister. The

1. Hallam's *Middle Ages*, vol. ii, p. 144, and note.

same privileges were gradually extended to the other churches, and thus a complete parochial system was established. But this was hardly the case in England till near the time of the Conquest."[1]

Manor of Selworthy.

The manor of Selworthy was in existence, probably, before its church. But the fact of no church being mentioned in Domesday is not conclusive evidence of none then existing, as Domesday was compiled for purely fiscal purposes.

At the time of the Conquest, Queen Edith held the manors of Luccombe and Selworthy. They had been granted to her by her husband, and had been at an earlier date the property of a certain Alric. Until her death in 1074, Queen Edith held large estates in Somersetshire, of a gross acreage of 30,468 acres, and of the yearly value of £253. At her death, these estates reverted, not by forfeiture, but as of right, to the king. In Domesday, Luccombe and Selworthy appear under the title of "Terræ Occupatæ Rege," and are thus described :—

	Saxon owner.	Value in Domesday.			Tenant in Capite.
Locumba.	Edeva Regina.	4	0	0	
Locumba.	Filetus.	2	0	0	Radulf de Limiseis.
Doveri.	Edeva.	0	7	0	Roger de Corcelle.
Seluerda.	Edeva Regina.	1	5	0	R. de Limiseis.
Hunnecota.	II Taini.	0	5	0	Duæ Nonnæ in elemosyni.
Hunnecota.	Aluric et Bristeuinus.	1	2	0	R. de Corcelle.
Alresforda.	Edricus.	1	2	0	R. de Limiseis.[2]

1. Schmidt, p. 206. F. Paul, c. 7.
2. Eyton's *Domesday*.

Mention is made of a-hundred-and-fifty goats (*capræ*) existing in the district of Luccombe, of seven *eques equestres* at Selworthy ; of a mill at Holnicote returning a profit of twenty denarii. Regarding Allerford, we have the note, "Ode filius Gamelino detraxit unam festinam."

Edith was the daughter of the famous Earl Godwin, and was married to Edward the Confessor, very much against his will apparently, in 1045. The historians favourable to the Godwin family are lavish of their praises, and speak of her as the "rose blooming in the midst of thorns." She was, no doubt, a clever, capable woman, and something of a scholar. Ingulphus tells us that when he was a boy, Edith would often stop him as he came from school, and make him repeat his lesson, and, having examined him in his Latin grammar, question him in logic. "I had always three or four pieces of money counted by her maiden, and was sent to the royal larder for refreshment."[1]

But this "fair rose" appears to have been both cruel and vindictive. She is accused, and in all probability rightly, of having caused Gospatric, an opponent of her favourite brother Tosti's tyranny in Northumberland, to be murdered within the precincts of her court ; and she took open part with Tosti against his brother Harold. It is also by no means improbable that she was in league with the Conqueror. At all events, when the Conqueror marched upon Winchester (the possession of the queen) after the battle of Senlac, he treated her with much respect, and claimed no further pay-

1. Lingard, i, p. 169. Ingulp., p. 62

ment from the city beyond the taxes the citizens had been in the habit of paying to the king.

Nor is it much wonder if this lady of the manor of Selworthy had but little affection for a husband who openly expressed his aversion to her, and who, when her powerful family were obliged to fly from the realm in 1051, at once stripped her of all her possessions and imprisoned her in the convent of Wherwell.

Possibly earl Godwin added to the possessions assigned to her in West Somerset by the king, as the Godwin family possessed large estates in this district. And it was his connection with this part of the world, probably, which caused Harold to make his unsuccessful descent on Porlock in 1052.

On the return of the Godwin family to power, Edith was released from her convent and her possessions restored to her. She remained in undisturbed possession of her estates until her death in 1075, when the Conqueror buried her with much pomp and circumstance, beside her husband in Winchester Cathedral.

Selworthy is mentioned in Domesday, but a fuller description of the manor is given in the Exeter Domesday :—

"Ralph de Limiseio holds Seleurda, which was held by Queen Eddiva on the day that King Edward was living and dead, and it was assessed to the geld for one hide. The arable land is sufficient for five ploughs. Ralph has there in demesne half a hide and two ploughs, and the villans have half a hide and three ploughs. Ralph has there seven villans, five bordars, two bondmen, one horse, two bullocks, four hogs, and sixty sheep. He has a mill which renders twenty pence, and forty acres of wood, five acres of meadow, and sixty acres of pasture. It is worth twenty-five shillings, and when he received it it was worth twenty shillings."[1]

On the death of queen Edith, the king exercised his undoubted right and bestowed the manors of Selworthy and Luccombe on Radulf de Limesei, in addition to large grants of land in other parts of Somersetshire and also in other counties, in acknowledgment of his military services. R. de Limesei appears to have lived at Maxtoke, in the county of Warwick, and to have married Hadewise, the widow of Nigel de Bradwell. The estate remained in the De Limesey family (see p. 27) until the death of Hugh de Limesey, *temp.* Henry III, who, dying without children, left, according to Mr. Savage, his two aunts his co-heiresses, viz.: Basilia, the wife of Hugh de Odingsells, (who died about the thirty-third year of Edward I,) by whom she had a son, John de Odingsells, living in the reign of Edward II and Edward III, and Eleanor, who married David de Lindesay.

The manor of Selworthy soon passed, possibly by purchase from these ladies, to the family of De Nonyngton, afterwards De Luccombe of East Luccombe, and from that period it has always formed part of that estate. In the reign of Edward I, the manor of East Luccombe was held by Sir Baldric de Nonyngton, a person of much importance in those days. He lived at Nunnington, in the parish of Wiveliscombe, and was returned in 1300 as holding lands in

1. Savage's *Carhampton*, p. 194.

the counties of Somerset, Dorset, and Southampton, to the yearly value of £40 and more. He was one of the knights of the shire for Somerset in 1298, and formed one of the jury appointed by the king to conduct the perambulation of the Forest of Exmoor in the March of that year. John de Radyngton, Robert de Escote, and Robert de Chubworthe, all, as was just, local people, were appointed as his fellow jurymen.

Sir Baldric was a great soldier. It is interesting to think of his calling his levies together for the Scotch or French wars; labourers from the rich lands of the Wiveliscombe valley, artisans from the little town itself, wild hill men from Horridge and Maundown and the Brendon Hills, and stalwart husbandmen from Selworthy and Luccombe. He left an only daughter an heiress, Margaret, and her descendants took the name of Luccombe, or de Luccombe, from the parish in which they dwelt. They also owned the manor of Stockleigh Luccombe, in the parish of Cheriton Fitzpaine, co. Devon. Of these estates Hugh de Luccombe died seised in the 16th Edward II, 1323.

The second Inquis. p.m. of Hugh Luccombe, 10 July, 19 Edward II, 1325, no. 61, gives the following details of his estate:

Extent of the knights' fees and advowsons of churches of Hugo de Luccombe, deceased, on the day of his death, taken at Donester, on the 10 July, 19 Edward II (1325), and the jury found: that the said Hugh had the fourth part of a knight's fee in Cloudesham, which John de Cloudesham holds in demesne of William Martyn, and it is worth per ann. 20s.; and the fourth part of a knight's fee in Dovery, which Geoffrey de Luccombe holds in demesne, and it is worth per ann. 20s.; and the fourth part of a knight's fee in Lynche, which John

Hewyssh holds in demesne, and it is worth per ann. 30s.; and fourth part of a knight's fee in Lynche, which the heir of Thomas de Estecote holds in demesne, and it is worth per ann. 30s.; and the fourth part of a knight's fee in Legh Wodecote (or cok?), which Lawrence le Tort holds in demesne of Nicholas Martyn, and it is worth per ann. 16s.; and the fourth part of a knight's fee in Harewode, which Nicholas de Harewode holds in demesne, and it is worth 16s.; and the eighth part of one knight's fee in Luccombe, which Roger de Roche holds in demesne, and it is worth per ann. 10s.; and the fourth part of one knight's fee in Luccombe, which Walter Wymende holds in demesne, and it is worth per ann. one mark; and the fourth part of a knight's fee, which the said Walter holds in demesne of Lawrence Tort, and it is worth per ann. one mark; and the eighth part of one knight's fee in Overeholte, which Lawrence le Tort holds in demesne, and it is worth per ann. half mark; and the sixteenth part of one knight's fee in Dovery, which Henry de Chullinch holds in demesne, and it is worth per ann. half mark; and the fourth part of one knight's fee in Dovery and Alreford, except the sixteenth part, which Robert Guerard holds in demesne, and it is worth per ann. 30s.; and the sixteenth part of one knight's fee in Luccombe, which John Fabyan holds in demesne, and it is worth per ann. half a mark; and the sixteenth part of one knight's fee in Nether Holte, which John de Holte holds in demesne, and it is worth per ann. half mark; and the sixteenth part of one knight's in Alreford, which Walter Bronnyng holds in demesne, and it is worth per ann. half a mark; and the sixteenth part of one knight's fee there, which the heirs of John Cadisser hold in demesne, and it is worth per ann. half a mark, in all issues about the true value.

They also say that the aforesaid Hugh held on the day on which he died in the same county, the advowson of the church of Luccombe, which is worth per annum about the true value of the same 20 marks, and also the advowson of the church of Selworthy in the same county, which is worth per annum about the true value of 10 marks.

Hugh de Luccombe left an only son, John de Luccombe, who died s.p. in the 19 Ed. II, leaving his sister, Elizabeth (who was born May 20, 13 Ed. II, 1320, and was baptised at Cheriton Fitzpaine), his heir-at-law. She married Sir Oliver St. John, and they had an only son, John, who died abroad in his father's lifetime, and on the death of Sir Oliver, in 1380 (13 Richard II), the manors and advowsons appear to have devolved on his brother, Henry St. John. Henry died in 1406, leaving his son, Edward, his heir-at-law. Edward, who was born 18 March, 1394-5, died after Hilary Term, 27 Henry VI (1448-9), leaving his son, William, his heir-at-law. William died in 13 Edward IV, 1473, leaving his sister Joan, who had married Nicholas Arundell, of Trerice, in the parish of Newlyn East, near Newquay, Cornwall, his heir-at-law. She died on the 5 June, 1482, and the manors, etc., descended in a direct line to the Arundells of Trerice, down to John, fourth and last baron Arundell, of Trerice, who was born 21 Nov., 1701, and succeeded to the family estates on the death of his father, on 26 Sept., 1766.

The first baron Arundell was Richard, a noted cavalier, who was created a baron 23 March, 1663-4. His son, John, the second baron, married Margaret, only daughter of Sir John Acland of Columb John, in the parish of Broadclist co. Devon, the third baronet of that name, and ultimately the heir of his brother, Sir Arthur Acland, fourth baronet, who died a minor and unmarried in 1672. The last baron Arundell married in June, 1722, Elizabeth, daughter of Sir William Wentworth, of Wakefield, Yorkshire, and sister of Thomas Wentworth, who, in 1711, was created earl of Strafford. It appears that on his marriage Lord Arundell settled all his manors in default of his own issue on his wife's nephew, William Wentworth of Henbury, in the parish of Sturminster Marshall, Dorset, in tail. Lord Arundell died in August, 1768, aged 66, leaving no issue.

The manors of Selworthy and Luccombe then devolved on the said William Wentworth, who barred his entail by recoveries suffered in Hilary Term, 9 Geo. III, 1769. Mr. Wentworth by his will, dated April 14, 1775, devised all his estates in Dorset, Somerset, Devon, and Cornwall, to his wife Susanna Wentworth, for her life, with remainder to his only son, Frederick Thomas Wentworth, for his life, with remainder to his (the said Frederick Thomas) first son and other sons in tail male, with remainder to his daughters in tail, with remainder to the testator's only daughter, Augusta Ann Kaye, then the wife of John Hatfield Kaye, for her life, with remainder to her first and other sons in tail male, with remainder to her daughters in tail; and subject thereto he devised the manors of Selworthy and East Luccombe (in Somerset), Stockley Luccombe (in Devon), and Degembris, Goviley, Thurlbeer, Ebbingford, otherwise Efford, Penshayes, and the barton of Garrows (in Cornwall), which manors and farms had formed the estates of the Arundells of Trerice, to Sir Thomas Dyke Acland, the seventh baronet, and he devised the "capital" messuages and farms of Henbury and Loscombe in Dorsetshire to his own right heirs.

William Wentworth died early in the year 1776,

and on the 22 June, 1776, his will was proved by his son, Frederick Thomas, in the Prerogative Court of Canterbury. His widow, Susanna, died in August, 1784, and was buried at Sturminster Marshall. The said Frederick Thomas, on the death of William, second earl of Strafford, of the creation of 1711, succeeded to the earldom. He married Elizabeth Gould, and died without issue on the 5 April, 1799, and was buried at Sturminster Marshall. Mrs. Kaye died without issue on the 23 April, 1802, and was buried in the parish church of Wakefield. On her death, the late Sir Thomas Acland, tenth baronet, and the grandson of the seventh baronet, entered into possession of the estates devised to the latter by William Wentworth ; and the present Right Hon. Sir T. D. Acland, the eleventh baronet, is now in possession of such parts as remain unsold.

Some fragments of a painted window exist in the east window of the north aisle of Selworthy Church. On one of these fragments is painted the shield of Nicholas Arundell of Trerys, and Elizabeth his wife, daughter and heiress of Martin Pellor. This Nicholas was the father of Sir John Arundell of Trerice, whose son, Nicholas, married Joan St. John, and the window was probably inserted by the last named Nicholas to the memory of his grandfather and grandmother, as before this St. John marriage the Arundells had no connection with Selworthy.

The arms of Pellower, of Cornwall,[1] are described as sable, a chevron or between three bezants, and these

1. Berry's *Encyclopædia Heraldica.*

form one of the quarterings on the above shield. They also form the last quartering in the shield on the brass in Stratton Church, Cornwall, to the memory of Sir John Arundell of Trerice, who died 25 Nov., 1560, and in his *Visitations of Devon*, Colonel Vivian states that Nicholas Arundell, Sir John's grandfather, married Elizabeth, daughter and heiress of John Pellor (John clearly a mistake for Martin) lord of the manor of Pellor.

By a curious accident, the advowson of Selworthy did not pass with the manor of Selworthy. The circumstance, however, was not discovered until many years after the late Sir Thomas had presented to the rectory. Sir Thomas then bought the advowson from the Rev. Robert Freke Gould the nephew of the countess of Strafford, and the devisee under the will of earl Frederick William her husband, of all the property at his disposal.

We find in the Bruton and Montacute cartularies, recently published by the Somerset Record Society, the following references to the family de Luccombe:—No. 66, Bruton cartulary.—Gift of William de Moyun of "his land of Bruwham." Amongst the witnesses is Ricardus de Locumba. No. 69.—Notification by William de Moyun to Robert, bishop of Bath and Wells, of lands given in almoin for the redemption of his sins. Ricardus de Locumba is a witness to this document also. No. 224.—William de Moyun confirms to the canons of Bruton in perpetual almoin the tithes of his miles at Codecombe (Cutcombe). Amongst the witnesses is William de Locumba. No. 394.—Charter by which William de Moyun grants to canons of Bruton his rights on various churches and ecclesiastical benefices in Normandy. One of the witnesses to this charter is William de Locumba.

MANOR OF BLACKFORD.

The history of this manor is not very clear, although the mansion house must have been at one time a place of some importance. In the thirteenth century it appears to have belonged to the Lovel family. "At Westminster, in the octave of Trinity, between Richard Luvel, querent, and John de Blakeford, impedient, for a messuage and three carucates of land in Blakeford and Wythele (Withiel Flory on Brendon Hill). Plea of warranty was summoned. John acknowledged the right of Richard or by his gift to hold of the chief lords of that fee, and he warranted against all men; for this, Richard gave John £20 sterling." (Somerset Fines, 33 Edward I.)

The very numerous places of this name in the west of England, make it very difficult to ascertain anything for certain of the early history of this manor. But, possibly, it may have been that manor of Blackford which in 1483 was granted to Sir Thomas Everingham, one of the knights of the royal body of the castle and borough of Barnstaple, and his heirs, as part of the estates of Thomas St. Ledger, for his services against the rebels.

At the beginning of the sixteenth century however the manor certainly belonged to the Lucar family, who held it for several generations, until, on the death of Antony Lucar, of Blackford s.p. in 1625, it passed to his sister, Cecile, wife of his neighbour, Charles Steynings, of Holnicote. The ancient dove-cot, a building of fifteenth century character, still remains intact; and within the memory of living men, "Torney Day," of Milverton, held a yearly court at Blackford on behalf of the owner, at which water rights were settled, fines paid, etc.

Manor of Allerford.

The manor of Allerford is thus described in Domesday:—

Ralph (de Limeseio, the same nobleman who held Selworthy of queen Edith) holds Alresford. Edric held it in the time of king Edward, and gelded for one hide. The arable land is five carucates. In demesne are two carucates and servants, and six villanes, and two cottages with one plough. There is a mill of fifteen pence rent, and six acres of meadow and twenty acres of pasture, and one acre of wood. It was worth fifteen shillings, now twenty shillings. This manor pays a customary rent of twelve sheep per annum to Carentone, the king's manor. Ralph still keeps up this custom.[1]

Collinson tells us that the de Limesey family held their property in this district for five generations. Ralph was succeeded by Alan de Limesy, Alan by Gerard, Gerard by John, and John by Hugh. The manor of Allerford was afterwards held of the De Mohuns the lords of Dunster.

The De Mohuns must have ruled over our district from the castle at Dunster, which William de Mohun

1. Collinson, vol. ii, p. 21.

had built in almost regal state, and we read[1] that when king Stephen endeavoured to reduce this turbulent baron to submission, he had to retire after a fruitless siege from before the stronghold which William "pulchrè et inexpugnatè in pelagi littore locarat." The manor of Allerford was held under the De Mohuns by the De Raleigh family of Nettlecombe, and in 4 Edward III, John de Ralegh held it of John de Mohun. It would appear to have passed to the St. John family some time in the latter end of the fifteenth or beginning of the sixteenth century.

Manor of Holnicote.

The manor of Holnicote does not appear to have been part of the estates of queen Edith, like so much of the hamlet of Selworthy was. In the time of king Edward two thanes, Alaric and Brictuin, held it of the king, when it was assessed to the geld for half a hide and half a virgate of land. "The arable land is sufficient for two ploughs and a half. There are four villans and one bordar." (These were settlers on the land, whose holdings were confirmed on the condition of their serving the lord of the manor for so many days a week according to the value of their holdings.) "There were sixteen acres of pasture, and the whole estate was valued in twenty-two shillings." A certain Abel de Hunecot held also half a virgate of land in Holnicote of the king, which "that king gave to Edith in fine and perpetual alms, because her husband was slain in the king's service." Abel must have been

1. *Gesta Stephani*, p. 41.

Edith's son or second husband. Besides these two lay owners, two nuns, Domesday informs us, held of the king in "free alms" two virgates and a half of land in Honecote. "The arable land is sufficient for two ploughs. There is one plough and five acres of meadow. It is worth five shillings." "Frank almoigne," *i.e.* free alms, was the tenure by which the ancient monasteries and religious houses held the larger portion of their lands. They were discharged from all secular burdens, but that of the "trinoda necessitatis," *i.e.*, "of repairing the bridges, building castles, and repelling invasions"; and they were bound to pray for the souls of the donor, his ancestors, and his heirs.

William de Holne held the manor in the reign of Edward I, and in the same reign, Savage tells us, Walter Barun (or Bidun) held a portion of it. Ten acres of arable and two acres of meadow land were held of the king in capite, by the service of hanging on a certain forked piece of wood the red deer that died of the murrain in the forest of Exmoor, and also of lodging and entertaining at the tenant's expense such poor or decrepit persons as came to him, for the souls of the ancestors of king Edward I. The manors of Bossington, Holnicote, and Blackford, with their woods and heaths, had been included by encroachment in the forest of Exmoor, and were disafforested at the perambulation made by order of Edward III, in 1297.

CHAPTER III.

Ancient Chapels in the Holnicote Valley.

BESIDES the churches of St. Mary's, Luccombe, and All Saints', Selworthy, there exist in the Holnicote valley two tiny mediæval chapels; and the ruins of a third, and perhaps even of a fourth chapel, are to be traced. On the south side of the parish and in the centre of the hamlet of Tivington there stands a little chapel, which an ancient will which contains a bequest to it tells us is dedicated to St. Leonard. The building was within recent times used as a storehouse and barn by the inhabitants of the cottage which is built against its east end. Some years ago it was repaired and used as a dame's school, and until recently it has been used during the week for this purpose, while occasional services have been held in it on week days and on Sundays.

As no occasion now exists for a dame's school in the hamlet, the little place has of late been used entirely for religious purposes, and has just been restored. It still possesses its ancient thatched roof, which is supported on moulded oak beams rising from behind a prettily moulded wall plate, which appears to

CHAPEL OF ST. LEONARD, TIVINGTON

be an old copy of a still earlier design. The roof was formerly open to the thatch; but of late years it has been boarded between the beams. During the recent restoration the outer jambs of a lancet window were uncovered in the east end of the chapel. And on the south side of the sacrarium a narrow window, hitherto built up, has been re-opened; and close beneath it the remains of the piscina were found. The east end and south side of the chapel, and the western doorway, are evidently the oldest portions of the building, and may be as early, possibly, as the fourteenth century. But the square-headed windows on the north side of the chapel must have been inserted quite late in the Perpendicular period.

The chapel is 29ft. in length, in the clear; 14ft. 6in. wide; 9ft. 6in. high to wall plate; and 18ft. high to apex of roof. The intersections of the beams were covered, until recent years, by bosses, decorated by figures of saints, etc.

No tradition exists as to who was the builder of the chapel; but it is another example of the multitude or small district chapels which before the Reformation existed in the outlying districts of our scattered agricultural parishes. The so-called mission chapels which are at the present time being erected in so many of our large country parishes are no new method of meeting a want which was recognised as fully in the Middle Ages as it is in the present time. The owners of manors lying at a distance from the parish church, used to build chapels for the use of themselves and their dependants, where the old, the infirm, and the very young could worship regularly. At the same time, all parishioners who were at all able to do so, were expected to attend the parish church occasionally, and especially at the greater festivals. And the old church path leading from many a lonely hamlet to the parish church, at one time well used, and kept in order by the church rate, bears witness to the fact that these chapels were not intended to supersede the parish church.[1]

Of this system, the hamlet of Tivington is a good example. There is the manor house, Blackford, at one time a place of much importance. There is the chapel, for the use of the lord of the manor and his tenants, situated in the midst of the hamlet of Tivington, which formed part of the Blackford estate, and there is the church path still to be traced, leading straight from the hamlet, by a long ascent of two miles or more, to the parish church.

Following the course of an old and very circuitous lane which runs down from the chapel, we reach the site of the old manor house at Blackford, and join the main road to Luccombe. Passing through the picturesque village, and leaving the newly-restored church of St. Mary and the rectory on the right, we ascend a steep piece of hill, at the top of which is a four-cross way. The road to the north leads to West Luccombe and Porlock; the one to the east to Holnicote; and the highway on the west climbs the side of the moor, at this point clothed with fir woods, towards Cloutsham and Dunkerry. And besides these four roads, a very ancient track leads off through the woods and along

1. *Newbery House Mag.*, 1890, p. 219.

RUINS OF ST. SAVIOUR'S(?) CHAPEL.

the moor, to the hamlet and church of Stoke Pero. This path is traditionally called the Priest's Path.

At the point where this ancient way branches off from the road to West Luccombe, we find the scanty remains of another tiny chapel, about two miles from the chapel of St. Leonard. A few mounds of earth alone marked the site of this building until recently, when the owner kindly gave the writer permission to excavate the ground plan of the chapel. At the depth of about two feet below the surface, and beneath the roots of a dead tree, some old knives were found, and a silver instrument, of which the use is uncertain. The chapel had for many generations been used as a stone quarry; but a few pieces of window jambs were found buried beneath the soil, and the footing of the walls was found to be fairly intact. A rise in the floor of the building, about two feet from the east wall, marks, perhaps, the original site of the altar. The chapel was 28 feet long in the clear, and 15 feet wide. Although so small, it had, apparently, three doors, as the chapel at Lynch has. It is difficult to guess at the object of these three doors, unless, indeed, they were of use for processions.

Like the chapel of St. Leonard, it is difficult to arrive with any certainty at the history of this building. A chapel dedicated to St. Saviour undoubtedly existed somewhere in the parish of Luccombe in the fourteenth century, for we find the following entry in Drokensford's Register, August 13, 1316:—Geoffrey de Luccombe to have chantry in chapel, "intra curiam suam, de Luccombe" served at his own cost, "salvo jure matris eccles."

If this entry refers to this ruined building, we thus get the date of its foundation. But "intra curiam suam" seems to imply a building within the manor or court house of Geoffrey de Luccombe. This chapel of St. Saviour appears to have been held in considerable repute, and to have attracted the devout offerings of the faithful. Thus, Thomas Coppe, of Selworthy, by his will, dated 20 Nov., 1533, leaves a "shepe to S. Savyour, as well as to the store of our lady of Luccombe."

But in 1548 no chantry is returned as existing in the parish of Luccombe. Probably, by that time, the churchwardens or others interested in the building, had prepared for the coming storm by selling the sacred vessels and furniture, and, perhaps, even the material of the chapel itself. It is difficult to see why the site of this chapel was chosen. There is no evidence of there ever having been any population in its immediate neighbourhood; and the lie of the ground forbids the supposition. The chapel, however, commands the first view coming from Luccombe, of the sea, and lies at the foot of the moor. It is possible that it was built, and masses ordained to be said here, by some pious person, to commemorate his escape from some great peril on the sea or on the moor. In the early Middle Ages our forefathers considered that wild tracts of moorland, like the hills above our valley, were the haunts of demons and dragons, and wayside chapels were sometimes built on the edge of the moor to keep these enemies of mankind at bay. When the writer was excavating the site, a very ancient person who happened to pass, assured him that her forebears had always known that a chest of gold laid buried beneath the building. He was not fortunate enough, however, to secure this interesting treasure!

Descending the hill to the picturesque banks of the Horner, we pass through the hamlet of West Luccombe, and following a footpath which crosses the main road from Minehead to Porlock at New Bridge, in about another two miles we reach the hamlet of West Lynch, which is separated by the Horner Stream from the larger hamlet of Bossington, which belongs to the ecclesiastical parish of Porlock. Here, in a very romantic situation, beside the Aller Water which just below this point joins the Horner, and close to an ancient house of an apparently late fifteenth century date, stands a pretty chapel of the Perpendicular period. Until the last few years it formed part of the buildings of the adjoining farm, and was used as a storehouse. But it has of late years been restored by Sir Thomas Acland, and has been used for Divine Service since the institution of the present rector of Selworthy. The chapel is 30ft. long, by 19ft. 6in. wide. It is 18ft. high to the wall plate, and 23ft. to the apex of the roof.

The chapel possesses a fine oak roof, with handsomely moulded beams. Most of the original bosses, all of which are of foliage patterns, still remain *in situ*. The detail of the chapel is all very good, and the east window is particularly noticeable. The piscina remains in a fairly perfect condition. On each side of the altar are two much mutilated brackets, which supported either figures of saints or a reredos. The building is probably of the same date as the south aisle of the parish church, *i.e. circa* 1520. The altar table at present standing in the chapel was removed from the parish church some time ago.

Nothing very certain is as yet known about the history of the chapel, nor has the writer been able to ascertain its dedication. It seems most probable that it was built as a chapel-of-ease for the use of the inhabitants of Bossington; and yet it lies just within the confines of the manor of Allerford.

Had the building, however, been destined primarily for the use of the Allerford people, it would have been built half a mile further up the valley. At the same time, the Raleigh family, who owned the manor of Allerford and property in Porlock parish as well, and who were great benefactors to the church in Somersetshire, may have founded a chapel here.

When the history of the manor of Bossington is given to the public, light, probably, will be thrown upon this point.

Various questions suggest themselves regarding these little chapels, at one time so numerous throughout the country. For whom were they intended? How were they furnished? Still more, how were they served? and what services were given in them?

We have seen above that these buildings were generally built by the owner of a manor lying at a distance from the parish church, for the accommodation of himself and his family, and as places where those of his tenants, who were unable to reach the parish church, might regularly worship. Many charters still exist, giving permission to private persons to have chapels

LYNCH CHAPEL.

From a Photograph by Mr. C. H. Samson.

within their houses, as *e.g.* to the above-mentioned Geoffrey de Luccombe, and to a certain Joan de Raleigh, to construct one within her manor house at Rowdon, in Stogumber parish.

In the late middle ages, noblemen delighted in the splendour of their private chapels. We read, for instance, that the earl of Northumberland, in the early part of the reign of Henry VIII, maintained for his chapel a dean, ten priests, and a choir of seventeen men and boys, whose surplices, it is noted, were washed sixteen times a year.

Prebendary Hingeston Randolph has recently given to the public some interesting particulars as to these chapels.[1] They are drawn from his investigation of the record of the visitations of the estates belonging to the bishop of Exeter, in the end of the thirteenth century and the beginning of the fourteenth. The Visitors, he tells us, found in the chapel of the manor of Norton, in the parish of Newton St. Cyres, in Devonshire, "a missal, without note, showing that the services were not generally, at all events, sung. A manual (an office book containing the services for baptism, extreme unction, etc.), a breviary, also without notes; a psalter in good condition, two sets of vestments, a chalice gilt within, two cruets, two bells for the dead, a vessel for the holy water, a 'pax board,' etc."

Such furniture, perhaps, might have belonged to Lynch chapel, before Henry VIII and Edward VI wrought havoc amongst the ecclesiastical buildings

1. *Newbery House Magazine*, 1890, p. 220.

throughout the land. And to this we may add that the chapel was probably furnished with oak stalls, as some small and very delicately moulded stall ends were recently found in the ancient house adjoining the chapel, which looked as if they might have belonged to the building.

Mr. Hingeston Randolph's investigation enlightens us, also, as to the services held in these chapels, and how they were served. The larger chapels had their resident chaplain. At Shute, in Devonshire, the chaplain, he relates, appeared before the Visitors and complained of the condition of the chapel, the roof of which was in so faulty a condition that mass could not be said there in wet weather; and yet the poor parson had to sleep in this half-ruined building for want of other accommodation.

It seems quite possible that Lynch chapel might have had at one time a resident chaplain; and that the tradition, that the pretty old house adjoining it was the "priest's house," may be true. In this ancient house the chaplain may well have lived, enjoying a stipend paid by the owner of the manor, or even by his congregation themselves.

But not every district chapel could have had its chaplain. How were the smaller buildings like Tivington chapel, and the one at Chapel Steep served? There were, Mr. H. Randolph informs us, existing in most dioceses at the end of the thirteenth century, and just anterior to the date of the building of St. Saviour's Chapel, at Luccombe, a number of clergy, "who were for the most part unbeneficed, and who were largely employed as curates-in-charge for non-resident incumbents, and sometimes as assistant curates. They were called chaplains; and there can be no doubt that the little hamlet sanctuaries, which were once so numerous in the land, were not unfrequently served by their means." "These Capellani were under the direct control of the bishop. And our episcopal registers show that it was an effectual control. The diocesan was accustomed to punish them when he ordered them to undertake the charge of any parish, and, as was sometimes the case, they refused to go."

From the researches of the same writer, we learn, not only how our manor chapels were served, but what the services at the three chapels in our valley probably were. The chapel of Norton in the parish of Newton St. Cyres was served by one of the abovementioned chaplains, whose stipend in this case was paid by the rector alone. These were the services he gave:—"On every Sunday he read to them out of the holy Gospel, sprinkled them with holy water, and distributed the blessed bread. On every Wednesday and Friday throughout the year he said mass in the chapel, and on Christmas and Easter days he gave them the full service (*plenum servicium*), by which no doubt was meant matins followed by mass. In Lent he received them to confession, and in his chapel he baptised their children."

Probably there would have been no preaching at these chapels, and, indeed, sermons were not invariably preached even in important churches on Sundays.

It is worthy of note that these little buildings, however small and humble the structure, were no mere mission rooms. In every case, they were especially built and arranged for the celebration of the one service ordained by Christ Himself. And it is pleasant to record that after a lapse of more than three hundred years, the Holy Communion is now once more regularly administered in the chapels at Tivington and at Lynch.

For the photographs which are here reproduced, the writer is indebted to Mr. C. H. Samson, of Taunton.

CHURCH OF ALL SAINTS, SELWORTHY.

CHAPTER IV.

Selworthy Church.

THE church of St. John the Baptist, Selworthy, consists of a nave, two aisles, and a chancel. A double flight of steps leads up to the churchyard from the high road. Three steps lead thence into the porch, and five more are ascended before the level of the church itself is reached.

The porch has two storeys, but the oak roof of the lower storey has unfortunately been removed, and a plain plaster one substituted for it. The heavy fifteenth century door, however, still remains at the bottom of the flight of steps which leads into the church.

On entering the church, the eye is caught by the font, with its curious movable covering of oak, carved with a linen pattern. The base of the font is apparently new, or at all events it has been much re-chiselled, but at the recent visit of the Somerset Archæological Society to Selworthy, the bowl was pronounced to be probably a Saxon one.

The greater part of the church is of the Perpendicular period, and the south aisle—the latest part of

the building—is dated 1527. In this aisle are some fine windows, with handsome tracery and transomes. It possesses also a beautiful oak roof of the waggon shape. The ribs, which are all delicately carved and ornamented at their intersection with finely executed bosses, spring from behind a deep and elaborate oak cornice. This cornice was until recently much decayed, but it has of late been well restored by the Selworthy Carving Club.

The chancel is approached by two steps, but the height of a piscina on the south wall of the south aisle indicates that the chancel has been raised one step, probably for making the vaults which exist under the east end of the aisle. During the restoration of the church in 1875, a painting of the Virgin and Holy Child was discovered under the east window of this aisle, and round the window were found floriated designs and portions of inscriptions in black letter. It was found, however, impossible to recover these paintings. It has been suggested that a carved altar-shaped stone of the Perpendicular period, which was appropriated in the eighteenth century for the tomb-stone of a certain Mary Hill, who now reposes beneath it, (as the inscription let into one of the panels declares,) was an altar to the Virgin, and stood beneath the group painted below the east window of the south aisle. Not only this aisle, but the whole church, was evidently covered with fresco painting when built, as painted devices have been found under the present limewash all over the church. Mr. J. D. Sedding, the late well-known London architect, considered that the sacrarium was the oldest part of the church. On each side of its plain and apparently early window are two niches for figures of saints, of different heights and of apparently different dates. The chancel was re-arranged in 1893 under Mr. Sedding's direction, and much improved. The steps to the sacrarium have been widened, the plaster removed from the roof and oak panelling substituted, and the seating altered. The post-Reformation altar table was removed several years ago to Lynch Chapel at the north end of the parish, and the present carved one presented by the Rev. H. Hoare, at one time curate of the parish. A beautifully carved oak screen, of which a few portions, sumptuously coloured and gilded, still remain, ran at one time across the church. We find that a certain John Horne, of Selworthy, whose will was proved in 1544, bequeathed xxs. to the making of this screen.

To the north aisle Mr. Sedding assigned a date of *circa* 1390. The roof is waggon-shaped, and was evidently never finished, as both bosses and carved wall-plate are absent. Carved bosses have been provided for this roof by the Selworthy Carving Club. Just below the chancel step, a narrow doorway gives access to the turret staircase, which originally led to the rood-loft. On the wall about this doorway, and also around the one above it which opened on to the rood-loft, vestiges have been found of many devices in fresco, such as cross-surmounted Ms, etc., and a large portion of the wall below the chancel was apparently ornamented with a design of fleur-de-lys. The plaster has recently been removed from the roof, displaying some handsome oak ribs, and the roof has been boarded with oak, felted, and re-slated. A doorway which had been secured by the customary great oak bar, was recently blocked up in the western end of this aisle.

Across the western end of the nave is an oak gallery, a good piece of eighteenth century carpenters' work, but which blocks the tower, and which, for many reasons, would be better away.

Close to the south entrance door a stone staircase in the wall leads up to the chamber over the entrance porch. This from the time of the Reformation until the beginning of the present century, appears to have been used as a lumber room, but it was then adapted to serve as a pew by the Hon. Mrs. Fortescue, grandmother of the present Sir T. D. Acland. This lady built the curious balcony which hangs over the church, and, in order to make the room more suitable for her purpose, raised and flattened the roof of it, and removed the external battlements. This alteration considerably mars the appearance of the porch from the exterior. The square head of the window appears at the same time to have been removed, and to have been replaced by an arched top. This room was retained for their use by the Acland family until the restoration of the church in 1875, when seats were allotted to them in the east end of the south aisle. The room is now used as a vestry. A second staircase at one time gave access to this room from the porch, but this was removed in 1875.

The tower, which is only forty feet in height and very massive, is approached by a relatively low arch, which is not in the middle of the west end of the church. The tower was evidently part of an earlier and smaller church, which was allowed to remain when the building with which it was first connected was swept away. Money, no doubt, ran short, otherwise we should probably have had at Selworthy a tower not dissimilar to the ones at Minehead and Dunster. The tower contains a clock chamber with a belfry above. Three of the steps of the staircase are formed of tombstones of an early date. Two bear incised floriated crosses, and on the third a portion of an inscription in Lombardic capitals is visible. The basement and belfry are lighted by two-light windows of an Early English character, and the clock-chamber by a narrow lancet window which is partially blocked up. A fine view is commanded from the flat leaden roof of the tower. The tower is solidly built of large blocks of ashlared stone, very different from the inferior masonry of which the walls of the church are composed, but both tower and church are at present covered with rough cast.

There is a pretty peal of bells on which are the following inscriptions :—

Treble bell. Come let us ring
for church and king.

W.E. 1757.

Second.—Prosperity to the Parish. W.E. 1757.

Third.—Peace and good Neighbourhood. W.E. 1757.

Fourth.—Wm. Evans of Chepstow cast us all. 1757.

Fifth.—Mr. Thomas Kent and Mr. Phillip Tayler, Churchwardens. W.E. 1757.

Tenor.—God preserve our king and kingdom and send us peace. W.E. 1757.

The tenor bell is said to weigh 18 cwt.

There is but little ancient painted glass left in the

church. The beautiful windows of the south aisle were evidently at one time filled with stained glass, but only a few fragments in the transomes remain. These windows have recently been filled with grisaille glass by Messrs. Beer, of Exeter, at a cost of about £100. The window over the altar was inserted in 1890 principally at the expense of Sir Thomas Acland, and is dedicated to the memory of the Rev. J. Stevenson, who died at the rectory at the advanced age of ninety-four, having held the benefice for sixty-three years. The window is the work of Messrs. Clayton and Bell, of London, and cost £170. In the east window of the north aisle are some pieces of painted glass, evidently of the fifteenth century. In the top tracery are (1) a pelican, (2) a very beautiful half-figure of our Lord blessing the cup, (3) a figure with its head surrounded by a glory, holding in its right hand a wafer surmounted by a cross, and with its left hand uplifted in the act of blessing. Below are represented the arms of Nicholas Arundell, of Trerys, (as a legend, wrongly placed, states,) and Elizabeth his wife, daughter and heiress of Martin Pellor. This Nicholas was the father of Sir John Arundell, of Trerice, whose son, Nicholas, married Joan St. John, the heiress of the manors of Luccombe and Selworthy.

There are a number of very quaint bosses on the roof of the nave and the chancel.

On the centre rib of the nave looking eastward we have—(1) a grotesque head, (2) a cross surrounded by a carved border, (3) a bishop in the act of benediction, with three Tudor roses on each side of him, (4) a Tudor rose, (5) a foliage design, (6) the exhibition of the Host by the Father. (This curious emblem is to be seen also on the tower of Minehead church.) (7) A head with pointed beard, wearing a diadem; (8) a Tudor rose, (9) a foliage design.

On right hand rib: (1) foliage design, (2) St. John the Evangelist with a scroll and a book, (3) a pilgrim with staff and wallet, (4) foliage, (5) St. John the Evangelist with eagle and book, on his right side a label with the inscription, "I am the Lord God," which is evidently a mistake of the German decorator's of 1875 for "Behold the Lamb of God"; (6) a winged angel displaying an open book, (7) St. Peter with his sword, (8 and 9) foliage.

On left hand rib: (1) foliage, (2) St. Christopher bearing the Child Christ, (3) the Blessed Virgin, crowned and seated, holding the Holy Child; (4) St. Catherine, crowned, with her wheel in her right hand and a sword in her left; (5) St. John the Baptist with a lamb beside him and in his hand a book, (6) St. Peter, with his keys in one hand and in the other a book, on the open page of which is displayed Our Lord's head crowned with thorns; (7) St. John the Baptist (or St. Agnes?) with a lamb beside him, holding an open book, on which is painted the crucifixion, with a kneeling figure on each side of the cross; (8) Tudor rose, (9) foliage.

The carving on the roof of the south aisle is well worthy of careful study. The large number of delicately carved bosses are mostly of conventional foliage or fruit design, but on the centre cross rib are five bosses bearing the five emblems of the Passion.

Coming to the chancel, on the centre rib looking

eastward we have—(1) a head, smooth-faced and young-looking, probably that of St. John the Baptist; (2) Our Saviour's head surrounded by a wreath, (3) the Holy Virgin crowned, (4) immediately over the altar a head and shoulders clad in a helmet and coat of mail. It is very probable that this figure may represent the founder of the church, or possibly it tells us that Alicia St. John rebuilt the church in memory of her husband. The helmet is of the type of the late fourteenth or early fifteenth century, and so corresponds with the date at which this lady was living as a widow in the valley.

On the right hand rib looking eastward we have—(1) A St. George's cross surrounded by roses, (2) St. Catherine's wheel surrounded by leaves, (3) a lamb with a cross and a label coming out of its mouth, (4) an eagle with a label coming out of its mouth, on which at one time there was an inscription; (5) a Tudor rose. These bosses are exactly reproduced on the corresponding rib on the other side of the roof.

On the right hand wall-plate looking east we have—(1) the cross of George, (2) a rose, (3 and 4) foliage designs, (5) a coat of arms, gules, a chevron engrailed arg., between three martlets arg., impaling az. three gerbes arg.; (6 and 7) foliage, (8) same coat as 5, (9 and 10) foliage, (11) same coat as 5, (12 and 13) foliage, (14) St. George's cross.

On left hand plate looking eastward: (1) cross of St. George, (2) same coat of arms as 5 on the right hand wall-plate, (3) foliage, (4) cross of St. George, (5) arg. a bendlet or, on a chief gules three mullets or, impaling az. three gerbes or. The dexter coat is that of St. John, of Selworthy and Luccombe, co. Somerset. The impaled coat, repeated five times in the chancel, is perhaps that of Comyn; (6 and 7) foliage, (8) same as 2, (9) St. George's cross, (10) foliage, (11) az., three mullets or, parted by a bar engrailed and within a border engrailed, impaling gules a chevron engrailed between three lions' faces or. The dexter coat cannot be assigned to any family: the sinister coat is that of De Luccombe. The various coats may represent various inter-marriages of the St. John family. But as they were recoloured in 1875, without the slightest reference to their original tinctures, it is hopeless to attempt to give any accurate description of them. (12 and 13) foliage, (14) St. George's cross.[1]

There are several brasses in Selworthy Church.

In the sacrarium are the following:

1.—On the north wall.

Epitaphium Gulihelmus Fleete pastoris gregis
Domini apud Selworthienis qui obiit
Quinto die Januarii. Ano Domini 1617.

Mortuus hic jaceo in terra tumulatus et urna
Funerei versus conditor ipse mei,
Londini natus, Winton nutritus et Oxon
Naviter edoctus cum grege Wicamico
Inde Somerseti Selworthia villa tenebat
Et coelo atque solo nomine digna satis

1. The frequent allusions to St. John the Baptist and St. John the Evangelist on the church roofs, seem further to connect the church with the St. John family. And yet St. John the Baptist was the patron saint of the Raleigh family of Nettlecombe, who for a considerable period held the manor of Allerford; and a rent charge was paid out of this manor towards the endowment of the chantry of St. John the Baptist in the parish church of Nettlecombe.

Quadraginta octoque annos puerosque senesque
Edocui vere dogmata Sacra Dei
Hisce locis hujus transegi tempora vitae
Nil superest nisi quod spiritus astra petat
Mortali hac vitâ transactâ certus ego sum
Quod mihi cum Christo vita perennis erit.

Here dead I lie in earth, entombéd in the grave
My funeralls in swanlike sort myselfe indited have
London my birth, my bringeing up Winton and Oxford had,
Where taught I was wth. Wickham's flocke ye grave and sad.
Thence Selworthye in Somersett this place of worth and fame
Mee kept for wholesome aire and soil most worthy of that name
Where forty years and eight I taught God's flock both young and old
And did to them as meete it was God's holy Word unfold.
And in these forenamed places all my time and life did spend
What now remaines but yt my soule above ye stars shall wend
For this my mortall life once o'er I know and I am sure
An everlasting life with Christ God will for me procure.

AMEN.

2.—

In Piam Memoriam
Andreæ Georgii Gilmore A.M.
Hujus Parœchiæ per IX annos
Rectoris
Qui obiit die XXIVº NOV. MDCCCLXXXII
LX annos natus
Obdormientes in Jesu Deus ducet cum Illo.

3.—On the south wall.

In this Chancel are deposited the remains of Hannah Brice wife of the Rev. Nathaniel Blake Brice who was buried March ye 20th 1767 aged 57 and four of their children viz:

SARAH was buried August 18th 1738 an infant
MARY was buried August 18th 1748 aged 5 years
NATHANIEL was buried March 20th 1770 aged 22
PENELOPE was buried Jan. 7th 1772 aged 38.

4.—

Underneath this stone lie interred
the remains of the
Rev. D. Williams
22 years RECTOR of this PARISH
who departed this life
the 1st day of Sept. 1802 aged 72
Magnus Homo. Acer. Memorabile.

5.—

In memory of
Rev. Theodor Muller
Rector of Selworthy from 1864
to 1873 who died at Minehead
January 2nd 1877 aged 77
a faithful preacher of the Gospel
a gentle loving Spirit
He patiently endured to the end
and has gone to his rest and reward.

6. South aisle under east window.

Heere lyeth ye Body of Phillip Steynings
Ye son of Charles Steynings of Holnicott Esq
who died ye 12th daye of Augusti ye yeare
Of Our Lord God 1634 and of His age ye 6th
moneth.

This Graves A Cradle where an Infant lies
Rockt fast asleep wth. Deathes sad lullabyes.

7.—

An Epitaph made in memory of that worthy gentlewoman Mrs. Margarett Steynings Widdow who died ye Xth day of March in ye year of Our Lord 1631 and of her age ye 70th.

Verte oculos quicunque venis paulisper et audi
Ut repetant gemitus moesta sepulchra suos
Ah jacet hic jacet hic specioso stemmate nata
Stemmate Pollardi nec generosa parum

Talis erat dum virgo fuit: Connubia nomen
Fecerunt Steynings. sic quoq dulce jugum
At Mors divisit tamen haud sine conjuge conjux
Quae nupta est Christo non viduata manet.

Gentle Spectator whatsoe'er thou bee
Stay heere awhile and see & sighe with mee
Ah here lies shee that lead a vertuous life
A Pollard's daughter and a Steyning's wife
And then a widow: now a wife again
Espoused to Christ her Saviour doth remaine
From Whom tho Death a tyme her body sever
Her soul with Him in blisse doth live for ever

TYMBE STONE KEEP WELL THY DUST TIS OF GREAT PRIZE
BUT GREATER FARRE WHEN FROM THEE IT SHALL RISE.

An account of this lady is given in the notes in this volume on the Steyning family. She was a member of the Kilve branch of the great west-country family of Pollard.

8.—

Here lyeth | the body of | Antony | Steynings | ye sonne of | Charles Steynings of | Holneycote | Esq: who died | ye 15th daye of | May in ye yeare | of Our Lord God | 1635 and of his | age ye 4th yeare |

9.—

Here lyeth the body of Cicely Staynings sometyme the wyfe of Charles Staynings of Holneycott Esquire by whom she had seaven sonnes and sixe daughters; She departed this lyfe in the fayth of Christ the XXITH daye of June in the year of Our Lord God 1647 and in the 47th yeare of her age.

Christ was to me both in lyfe and in deathe advantage.
Here lyes intoombed in dust together
A tender sonne and loving mother.

Philip Stenynges Esquiere married unto Alice Ffrie daughter of William Frie of Membrie Esquier by whome he had nyne sonnes and five daughters departed this life the fiveteenthe daie of January in ye yeare of Our Lord God a thousand five hundred fourscore and nyne.

Egregias animi dotes vel munera mentis,
Si spectes, si qui sit donis preditus istis.
Nobilis est, (vere sunt nobilitatis origo.)
Tunc vere clarus fama et virtute Philippus
Stenninges, qui claris ab avis sua stemmata ducens
Æquavit semper nomen virtutibus amplum.
Discite ab hoc uno, generosi, agnoscere Christum.
Discite ab hoc rectè vivere, ritè mori.

If inwarde gifts of minde thou doe respecte
If he innobled be that soe is decte
For soe some saie true nobleness is got
Then well may Philip Steninges have that lot.
Who coming of most ancient line and race
Did ever equal it with virtues grace
O learne of him all gentils Christ on high
O learne of him to live and well to die.

Prosopopeia defuncti ad lectorem tetrasticon ejusdem.

Qualis tu nunc es jamdudum talis habebat
Qualis ego nunc sum, tu quoqtalis eris,
Ergo tuae semper memorare novissima vitae,
Non moriere, deo vivere certus eris.

Such as thou art suche one some tyme was I
Such as I am shalte thou be truelye
Remember still therefore thy endinge daye
Thou shalt not die but live with God alwaie.

The tradition holds in the parish that the beautiful south aisle of our church, in which the Steyning brasses are placed, was built at the sole expense of this ancient family, who held the manor of Holnicote from time immemorial, and who were also possessed of large estates in Overstowey and other parishes. It is quite clear that they built for themselves a vault under the east end of the south aisle, and the relative position of the piscina to the floor appears to indicate that they raised the floor of the aisle in order to accomplish their purpose more satisfactorily. The family is now extinct in the direct line, but are represented through the female line by the Trevelyans of Nettlecombe Court. Amongst the Trevelyan papers are many letters from members of this family, and a pedigree going back four generations from Philip Steynings. It is not, however, quite a correct one.

11. On the floor at the west end of the nave is a small brass.

"Here lyeth the body of Judith Horne deceased 26 June, 1632."

The name of Horne is connected with Selworthy parish from very early times.

12, 13, 14. On the east wall of the north aisle we find the following brasses :—

Robert Siderfin Gent: who died Jan: 20th, 1714 aged 25.
Walter Siderfin Gent. who died March 21 1731 aged 40.

In memory of John Clarke of West Lynch in the parish of Selworthy, who departed this life 26 Feb: 1796 aged 90 years.

In memory of Mary Clarke wife of John Clarke jun: of West Lynch in the parish of Selworthy who departed this life 12th Jan: 1795 aged 48.

These last two brasses were taken up from the floor of the middle aisle, during the church restoration in 1875.

Returning to the south aisle, we find under the east window a stone with the following inscription, with a skull cut beneath it :

Under here lyeth
Mr. Courtenay Oram
A.M. and Fellow of
Caius College in Cambridge
Who died the 14th day
of Aprill ANo. Dom : 1687.

On the south wall of this aisle we find the following monuments, mostly of marble.

1.—

Sacred
to the memory of Charles Staynings Esqre.
of Holnicote in this parish of yt ancient family
and of Susanna his wife Daughter to Sir Nicolas
MARTYN of Oxton in the County of DEVON
She departed this lyfe the 8th day of May 1685
He the 4th day of December 1700 aged 78 haveing
made and ordered the following verses to be written
on his monument

Here lyes Charles Staynings by his wife
Who loved him as she did her lyfe,
As hee did her their loves increased
Till that sad day his wife deceased.
To whom her husband now is gone
Both lived together thirty years and one.

This was erected by Willm. MARTYN, ESQre. his
Heir and sole Executor in TESTIMONY of his
profound respect and gratitude Anno 1701

Above the inscription are emblazoned the arms of Steynings and Martyn.

Arg : a bat sable displayed.

Arg : two bars gules.

2. This is a very stately monument which bears the following inscription.

Near this place
is deposited the Body
of WILLIAM BLACKFORD
late of Holnicote in this parish
Esq.
and also ye Body of HENRIETTA
his wife
He was the eldest son and heir
of WILLIAM BLACKFORD
of the same place Esqre:
By ELIZABETH the daughter of
JOHN DYKE
of Pixton in the parish of Dulverton
in this county Esqre.
He died the 20th of March 1730
in the 37th year of his age.
She was one of the daughters
and coheirs of JOSEPH COLLET
late of Hertford Castle
in the county of Hertford Esqre:
and sometime President
of Fort St. George in East India.
She died the 13th day of September
1727 in the 23 year of her age.
HENRIETTA BLACKFORD
their only daughter and Heir
died the 6th day of December
1733
in the seventh year
of her age.

Arms: gules a chevron argent between three etoiles or; on an escutcheon of pretence sable a chevron argent between three horses argent passant, on chevron three orles sable. Crest: a negro's head.

The elder William Blackford was a Master in Chancery, who settled at Dunster, and bought the Holnicote estate of Charles Staynings's heir, William Martyn. On the death of the poor little girl-heiress, who, bereft of both her parents and left alone in the world, was but badly looked after, we expect, the estate passed to the Dyke family of Pixton, from whom it came through an heiress into the Acland family.

3. A marble monument carved by Chantrey, on which are sculptured two heads, and beneath them a sextant across a copy of Heber's hymns, bears the following inscription :—

CHARLES BALDWYN DYKE ACLAND,

Third son of Sir Thomas and Lady Acland, was born November 1st, 1812, entered the Naval Service in the fourteenth year of his age on Board of H.M.S. Helicon, under the command of his uncle, Captain Charles Acland. Like him, in the cause of humanity, fearlessly exposed his life to the deadly influence of African Fever: and so died, full of faith and hope and devout affection, May 10th, 1837, off the Bight of Benin, and was buried in the island of Ascension. This affliction was made known to his parents on the 17th day of July following, and on the 31st of the same month it pleased God to remove from the bosom of their family, in the tenth year of his age, their youngest child.

DUDLEY REGINALD DYKE ACLAND

a good little boy early ripened for heaven, by the mercy of Him who would have little children suffered to come unto Him "and He took them" and "Blessed them."

"The Lord gave, the Lord hath taken away, Blessed be the name of the Lord."

4. A companion monument by Chantrey representing a curtain drawn back, and showing, beneath,

the head of the officer to whose memory it was erected, has the following inscription :—

Charles Richard Dyke Acland
third son of Sir Thomas Dyke Acland, Bart.
died at the Cape of Good Hope April 23, 1828,
Commander of H.M.S. Helicon
in the thirty-fifth year of his age

The battle's rage o'erwhelmed thee not nor ocean's stormy wave
Though kindred tears may not bedew thy distant early grave
In Delagoa's fatal bay the fever's burning zone
To save the captive's life from bonds, thou freely gavest thine own.

Oh nurtured in this quiet vale in justice, mercy, truth,
How well thine after years redeemed the promise of thy youth!
With rectitude of purpose blest, faith simple and sincere,
The kindness of a manly heart, the strength of godly fear.

Son, brother, husband, best beloved, we mourn thee not unblest;
Dear is the hope that thou hast gained the haven of thy rest;
Their steadfast love who walk in faith nor death nor time destroy,
And they who sow to God in tears, shall surely reap in joy.

In the north aisle is a monument to three generations of the Stoate family.

There are no tombstones of great antiquity or of much interest in the churchyard. The yew tree on the eastern side of the church was planted by the late Sir T. D. Acland, on March 26th, 1860, being the ninetieth birthday of the rector, and the yew tree on the western side was also planted by the late baronet on March 29th of that same year, which was his own seventy-third birthday.

The Commissioners of second year king Edward VI,

report in their survey, "The lights and obits founded within the parish church of Selworthy, are yearly worth in lands, tenements, and other hereditaments in the tenure of sundry persons (as may appear particularly more at large by the rentall of the same), xiiij*s.*"[1]

These lands and possessions were as follows :—

"Land and possessions given as well to the use and maintenance of divers lamps and lights burning in the parish church there, as for the observance of an annual obit there.

"Annual rent from the revenues of certain land there, parcel of the possessions of the late dissolved house of St. John of Buckland, in the county of Somerset, as the price of vij lbs. of wax at the rate of v*d.* per lb. per ann.,—ij*s.* xj*d.*

"Money annually paid from the same land per ann. —iiij*d.*

". . . Brattons gent., renders annually from his land and tenements lying in Estlinche for a lb. of wax, per ann.,—v*d.*

"John Arundell, Kt., renders annually from the revenues of his land and tenements in Honycote, for half a lb. of wax,—ij½*d.*

". . . . . Hensley, gent., renders annually from the revenues of his land and tenement in Honycote, for half a lb. of wax,—ij½*d.*

". . . . Whyttyns, gent., renders annually from the revenues of his land and tenement called Atwill for wax, per ann.,—vj*d.*

". . . . Sydenham, gent., renders annually from his lands at Brosington (Bossington) for wax per ann.,—iij*d.*

1. *Somerset Chantries*, p. 40.

"Richard Horne holds an acre of arable land in Allerford, and renders per ann.,—xx*d.*

"Rent of a house and a virgate of land, with a little garden, per ann.,—iiij*s.* ij*d.*

". . . . Stevinges, gent., renders annually from the revenues of the manor of Honycote in ready money, per ann.,—ij*s.*

"The churchwardens of the parish church of Selworthie hold a house there commonly called the Churchhouse, and render per ann.,—xvj*d.*

"Total—xiiij*s.*

"Deduct in Rent resolute to John Arundell, Kt., for free rent of the house called the Churchhouse, per ann.,—j*d.*

"Rent resolute to . . . . Steyninge for free rent of the house containing a virgate of land with a little garden, per ann.,—j*d.*

"Total—ij*d.*

"And remain over per annum,—xiii*s.* x*d.*"[1]

The church house, which stood on the south side of the church, on the other side of the present road, had been purchased by the parish authorities in the reign of Edw. VI, together with a cottage and about half an acre of land at Allerford, from Edward Crosse of Nettlecombe. From the date of its purchase it was probably used as a refuge for the aged poor of the parish. It existed to within the memory of living people. "'Twas a fine girt house, sure enough, nigh as long as the church, and 'twas a mighty pity 'twas pulled down," is the description of it by an ancient inhabitant. It was divided at the time of its re-

1. *Somerset Chantries*, pp. 217, 218.

moval into four tenements, and we find that the average number of occupants was not generally more than four, although sometimes, no doubt, a whole family (and overcrowding of this kind was the blot on a system which was not only economical, but had many other advantages over our workhouse system) was at times crowded into one of these tenements.

The poor house and its occupants were under the management of the overseers. They put an officer in charge of the house who was responsible to them, and whose accounts were very carefully kept. The expenses of the house was met by a yearly rate. In 1740, William Slade was the "master" of the house, at a salary of £4 4*s.* per year. His bill for the cost of the house, *i.e.* maintaining its occupants, etc., for that year, was £35 19*s.* 5*d.* This outlay, however, does not appear to have included clothing. Besides the expenditure on the poor house, the overseers gave relief also to poor people not in the house, in occasional and also in fixed sums. Twenty people in 1740 received occasional relief; and a little later we find several people receiving a regular quarterly dole of five shillings. Besides the poor rate, the poor of the parish were entitled to a sum of fourteen shillings per year, the interest of a sum of money which has long since disappeared, and which was divided amongst them in such manner as the overseers thought fit.

Descending from the church to the rectory, we pass the fifteenth-century tithe barn, a somewhat handsome building. Against the road is a small window, now blocked up, having a label carried partly round it. The label at the point of the arch supports a sheaf of corn, and rests, on one side on a lamb, and on the other on a pig. These three carvings are said to be emblematical of the three principal forms of tithes. The late Lady Acland told the writer that she had seen the tithe corn put in through this window before the Tithe Commutation Act was passed. In the west gable end of this building there is a pretty window of local red stone of the same date as the building, and beneath it is a moulded oak one with heavy iron bars, of apparently about the same date. The rectory house is a picturesque building built in two sides of a square. Some parts of it are said to be of great antiquity, but it has been much altered. During recent repairs the remains of a narrow stone staircase were found in the wall of the south wing, which is nearly four feet thick.

Mr. D. Williams tells us that when he succeeded to the benefice of Selworthy in 1780, he found the buildings belonging to it in a very ruinous condition, and, alas, "the dilapidations had been assessed by Kingdon, 'a friend of Mr. Willis,' (the previous rector) and £82 paid down, but the money was not sufficient to pay half the damages." The west wing had to be pulled down nearly to the ground and re-roofed. A stone central wall four feet thick, running across the house for its whole height, seems to have been the cause of much difficulty, and "the only parlour belonging to the house" was made into a brewhouse. A square and high-walled court at this period shut in the back of the house, while an orchard, surrounded by a high hedge, lay in front of it. Mr. Williams pulled down this hedge, as "interrupting one's prospect." The meadows attached to the glebe were at this time drained, as well as "guttered and watered in the modern fashion," by which improvement it was hoped the rent would be "considerably advanced." Mr. Williams repaired the timbers of the chancel roof, and "tiled it anew from end to end, and whitewashed the chancel inside," for the apparently modest expenditure of £7. Mr. Williams records the planting of many firs and beeches about the house, and the sowing of acorns in the portion of the wood below the house, which, to the extent of some seven acres, then belonged to the rectory. This wood was included in an exchange of lands which took place between the last baronet and Mr. Stephenson.

CHAPTER V.

Rectors.

THE benefice of Selworthy, in the taxation ordered by pope Nicholas (1291), was valued at six marks and a half. In Exton's *Thesaurus* we find a payment from the church of All Saints at Selworthy of xl*s*. to the abbey of Athelney, and Dugdale in his account of the property of Athelney Abbey, has: "Selworthye, Penc̓ Rc̃orce 2 : 0 : 0."

It is probable that this payment represented a charge made upon the benefice in favour of the abbey of Athelney, by Richard de Luccombe, *circa* 1200. This payment was confiscated when the abbey was dissolved. Until recently it was paid annually to a family of the name of Tyrrwhitt, but within the last few months this ancient pension has been purchased by Sir Walter Orlando Corbet, bart.

Besides this payment to the abbey of Athelney, another payment of twenty shillings is yearly paid from the benefice of Selworthy to Eton College. This was originally a charge by Ralph de Limeseio (or Roger de Curcelle, who held Holnicote at the time of the Conquest) on the manor of Selworthy in favour of the priory of Stoke Courcy. The church of St. Andrew and much land in Stoke Courcy were presented to the abbey of Lolley by William de Falaise, (*temp.* Henry II) and a prior and some monks were sent thence to settle at Stoke Courcy, and continue the new priory as a cell to that foreign house. The priory was suppressed with other alien priories by Henry VI, and given to his newly founded college of Eton. This payment is now made to the Merchant Venturer's Company of Bristol.

Another payment of £1 4*s.* is made to the rector of Luccombe for "Boar Tithing." First fruits to the amount of £1 6*s.* are paid yearly to the Queen Anne's Bounty; and annates, procurations, etc., are yearly due to the archdeacon of Taunton.

The living is valued in the king's book at £12 15*s.* 4*d.* The *Valor Ecclesiasticus* has the following particulars concerning the benefice.

1535. Richard Denyse, rector.

Annual value of the demesne or glebe lands	£1	6	8
Tithes of wool and lamb	3	3	4
Predial tithes	8	0	0
Personal tithes and other casualties ...	3	15	0
	16	5	0

Out of which sum there is paid :—

To the abbot of Athelney	£2	0	0
Dean and Chapter of Eton	1	0	0
Archdeacon of Taunton	0	9	8
	3	9	8
Clear	12	15	4
Tenths	1	5	6½

In 13 Edward II, 1326, Hugh de Luccombe, then recently deceased, was found to have been possessed of the advowson of this church. By another inquisition, taken in 4 Richard II, 1380, Oliver de St. John and Elizabeth his wife were found to hold the advowson of the church of Selworthy as of the honour of Pinkney.[1]

We subjoin a list of rectors up to the present time, to which we are for the most part indebted to Rev. F. W. Weaver's *Somerset Incumbents.* A few vacancies have been filled up from other sources.

1310. JOH. DE ROGES. *(Drok. 32.)*

1317. THOM. LE DENEYS, on the resignation of J. de R. *(Drok. 152, 19.)*

1364. Sept. 10. JOHN HATCH, on the death of T. le D.; presented by Sir Oliver St. John. *(Islip's Reg.*, f. 42a.*)*

1402. Feb. 20. JOH. RUSSEL, on the death of J. H.; presented by Henr. Sentilon dom. de Esteluccombe. *(Bowet, 22.)*

1434. Feb. 24. THO. BARRY, LL.B., on the death of J. R.; presented by Ed. Seynt John. *(Staff.*, 106.*)*

1468. Aug. 4. THO. PAWLYN, on the death of T. B.; presented by Will. Saynt John, arm. *(Still.*, 14*)*.

1473. Nov. 10. THO. STEYNING, on the death of T. P.; presented by Alicia, relict Will. S. John, arm. *(Still.*, 42.*)*

1 *Hundred of Carhampton*, p. 186.

1485. Feb. 21. JOH. COLYNS, on the death of T. S.; presented by Joh. Fogg, mil., Custos Rob. Arundel, Trerice, filii Joh. Arundel, Trerice. (*Still.*, 131.)

1492. Oct. 27. RAD. HENKES, on the death of J. C.; presented by Joh. Arundel, Trerice, arm. (*Fox*, 5.)

1503. Dec. 29. THO. SMYTH, on the death of R. H.; presented by Joh. Arundel, Trerice, arm. (*Vac. King*, 2.)

1535. SIR RICHARD DENYSE (*Valor Eccles.*)

1540. SIR HENRY PUGGSLEY.[1]

1544. SIR WILLIAM MORLE.[1]

1549. SIR WILLIAM NICHOLS.[1]

1560. SIR ROBERT COOPE.[2]

1570. Jan. 3. WILL. FLEETE, on the death of R. C.; presented by Elisab. Regina. (*Bark.*, 31.)

1617. Feb. 25. HEN. BYAM, on the death of W. F.; presented by Joh. Byam, rector de Clatworthy, a.c. per Joh. Arundel de Trerice in com. Cornubiæ. (*Lake*, 5.)

1669. July 23. JOH. WOOD, on the death of H. B.; presented by Geo. Hayman et Tho. Fugar. (*Peirs*, 130.)

1. These three names were given to the writer some years ago by a late eminent antiquary, but unfortunately without his authorities for his statement. They must be therefore received with some doubt. Puggsley appears to have been curate of Porlock in 1538.

2. Sir R. Coope is mentioned in contemporary wills as being Curate of Selworthy.

1687. Oct. 25. SOLOMON COOK, S.T.B., on the death of J. W.; presented by Joh. Arundel. (*Ken*, 6.)

1692. June 16. JOH. GAYLARD, A.M., on the death of S. C.; presented by Joh. dom. Arundel de Trerice. (*Kidder*, 2.)

1724. June 15. RIC. PERCIVALL, LL.B., on the death of J. G.; presented by Joh. dom. Arundel de Trerice. (*Hooper*, 50.)

1725. Feb. 4. WILL. WILLIS, on the resignation of R. P.; presented by Joh. dom. Arundel de Trerice. (*Hooper*, 56.)

1730. NATHANIEL BLAKE BRICE, on the death of W. W.; presented by Joh. dom. Arundel de Trerice.

1780. Oct. 28. DAVID WILLIAMS, on the resignation of N. B. B.; presented by the representatives of Joh. dom. Arundel de Trerice.

1802. JOSHUA STEPHENSON, M.A., on the death of D. W.; presented by Sir T. D. Acland, bart.

1864. T. MULLER, on the death of J. S.; presented by Sir T. D. Acland, bart.

1874. A. G. GILMORE, M.A., on the resignation of T. M.; presented by Sir T. D. Acland, bart.

1884. F. HANCOCK, M.A., S.C.L., on the death of A. G. G.; presented by Sir. T. D. Acland, bart.

The first of the rectors mentioned on our list was a member of the ancient family of Roges of Porlock, of whom a full account is given in prebendary Hook's recently published history of the church of St. Dubricius at Porlock.[1] We find that John Roges, who was perhaps a brother of the Simon Roges who, in 1306, held the town and advowson of Porlock, was instituted to Selworthy in 1310. In the bishop's Register he is described as John de Roges, and as holding the two sister benefices of Selworthy and Luccombe; for in the next year, 1311, John Roges was presented to the benefice of Luccombe by John de Luccombe. To this benefice Jo. de Wamberge had already been inducted in the March of that year by the archdeacon of Taunton, on the presentation of Lady Joan de Luccombe,[2] and a contest as to the patronage ensued between the two rival patrons. It ended in the bishop commending the benefice to Roges, who swore to indemnify the bishop both in the king's court and that of Arches. Roges held the benefice of Selworthy until 1317.

In connection with the family of Roges, we find that the bishop "at Whetecumbe juxta Frome," admitted George Roges acol. to the rectory of Porlock, patron Henry Roges filius, in 1310.[3] In 1311, one year for study is granted to the rector of Porlock at the request of Robert Fitzpaine.[4] In the case of very young rectors, these licences to study away from their cures were very common. Fitzpaine was probably some relation of G. Roges, as in 1318 we find this same Roges rector of Staple Fitzpaine on the presentation of Robert Fitzpaine. Roges appears to have exchanged benefices with William de Wengrave, who

1. *A History of the Ancient Church of Porlock.* Rev. W. Hook, M.A.
2. *Drokensford Register*, p. 1.
3. *Ib.* p. 36.
4. *Ib.* p. 47.

had been instituted rector of Staple in 1310. This Wengrave was presented to Witheridge (Devon) by R. Fitzpaine in 1317.[1] In 1318 the bishop's Register notes a dark shadow on the life of G. Roges. But it is sufficient to say that he confessed his sin, bound himself over in the sum of £10 to abstain from bad company in future, and was at his own request fined the sum of five marks.

The family of Roges must always have been of importance, for in 1188 the Lady Alicia de Roges gave the church of Winsford to bishop Reginald for St. Andrew's Church at Wells, and in 1410 we find Christiana Roges sub-prioress of Canonsleigh Priory, near Wellington. "Holcombe Rogus no doubt takes its name from this family. The name is said to have been corrupted into Rogers, but this, however, is not probable, as the hard 'g' in Roges would not become soft."[2]

John Hatche, who was inducted to the benefice of Selworthy on Sept. 10, 1364, was in all probability a member of the family of Hacche, then flourishing at Aller, near South Molton.

The institution of Thomas Steyning, on the presentation of Alicia, widow of William Saynt John A.M., on the 10 Nov., 1473, possibly shows that the Steyning family, with whom the fortunes of the parish were so long connected, were already settled at that period in the parish. A question seems to have arisen at this time about the payments to the abbey of Athelney

1. *Drokensford Register*, p. 126.
2. *Canonsleigh Priory.* F. T. Elworthy.

and the priory of Stoke Courcy before-mentioned, and the patronage of the benefice.[1]

Alicia Saynt John claimed the patronage of the benefices of Selworthy and East Luccombe, which were held together in demesne, "ut de feod. stalliato," and John Fogg, mil., who was acting on Alicia's behalf, seems to have been successful in establishing that lady's right.

On the death of John Colyng, Ralph Henkes was presented by John Arundel, and was instituted (by proxy of John Glover) at Wells, and inducted by the archdeacon of Taunton, Oct., 1492.[2]

For a hundred years the rectors of Selworthy seemed to have pursued very quietly the even tenour of their ways, leaving no mark behind them. The list gives no hint of any sudden changes, and we wonder how they passed through the stormy times of the Reformation. With William Fleete, instituted on Jan., 1570 on the presentation of the crown, we are on firmer ground. From his brass, still in the chancel of Selworthy Church, the inscription on which is recorded in Chapter IV, we learn that he was educated at Winchester and New College, and that he lived at Selworthy forty-eight years. In his time the chalice still used in Selworthy Church was purchased from John Legh, a noted silversmith of the period at Exeter.

William Fleete was a friend, possibly a school friend, of the famous bishop Montgomery, whose history is

1. "Processus inquisicionis factæ de et super jure ecclesiæ parochialis de Selworthy." Bishop Fox's Register, p. 18.

2. Bishop Fox's Register, p. 20.

treated fully in Chapter VIII. We shall see how the vicar of Chedzoy, as he was then, ran Fleete's mare for him one winter, and how Mr. Montgomery sent the rector of Selworthy a medicine to cure the "melancholy" from which he suffered. The quick-witted statesman, even then in the rush and turmoil of the political life of the day, sympathised, perhaps, with Mr. Fleete's somewhat dull life amidst the lonely coombes of West Somerset, somewhat as Aratus mourned for the poet-schoolmaster Diotimus.

"I mourn for Diotimus who sits among the rocks
Beating their A B C into infant Gargantuan blocks."

And yet Mr. Fleete was not entirely without neighbours. At Porlock, sturdy Robert Brocke, who held as tightly to his benefice during those troubled times as the vicar of Bray did to his, had been obliged at length to give way to Thomas Washington, A.M. At Luccombe was canon John Bridgwater, a notable man in his time, who was succeeded in 1573 by Will. Maskall; and after Maskall quickly followed Laurence Byam, the father of Henry Byam the most famous ecclesiastic our valley has produced.

At Holnicote worthy old Philip Steyning, the vigorous head of a vigorous family, was living in the old manor house, the gateway of which alone remains. He had married a daughter of William Frye, of Membury, near Axminster, a man of large possessions and ancient family, whose picturesque old home has only of recent years been burnt down. No doubt there was much coming and going between the two houses at Membury and Holnicote, and Mr. Fry would have had much to tell of the great Devonshire men so much at that time to the fore. Perhaps he would have brought with him a few of the curious tubers which Hawkins or Raleigh had brought from South America, for trial in the valley, and thus first introduced potatoes amongst us; or we can picture him relating some of the wonders he had seen on board the ship of his neighbour, Drake, when in 1580 that high admiral returned from circumnavigating the world; or narrating how great a favourite at court Sir Walter Raleigh had become; or holding his audience spell-bound as he told of the doughty deeds of Martin Frobisher.

Henry Byam, the son of Laurence Byam, who succeeded Mr. Fleete, was born at Luccombe in 1580. In 1597 he entered at Exeter College, and two years afterwards obtained a studentship at Christ Church. He was a brilliant scholar, and soon became a famous preacher. In 1612 he took the degree of B.D., and in 1614 he succeeded his father as rector of Luccombe on the presentation of Edward Byam, advocatione concessâ pro hac vice per Joh. Arundel, A.M. He married a daughter of William Fleete, whose benefice he added to his own by the presentation of his brother Joh. Byam, rector de Clatworthy, a.c. per Joh. Arundel de Tresise (Trerice), on the death of Mr. Fleete in 1617. Henry Byam must have been sixty-two years of age when the great rebellion broke out, but he at once became a marked man on account of his strong royalist opinions.

The prominence of Byam probably helped to bring the storm upon our valley, which at so early a date in the civil war broke over it. We can imagine how he urged Mr. Steyning at Holnicote to be true to the king, and both in the pulpit and out of the pulpit exhorted the yeomen and labourers of Selworthy and Luccombe to do likewise. He not only bore the principal part in raising a regiment of cavalry on the king's behalf, but his five sons were all officers in the royal army. On the outbreak of the civil war, "hunc seditiosi cum rebellare cœpissent, comprehenderunt, atque in publicam custodiam incluserunt," he was at once seized by the parliamentarian party, thrown into prison, and his property confiscated. The name of "Henry Byam, clerk," appears amongst the list of Somersetshire men who compounded for their estates. The sum he paid to the Sequestrators as composition was £49 4*s.* 8*d.*

Byam appears soon after his seizure to have found means to escape and to join prince Charles at Oxford, where he was made a doctor of divinity. He accompanied that prince in his flight from England, and was with him in the island of Scilly and then of Jersey, and he remained at Jersey until that island was reduced by the parliamentarian forces. Hearing of his safe escape from the country, his wife and daughter gathered together all the property they could, and endeavoured to escape from the persecutions of their Puritan guards, and join him. They reached the sea-board safely, but their boat went down in a great storm which caught them in mid-channel, and Mrs. Byam and her daughter with their maidservant, were drowned.

Hamnet Ward, prebendary of Wells, the editor of Byam's sermons, speaks of him as "the most acute and eminent preacher of his time." His sermons are certainly very racily written, and full of curious learning. Of those extant, "most of them were preached before his majesty king Charles II in his exile," in the "island of Jersey," at "St. Hiliar," and elsewhere. They are full of the political thought of the day, and of unsparing denunciations of the ruling power in England. Here is a sketch of the predominant parties of the time, in which Byam compares Charles II to Josiah crowned after the death of Amon :—

"Where be those of his people we would have him brought unto (to crown him)? Shall the Presbyterians be the men? 'Twere strange they should. They that brought the first fewel to that prodigious fire: they that swore against him, fought against him, betrayed, sold their Innocent Master; they that disavowed that cement, by which the church of Christ hath been firmly knit together ever since there was a Church Apostolick upon the earth: I mean the Episcopacy. The Independents can be none of them. They have cut themselves off from all Communion with the Holy Catholic Church by their professed factious fractions and independencies. They cut off that Sacred Head, and, *quantum in ipsis*, all future hopes, that Root and Branches should ever bud forth and sprout again. Both these have sold themselves to work wickedness. And though their heads look several ways, like Samson's foxes, yet each carries fire in his tail to burn the Church and Commonwealth. Both Anti-Monarchical and the kingdom's bane: both can agree together to divest the Lion of Judah from his innate and just authority. To give these men the capital Right Hand of fellowship, to joyn with either of these, were to partake of their Sins, and render ourselves guilty of that Sacred Blood their hands have spilt. Where are those people that our Judah must be brought unto? What? to Complyers and Compounders, whose moneys have fermented these wars, and their examples have encouraged the rout of Rebels in their wickedness! I fear these are some of Gomer's Children in the first of Hosea. Sure in that glorious martyr's phrase if not imbude yet are they besprinkled with Royal Bloud. Oh poor Compounders! I pity their case. God give them grace to relent, repent, and make their composition with God too. But truly they are in sad condition! Laodiceans, nor hot nor cold; vespertilios or Bats, nor mice nor birds; Populus and no Populus: I am sure not Populus suus; never cut out to be Martyrs for religion, not truly loyal to their Sovereign."

And in his sermon on "The Danger of Ignorance," Byam breaks out:—

"'Prodidistis, Abnegastis, Trucidastis,' betraying, denying, killing the Lord's Anointed; more traitorous than Judas, than Peter; more killers than Pilate, and all under the Cloak and vizard of Religion. A Cloak and a short one, 'tis not *ad tales*, none of those *στόλαι* the Scribes did wear, or if it be, a cloven foot will be seen under it, and too much of the Devil will appear. The Cloak is Religion, but such a Cloak, such a religion as is pernicious and destructive to Church and Monarchy. All ornaments, Donatives, all Anathemata, all consecrated things . . . these all have the pretenders to this new reformed, refined religion seized upon . . . Episcopacy, the constant practice of all Christian Churches from the Apostles down to these very dayes: yet do our Hesterni cry down this for Anti-Christian; and suppressing one Pope at Rome, they labour to erect a world of Popes in every place. Sure, if we would look upon the end of many of our Incendiaries and bloody Traitors slain, shot, hanged, or otherwise cut off, we might see with what fears and terrors of conscience they took their part in it. Their Souls were required of them as 'twas said of his, in *Luke* xii. God knows much against their wills."

It appears to argue much for the clemency of Cromwell and his party after the Commonwealth government was established upon a sound basis, that Dr. Byam appears to have been allowed to be at large at Luccombe and Selworthy once more. We find him preaching the funeral sermon of Colonel Deyer, of Brushford, in 1654; and an eloquent discourse on "Baptism" in 1656, "upon Thursday the 19th day of March, at the Christening of T. L., son and heir to Fra. Luttrell of Dunster Castle, Esquire." The mother of this child was a co-heiress of John Tregonwell, and married, secondly, Sir Jacob Bancks. She lies buried in the Bancks aisle of Milton Abbey Church, in Dorsetshire.

A sermon of some interest is one entitled "A Return from Argier.—A sermon preached at Minehead in the county of Somerset, the 16th of March, 1627, at the re-admission of a Relapsed into our Church." The poor creature, who appears to have been taken prisoner by the Turks and compelled to profess the Mahommedan religion, and then to have escaped and returned to Minehead, seems to have had to endure this long discourse standing in the church of St. Michael, clad in the Turkish costume in which he had escaped. The preacher addresses him directly in one part of his sermon :—

"You whom God suffered to fall, and yet of His infinite mercy vouchsafed graciously to bring home, not only to your country and kindred, but to the profession of your first faith and to the Church and Sacraments again: let me say to you (but in a better hour) as sometime Joshua to Achan: 'Give glory to God, sing praises to Him who hath delivered your soul from the nethermost hell.' When I think upon your Turkish attire, that embleme of apostacy and witness of your wofull fall, I do remember Adam and his figleave breeches:

they could neither conceal his shame, nor cover his nakedness. I do think upon David clad in Saul's armour. How could you hope in this unsanctified habit to attain Heaven ? "

Dr. Byam would seem to have been hard upon the poor Minehead lad, who probably had to embrace the creed of Islam or die ; and we are glad to see that the preacher protected him against the witticisms of the young Minehead of the day.

" Let not what is said or done encourage any of you to rejoyce in your neighbour's fall nor triumph in his misery."

Dr. Byam denounces the "unspeakable Turk" in the strongest language, and declares him " with the learned Zanchius and many others" to be "the Antichrist of prophecy," for

" he reigneth in that seven-hilled city of Constantinople, and sitteth in the very Temple of God. Hierusalem is his, and a great part of the World runs after him." He is "the very scourge and plague of Christendom and Hammer of the world, who shares his lies with the Devil. The one seek the body, the other the Soul. Oh might I live to see the time when our Roberts', Godfries', Baldwin's would set foot in stirrop again, and might I be one of the meanest Trumpetors in such an holy expedition."

Here is a passage from his sermon on colonel Deyer, who "died early of consumption" :—

" We have a consumption as he ; his was *patens* ours *latens*, and the more dangerous ; his *in januis* ours *in insidiis* : his was open, our's in secret, and yet not so secret but every man may run and read the Character of *Declining* writ on our foreheads, and every limb can tell there's something works within it to our end ; and every day can tell another we are worse than when he found us."

His editor has preserved for us the Latin address which the rector of Luccombe delivered in St. Mary's, Oxford, on his taking his degree in 1612, and also a Latin sermon, entitled "Osculum Pacis," preached at a visitation of Dr. Jos. Hall, bishop of Exeter, of which cathedral Byam was a canon. Mr. Ward includes in the volume his own funeral sermon on Dr. Byam, which is entitled "The Testimony given to the Reverend Dr. Henry Byam at his Burial in the Parish Church of Luckham in the County of Somerset." In the quaint euphemistic language of the day, Ward tells us that the dead man's life was:

"like a garden of spices replenisht with all the graces and vertues that can adorn a Christian, 'whence' you may gather yourselves such Posies of spiritual flowers as may serve to perfume all your Actions as long as you live. During the time of the late unhappy rebellion what could he do? how could he suffer more than he did? at his own charge (as far as he was able) raising both men and horse for the King, engaging his five sons (all that he had) in that just quarrel; exposing all his estate to rapine and plunder, his children to distress and danger, and himself to many grevious shifts and exigencies, hunted up and down by his and the King's enemies as a Partridge upon the mountains, forced to fly and hide himself in by-places and corners of the Country; and at last at that great age to cross the Seas for the safety of his life. And all this he did only that he may keep a good conscience not out of any base or greedy desire of reward: for after his Majestie's Return, when he might easily have obtained what he would have askt, he contented himself with what His Majesty was pleased freely to bestow upon him; but had not his own modesty stood in the way, 'tis well known his Majestie's bounty towards him had not rested here, but he must have died a Bishop."

Charles, in fact, neglected him after the Restoration,

as he did so many of those who had suffered most for him.

Mr. Ward thus sketches Byam's character for us:—

"Come here now from the Court into the Country, where we shall find him as much in the affections of the people as in favour with His Prince (respected by the nobility and gentry, honoured by the Commonalty, reverenced by the Clergy, and generally beloved by all). And good reason there was, for besides his excellent, good, sweet and obliging nature and disposition, which drew to him the affections of all that had the happiness to converse with him, his free, hearty entertainments and constant bounteous hospitality challenged a respect from all, *semper aliquis in Cydonis domo* may truly be applied to him: for his house was Bethlehem, a house of Bread, where the rich were sure to find divertisement and the poor relief. Yet was he far from a wasteful prodigality as from a bare penuriousness. His Bounty allayed with that *Vetus Parsimonia* so much heretofore esteemed and still exercised by all wise and sober persons: after he had taken enough for himself, his friends and his poor neighbours, he carefully laid up the remainder wherewith he hath made a competency for his Family, which being so honestly gotten, and so honourably saved, will doubtless carry God's blessing along with it as it had his."

Part of Dr. Byam's estate was a considerable amount of land in Luccombe, Stoke Pero, and Porlock, probably purchased by him. A portion of this property passed to his daughter, Mrs. Wood, whose husband succeeded Dr. Byam in the two livings of Selworthy and Luccombe, and, until quite recent years, their descendants possessed property in Luccombe.

"Nor was his Religion towards God less than his Loyalty to his Prince, or his charity to his neighbour; it lay not so much in the tongue as in the heart. He was a true Nathaniel in whom there was no guile; and have you heard of the patience of Job? why such was his. I can compare it to no other. God was pleased to afflict them much alike: Job was cast out of his own house, so was he; Job was plundered of his cattle by the Sabeans, and so was he of all that he had, worse than the Sabeans, if possible, by the rebellious Sequestrators; Job lost his children, so did he, only in this his misery was not so great, Job's children were taken away rioting in a Banqueting House, but his died honourably in the service of their Prince; Job was afflicted in his wife too, and so was he, but in a quite contrary manner, Job in having the worst of wives, he in losing the best. But the manner of his losing her could not but add much to his sorrow, for she was snacht out of the world in a tempest and swallowed up quick by the merciless waves, having all the remainder of the treasure he had about her to a very considerable value; and a far greater treasure in her arms than that, even his young and darling daughter, who chose rather to embrace Death than leave the embraces of her tender mother, and so both sunk together, with a maid-servant that attended her, into the depth of the sea. There are some, I think, at this time present, who were then with her, who remain the monuments of God's mercy in their deliverance, and faithful witnesses of the truth of what I speak."

It seems strange that Mrs. Byam and her child and her maid should alone have been drowned, whilst the rest of the ship's company escaped without hurt.

Dr. Byam had reached the ripe age of eighty-nine years, when he passed to his rest in the long old white rectory house at Luccombe, which a few old folk still remember, beneath the shadow of the tower of the ancient church which he had loved so well and served so faithfully. The quaint old house must have had many a tale to tell of those stormy times: of the sudden surprise when the house was surrounded by noisy Parliamentarians sent to drag its master to prison; of Mrs. Byam getting quietly together such goods as she could and slipping off with child and maid, alas! to her death; of the pompous sequestrators seizing and sealing up all the property of Dr. Byam that they could find; of the desecration of the church by the dragoons of Waller; of a long sad time when the parish was without anyone to visit their sick or bury their dead, and good Mr. Turberville, J.P., of Gauldon in the parish of Tolland, married such poor souls as sought his unsanctified assistance!

A handsome monument exists to Byam in Luccombe Church. Until the recent alterations it stood above the vestry door now removed. It bears the following coat:—Arg. three boars' heads erased vert., and the following inscription from the pen of prebendary Ward:

"Non procul hinc sub marmore congenito, sepultum jacet corpus Henrici Byam ex antiquissimâ Byamorum familiâ oriendi: Sacro sanctæ theologiæ doctoris insignissimi hujus ecclesiæ et proximæ Selworthianæ rectoris, pastorisque vigilantissimi: ecclesiæ cathedralis Exoniensis canonici, ecclesiæque Wellensis prebendarii serenissimæ Majestatis Caroli secundi regis Capellani et concionatoris ordinarii, necnon ejusdem (sæviente illâ tyrannide, et semper execrandâ fanaticorum rebellione) terrâ marique comitis exulisque simul. Ex meliore luto ejus constructum corpus post annos tandem, octoginta et novem anno salutis millesimo sexcentesimo sexagesimo nono morti non triumphanti quam invitanti placide cessit. Sed extat adhuc viri hujus optime celebrius multo hoc et ornatius ornamentum, non marmore perituro, sed typis exaratum perpetuis scripta: scilicet ejus plane divina: ubi animi vires, et summum ejus ingenii acumen; intueberis simul et miraberis. Lugubrem hunc lapidem honoris et reverentiæ indicem posuit filius ejus obsequentissimus Franciscus Byam: Instauratum a Mariâ et Cecilia Wood, Anno Dom. 1713. Instauratum iterum a.d. 1862 ob honoris et Reverentiæ causâ a quibusdam ejusdem nominis et perantiquæ familiæ oriundis scilicet a fratre defuncti Edwardo de Litter et Castle Lyons in Hiberniâ Rectore Ecclesiæ Cathedralis Clonensis Cantore et Prebendario de Lismore. Hic Edwardus Byam sepultus erat apud Castle Lyons A.D. 1639."

The family of Byam is of Welsh extraction, and claims royal descent. Laurence Byam may very possibly have been a son of Thomas Byam, who was expelled from his prebendal stall at St. Paul's on the accession of Mary. Laurence Byam married in 1578 a daughter of Henry Ewens, of Capton in the parish of Stogumber, by whom he had the three sons above mentioned: (1) Henry, (2) John, rector of Clatworthy, and a great sufferer in the civil wars; and (3) the above-named Edward. And three daughters, from one of whom (Mary) the Pierce family, late of Bratton Court, are descended. Henry Byam, by his marriage with Susan, daughter and co-heiress of Wm. Fleete, in 1615, had issue five sons and four daughters, viz.: (1) William, (2) Henry, (3) Francis, (4) John, (5) Laurence, (6) Mary, (7) Susan, (8) Cecily, and (9) the young child drowned with her mother on their flight from Luccombe.

Dr. Byam's will is dated the 30th of April, 1669, and was proved in the prerogative court of Canterbury. He names his sons William and Francis his executors, and to them he bequeaths various lands lying in Luccombe, Porlock, and Stoke Pero. Francis, the third son, proved his father's will, and erected the monument above-mentioned to his memory.

"Henry the second son was slain in the king's service at sea; and John the fourth son in the same service in Ireland. No account remains to us of Laurence, the fifth son. Susan Byam, the second daughter, married William Dyke of Kings-Brompton, whose estates descended ultimately to the Acland family."[1]

Cecily Byam, the third daughter, married the Rev. John Wood, her father's curate, who succeeded him in the two benefices of Luccombe and Selworthy. Five sons were the issue of this marriage. (1) John, (2) Henry, (3) Charles, (4) Laurence, (5) Byam; and two daughters, Mary and Cecilia, who are mentioned as having restored their grandfather's monument in 1713. A Byam Wood, a man of considerable property, was living at Luccombe in 1741, in which year he had a son baptised. He left his property to his widow, who in turn bequeathed it to a maidservant, Mary Gillman.[2] Some members of the family seem to have lived at Minehead, where, indeed, Wood is still not an uncommon name. A curious entry in the Selworthy Registers tells us that in 1761, George Wood was buried the 24th day of May, Jenny Maria Wood the 31st of May, Betsy Wood the 2nd of August, James Wood the 13th December, all of Minehead. The whole family seem to have been destroyed by some mysterious ailment.

In 1692 John Gaylard was presented to the benefice by John, lord Arundel of Trerise, and in 1714 to the benefice of Winsford by John Balderston. It is curious that this John Gaylard should be described as William Gaylard on the cover of the second book of

1. *Hundred of Carhampton*, p. 176. 2. *Ib.* p. 177.

Registers (*see* Chapter VI). His son, John Gaylard, obtained a fellowship at Emanuel College, Cambridge. In 1728 he left Cambridge to become master of the Cathedral School at Wells, and in 1733 he was made headmaster of Sherborne School.

John Gaylard, senior, held the living of Selworthy for thirty-three years, and died in March, 1723; and on the 17th March in the following year his wife Susanna followed him to the grave.

Richard Percivall, or Perceval, who succeeded to the benefice on the death of John Gaylard, must have been a member of the very ancient family of that name who held the manor of Eastbury in Carhampton from very early times, and with it the advowson of Exford. The patronage of this living seems to have been in their hands from a date prior to 1318 to the time of the Commonwealth, and in 1318 we find a certain Richard Perceval presented to the benefice by his mother Domina Johanna Perceval.

Of William Willis, Nathaniel Blake Brice, and David Williams, little is known beyond the fact, recorded in Chapter VI, that Mr. Brice was "curate" of Selworthy from the year 1730 to the year 1775, and that he died at his "paternal living of Aisholt in 1790, May 31st, after being curate of Selworthy forty-five years, and resident on his living fifteen years more. He departed this life in the eighty-third year of his age, after a lingering illness of three months." "He was a stout man of a warm temperament; soon angry and soon pacified," is the testimony to him of his successor, David Williams.

David Williams died in 1802, and was succeeded

by one who is still held in affectionate remembrance by many of the elder inhabitants of the parish, the Rev. Joshua Stephenson. Mr. Stephenson had been Sir Thomas Acland's tutor at Oxford, and was by him appointed to the living. Still old folk in the parish love to tell of the kindly old rector surrounded by groups of children competing for the sweets and threepenny pieces, of which they knew his pockets were never empty. It is recorded of him that, rain or shine, he always carried an umbrella of portentous size. When asked why this article was his unfailing companion, he confessed that his dread of cows was unconquerable, and that if, when walking alone, he met any of these dangerous creatures, he opened his umbrella and retired behind the shelter thus afforded until the peril was overpassed. Mr. Stephenson held the living of Selworthy for sixty-one years, and died unmarried at the great age of ninety-two.

The author of *A Tour in Quest of Genealogy*, in describing his visit to Holnicote in 1809, draws this pleasing picture of Mr. Stephenson:

"And last, though not least in the estimation of such as would relish benevolence without parade, and piety without cant and austerity, we had likewise a clergyman of our party, the rector of the parish, a scholar, a gentleman, and a Christian, a rare union, but the benefit of which, owing to his meekness, his modesty and retired habits, is not as widely diffused as it could be wished . . . . . The worthy rector of Selworthy is unwearied in the discharge of his pastoral duties." And again, "we passed a few truly Attic hours in his parsonage house, that most happily unites elegance and comfort, giving by a discussion of a variety of interesting subjects, zest to our wine."

CHAPTER VI.

Selworthy Registers.

THE history of genealogical records can be traced back to the earliest times. The Patriarchs interested themselves in writing them down, perhaps on those tablets of terra cotta, specimens of which still exist, by means of which the ordinary business of life was transacted in Abram's time with the greatest exactness and decorum. The Egyptians were devoted to exact statistical knowledge; and the idea of an enrolment and registration of the people of Israel was no new one to Moses, when God bade him take the sum of the children of Israel at Sinai, a numbering which was repeated some six months later, when the people were enrolled under the three distinct heads of (1) tribe, (2) family, and (3) their father's house. The laws of Greece and of Rome, too, provided for the careful registration of births.

But with the falling to pieces of the splendid organisation of the Roman Empire, the system of registration disappeared, and throughout the Middle Ages no records of this kind were kept, except by the religious houses of the benefactors whose obits they were bound

to observe. It was to that powerful ecclesiastic, cardinal Ximenes, archbishop of Toledo, that we owe the present system of registration. The law of the church which disapproved of marriage between those spiritually related, was at that time the cause of much scandal, owing to the ease by which divorces could by its help be obtained. The law took its rise from a regulation laid down by Justinian, that no man might marry a woman to whom he had stood godfather. This regulation was extended by the council of Trullo to the mother of the baptised infant, and rapidly grew to an extravagant pitch. It was only necessary to prove some degree of spiritual relationship, and release from the marriage bond at once followed. The archbishop, in order that these scandals might be put an end to, in 1497 ordered the registration of births through his diocese, and also decreed that the names of the sponsors should be set down at the same time.

Mr. Chester Master, in his interesting book on Parish Registers, tells us that the last divorce for spiritual affinity in England was enforced in our own neighbourhood. Thomas Luttrell, a cadet of the Luttrells of Dunster Castle, had in the reign of Edward V been contracted to Margaret Hadley, the infant heiress of Withycombe Hadley, notwithstanding that she was the goddaughter of T. Luttrell's mother, Mrs. Margaret Luttrell. In the eye of the church this made the young people spiritually related to each other as brother and sister, and therefore canonically incapable of marriage. A sentence of divorce and excommunication was decreed against them. Pope Paul IV was appealed to for a dispensation, and by his command the Grand Penitentiary the cardinal of St. Angelo, released the unhappy pair from their sentence in 1558, on the understanding that they should be re-married. The marriage, however, did not take place until the Roman Catholic Bishop of Bath and Wells had been deposed from his see for refusing to take the oath of supremacy to Elizabeth, when the proceedings at Rome appear to have been quietly ignored, and the two young people were married at East Quantoxhead on August 7th, 1560.

From Spain the system of registration crossed into England. Thomas Cromwell, the astute minister of Henry VIII, had had opportunities during a residence abroad of observing its usefulness, and in 1538 he obtained Henry's permission to establish registration in England. At once a storm of indignation arose, as the scheme was looked upon as an excuse for the imposition of fresh taxes. Our own West Country forefathers were particularly opposed to it, and it was made one of the grievances which in April, 1559, lit up the flames of a civil war which spread from the Land's End to Honiton, and cost Courtenay, marquis of Exeter, and the old countess of Salisbury their heads. Cardinal Pole ordered the addition of the names of sponsors, an order which is still legal.

It took thirteen years for the advantage of the system to be fully realised, but in 1597 the Convocation of the clergy of the province of Canterbury passed a resolution declaring the great importance of registers.

The seventieth canon provides that "in every parish church and chapel within this realm a parchment book

N

shall be provided wherein shall be written the day and year of every christening, wedding, and burial which have been in the parish since the time the law was first made in that behalf." This book was to be kept in a "sure coffer" with three locks and keys, one for the rector, and one for each churchwarden, and the register was not to be taken out except in the presence all three of these officials. On every Sunday the book was to be written up and then returned to its coffer. And within a month of Lady-day a transcript of the entries for the year was to be transmitted to the bishop. Of what priceless value would these transcripts be if they had been properly taken care of and arranged!

Each parish priest had on institution to sign a declaration that he would keep the registers carefully, and the system worked smoothly till the civil wars disorganised the church and country. During that troubled time some parish registers were not kept at all, or but in the most irregular fashion. "1643 bellum, 1644 bellum, 1646 bellum. Interruption, Persecution," is the compendious entry which in one parish register stands in place of three whole years' record.

Cromwell did what he could to restore order. He appointed lay officers called "Registers," who kept the books carefully as far as they could, but they could not often get the people to come and pay the fee which they were entitled to charge for each entry; and on the return of the clergy these books in many cases were carried off by the "Registers," and in more than one instance destroyed by the clergy themselves. One of these fates perhaps befell the Selworthy register for the Commonwealth period.

Registers differ very much in interest and value. In some fortunate parishes these records are found going back to the very year in which they were first ordered to be commenced by Cromwell; in others only the records of comparatively recent times are to be seen. Very frequently no doubt at the end of the Civil War the victorious Parliamentarians made as short shrift with the parish papers as they did with all that was beautiful and easily destroyed in many parish churches. It was a sad time for the nation at large! Even libraries did not escape the contempt which those in power held for all culture and refinement, for the precious contents of the Bodleian at Oxford were shipped out of the country, and its shelves sold for firewood.

Registers, too, differ much in condition: some have always been well preserved, and gladden the eye of the antiquary by their perfection: others are found torn, dirty, dog's-eared, and clipped—sad testimonies to generations of careless custodians. These records sometimes contain much interesting matter beyond their priceless material for parochial history in the entries required by law. In a parish known to the writer, where the present incumbent is the ninth of his name who has held the living, the volume which contains the registers for some 200 years appears to have been used as a kind of family note-book. Inscriptions in Hebrew, Greek and Latin verses, pious aspirations, and notes on local matters are thickly sprinkled over its vellum pages. "House robbed last night, self and servant bound," observes one old gentleman laconically, about the beginning of the eighteenth century; another worthy relates the ceremonial of the laying of the foundation stone of a new rectory-house by his youngest son; another the number and height of the trees he had planted around his churchyard; while yet another considers the previously unheard-of failure of the rectory well, a fact worthy of record in the parish books.

The carelessness with which until late years these priceless books have been kept is inconceivable. The early registers, for instance, of an important parish in a neighbouring county were lately found by an antiquarian archdeacon in the deed chest of another parish. We hear of registers turning up for sale in booksellers' shops (as in the case of the Cwm registers, which were recently advertised for sale in a bookseller's catalogue), and of their being swept out from the church with the litter from a heap of refuse. "Will it be believed that, according to a catalogue of the effects of a Sir Peter Thompson, who died in 1815, 'The parish registers of St. Mary, Woolchurch Haw, were sold for £2 12s. 6d.' (about the same price as that at which those of Cwm were valued the other day); that at the end of the last century, the rector and churchwardens of a place in Kent, one day after dinner committed the registers up to date to the flames; that at another place the registers were sold at a bazaar; and that those of Christchurch, Hants, were cut up for kettle-holders by the curate's wife? This shameful list might, we conceive, be extended very considerably. So lightly in times past have records been held, which are now recognised as stores of valuable data for the genealogist, for the statistician, for the student of the life of the people."[1]

1. *Church Times*, January 24, 1890.

And in some parishes these interesting records are still mouldering away unheeded in damp iron chests, and thus memorials and materials for local history, which cannot be replaced, are gradually disappearing.

Hands not always of the tenderest or most careful kind have made some havoc with the registers of the parish of Selworthy. The registers are contained in ten books, the oldest of which is sadly mutilated. With the exception of a recently discovered fragment belonging to the Elizabethan period, the registers begin only with the year 1672. Where are the earlier ones? The books containing these must, we fear, have been destroyed during the troubled thirty years preceding this date, when the parish generally seems to have suffered much at the hands of the Puritans. At that time, no doubt, the painted windows of the church were dashed out, the delicate paintings, traces of which are still to be seen on the walls of that portion of the fine old church which formed the lady chapel, plastered over with whitewash, the stone altars cast out, and the very capitals of the pillars defaced.

Possibly, from some unexplored recess, or in the depths of some bookseller's shop, the lost volume may yet come to light; but this seems hardly probable. The first volume of registers still possesses its original vellum covers, but they are very soiled and torn. On the outside of the covers are many calculations of different dates, and the following note: "W. Galard became Rector of Selworthy June the 6th, 1692; Rector there 31 years. William Galard was buried the 10th day of March, 1723." The book is entitled

"The Register Bookk of Selworthy, 1673," and under the written title come the signatures of:

JOHN WOOD, *Rector.*
THO. BORASTON, *Curate.*
GEO. HENSLY, } *Churchwardens.*
WILL. WITHICOMBE, }

The earliest existing baptismal register of Selworthy has been somewhat carelessly kept in days gone by. The first entry as to position, is that of the baptism of one Mary Taylor, in 1712, but at the bottom of the page follow the records of the baptisms of John and William Knight, in 1668 and 1672 respectively, and on the following page come entries concerning the Coffin and Siderfin family, dated as early as 1653. The rest of the second page is filled by the following entry, which is worth transcribing:

"Whereas Charles Staynings Esq., of Holnicote, in the parish of Selworthy, did give unto the poor of the parish of Selworthy by his will nuncupative, who died in the year of our Lord 1652, twenty pounds, whereunto his son Charles Staynings of Holnicote in the parish and County aforesaid hath in the yeer 1660 April the tenth given ten pounds more, which said thirty pounds with the full interest hath been and is fully satisfied from time to time to the day of the date hereof to the severall officers Churchwardens and Overseers of the poor of the parish of Selworthy for the time being, And now the said principall summe of thirty pounds is received by us the Churchwardens and Overseers of the poor for the use of the parish aforesaid the nineteenth day of January in the yeer of our Lord above said. In witness whereof wee the

Churchwardens and Overseers of the parish of Selworthy have set our hands the day above said.

Witness—

JOHN WOOD, *Rector.* THOMAS TRILL, } *Church-*
ELIAS HALSEY. JOHN HAYWARD, } *wardens.*
THOS: BONASTON.

The mark X of GEO. HENSLEY.
The mark X of WILLIAM WITHICOMB,
Overseers."

No trace of this bequest now exists.

The baptismal register in the first book ends with the year 1721.

During this period the register is perfect. There is nothing particular to note in it save the occurrence of names still with us, or familiar to us, showing the antiquity of many of the Selworthy family names.

The name of one ancient Selworthy family, that of Coffin, occurs frequently. One of the family, in 1663, subscribed seven shillings and six pence to a Benevolence to Charles II. This family lived at Allerford, and seem to have held some position in the parish. They were probably a branch of the old Devonshire house of Coffin of Portledge.

The second book of registers of the parish of Selworthy is a vellum folio of the same size as the first volume—viz., about fifteen inches by ten, and is in fairly good preservation, except that the margins have been cut for re-binding. On the cover is written: "A Register Book for the Parish of Selworthy, 1720.

JOHN GALARD, *Rector.*

JOHN BEAGUE, } *Church-*
ROBT. BRYANT, } *wardens.*"

The following notes also find a place on it: "William Stoat, married to Mary Snow, ye 16th of July, 1721." "Memo[nd]—John Dyke Acland, Esqre., born Jan. 21, 1747." "Bryce, curate of Selworthy, 1733." On the paper fly-leaves within the cover are the following notes: "Miss Henrietta Blackford was buried 11th of Jan., 1733, by Thos. Blackwell, Rect[r] of S. Clement's Danes, London." This lady was the last of the ancient family of Blackford, owners at one time of Holnicote. Below is another note: "Mem.—Thomas Dyke, son of S[r] Thomas Dyke Acland and Dame Elizabeth, his wife, was born Fryday, ye tenth of April, in Holnicot House, five minutes after one o'clock in ye afternoon, and was privately baptised ye eighteenth of the same month by Nath. Brice, curate of Selworthy, xxx., in ye year of our Lord one thousand seven hundred and fifty-two." This, with the note on the cover, is the first entry in the registers concerning the Acland family. On the opposite page is written: "Memo.—Lady Dyke Acland, died ye 33th June, 1753," and below: "Thomas Knyton, bapt. ye 21st June, 1753." On the next page are the following entries: "D. Williams, curate of Selworthy, 1775," and below: "Nathaniel Blake Brice, curate of Selworthy from the year 1730 till the year 1775, died at his paternal living of Aisholt in 1790, May 31, after being curate of Selworthy 45 years, and resident on his living 15 years more. He departed this life in the 83rd year of his age after a lingering illness of 3 months. He was a stout man, of a warm temperament, soon angry, and soon pacified. William Slade, Mr. Brice's clerk at Selworthy for about 40 years, died on Whit Sunday, the 30th June, 1790, in the 80th year of his life. William Slade was a strong hail man, and continued in the employment of a gardener to Sir Thomas Acland until he died. The curate and the clerk, after having lived many years together at Selworthy, at last finished their respective courses within a month of each other."

There is little of importance to notice in the baptismal entries in this second volume of registers, save the way in which many names still familiar to us run back generation after generation, as is indeed also recorded on the tombstones in our churchyard. The entry quoted above relating to the birth of Thomas Dyke, son of Sir Thomas Dyke Acland and Dame Elizabeth, his wife, shows that that family were then beginning to reside regularly at Holnicote.

The third register book of the parish of Selworthy is a long paper book, bound in vellum, $16\frac{1}{2}$ inches long by $6\frac{1}{2}$ inches wide, well written and well kept. On the inside of the cover are numerous entries. Among them is the following: "N.B.—An exact copy of the Register is to be taken for every year ending the 25 March, to be presented at the Archdeacon's Visitation; it must be written word for word on Parchment, and that on one side only." Then come records of some baptisms omitted in previous years. Then "The Revd David Williams, buried Sept. 8, 1802, 22 years Rector of this Parish, succeeded by the Revd Joshua Stephenson, M.A., late of S. John's Coll., Cambridge. Inducted Decr 11, 1802." Then follows in Mr. Stephenson's handwriting, under date May 26, 1813, "A List of the Registers extant at Selworthy prior to those of 1813:

"No. 1. Contains *Baptisms* from April 25, 1672, to July 2, 1721. *Marriages* from May 5, 1673, to March 20, 1721. *Burials* from April 4, 1673, to February 11, 1721.

No. 2. *Baptisms* from August 19, 1721, to December 28, 1777. *Marriages* from April 11, 1721, to February 7, 1754. *Burials* from March 26, 1721, to July 13, 1777.

No. 3. *Baptisms* from February 2, 1778, to December 20, 1812. *Burials* from April 4, 1778, to November 29, 1812.

No. 4. *Marriages* from October 2, 1775, to December 25, 1812."

When Mr. Stephenson made this list he was evidently unaware of the small and mutilated fragment on paper of the Elizabethan register.

At the end of this third volume are the following curious entries: "Sir Thomas Dyke Acland went to London the 4th of May, 1794; was taken ill in the way thither, and on the 17th day of the same month ab[t] 6 o'clock in the evening died; he was brought down to Broadclist to be buried in the vault of his family.

Hic finis fatorum Priami hic exitus illum
Sorte tulit!——Vale. Vale. Vale.
Nec meridies nec Aurora unquam vident ejus ora.
Reliquit nobis cornu, canes, tandem quiescant ejus manes."

"Sir Thomas Acland married Harriet, only daughter of Sir Rich[d.] Hoare, Bart. He left behind four children and his amiable widow . . . . . Sir Thomas came to the estate and title on the death of his nephew, and he enjoyed it about 9 years."

The names mentioned in the register are for the most part still familiar to us; but some names, such as Taylor and Elsworthy (the same name, we presume, as that of the founder of the Ellsworth Timberscombe Charity), which seem at one time to have been prominent here, have disappeared. In 1801, June 21, occurs the baptism of Arabella, daughter of Peter Hoare, Esq., and in 1812 the register closes in consequence of the Act of that year for "The better regulating and preserving Parish and other Registers of Births, Baptisms, Marriages, and Burials in England." This Act provides (1) for the keeping of registers by the officiating minister; (2) the provision of the necessary books by the parish; (3) for the keeping of the registers in separate books; (4) it also orders the register books to be kept by officiating ministers in an iron chest provided by the parish; and (5) declares false entries, false copies of entries, the altering or destruction of a register to be a felony punishable by transportation for fourteen years, etc., etc. The succeeding (and fifth) register measures 10 inches by 15½ inches, and is in good condition. The first entry is dated the 1st of January, 1813, and the last July 19, 1857.

The marriage registers of Selworthy at present existing, like the baptismal registers, do not commence until after the Restoration. Perhaps those bold dragoons of Cromwell's who, when quartered upon Holnicote and the parish at large, did not allow peaceable men, as the Squire Stayning of the day so pathetically laments, even "to eat hay with their horses," used them for wadding for their muskets! It would almost appear that they may have done so, to judge from the mutilated portion of the Elizabethan burial register which has recently been discovered. But at all events the earliest marriage at Selworthy of which we have any public record took place on the 5th of May, 1673. It is that of one Edward Williams with Christian Burges; and in the same year were married John Dunscomb and Mary Watts, and James Blanchflower, of Weindon (is this Whydon?), and Allice Farrole. In the following year we find again the old familiar Selworthy names of Taylor, Beague, Giles, Withycombe, Spurrier, etc. Under the year 1677 we have the note—"Thomas Long had a son baptised ye 30th May, 1735"; and under the year 1691—"Mem: John Galard became Rector of the psh. of Selworthy ye 6 June, 1692." Under the year 1694, amidst many flourishes, it is announced—"Be it remembered y[t] John Thorn came into * * * * [some words obliterated] and became the psh. Clarke of Selworthy on Christmas Day in the year of our Lord 1694." We notice some curious surnames, such as Quirk, Question, Gelliben, Leany, etc., and some Christian names which sound strange to us now, as Welmoth, Johan, etc. The first book of the marriage registers closes with the marriage of William Taylor and Dinah Court, 20th, May 1720.

After 1754 the marriages are contained in separate books. The first book is arranged according to a form ordered by Parliament, in an Act which came into operation on March 25, 1754. It is a handsome parchment volume, rather more than 13 inches long by 8½ inches wide, and is in perfect condition. The banns of marriage are entered in it; and then follow the attested entries of the marriages themselves. The register commences with the marriage of John Thorn and Betty Goodgroom, which was solemnised on February 3, 1755, by the rector, Nathaniel Brice. By this time the contracting parties had to witness the entry of their marriage, but it is curious to note how very few could sign their names. It would not be too much to say that seventy-five per cent. could only affix their mark. Some entries are curious—*e.g.* the marriage of John How, "Sojourner," who, in 1761, while but a visitor in the parish, won away from the local swains, the heart of fair Miriam Gooding! In 1770, we get the entry of the marriage of John Coffin (who signs his name in clerkly fashion), and Betty Devonshire, by one John Anthony, minister. After 1770 the entries are more frequently signed by the happy pair. Education in Selworthy had at length evidently made a start! The last entry—the marriage of Thomas Long and Ann Vicary—is dated May 6, 1775, in which year the rector, in whose writing are all the rest of the entries in this book, Nathaniel Brice, retired to Aisholt, and was succeeded by the Rev. David Williams.

The next book of the marriage registers is an equally handsome volume, measuring 10 inches by 14½ inches. It is well bound, and on the cover is a red label, on which is printed in gold letters: "James White and Robert Siderfin. Churchwardens." The register opens with the marriage of Robert Leigh, of the parish of Dulverton, and Elizabeth Hyett, of Selworthy; and the entries are discontinued in 1812, when a new form for the registers was put out by the Government. The first marriages were solemnised by the aforesaid D. Williams,[1] who signs himself in the old manner, "Curate" of Selworthy, "minister," "pastor there," etc. His record of the alliance of Henry Hawkins and Joan Giles, on April 3, 1802, is very infirm, and the marriage of Simon Berry, on April 3, 1803, was conducted by the Rev. Joshua Stephenson, who held the benefice for sixty-one years.

According to the list of the late Rev. J. Stephenson before alluded to, the burial registers begin in the same year as the baptismal and marriage records. He could never, as stated above, have seen the earlier one, lately discovered. It is unfortunately on paper, and in a sadly torn and decayed condition. These pages begin with the year 1571, and above the first entry is the following note: "Willyms ffleete intravit in possessionem Selworthiæ." An account of William Fleete is given in Chapter V. The first burial entry in this register is that of George Nicoll, the 4th Januarye, 1571, and next comes that of Julyan, daughter of Walter Baker. In Februarye, John Horne and Joan, the wife of John Cole, were buried; in Marche, ... Sporier, Thomas the son of William Rodden, and George Upham. The entries for the rest of this year are almost entirely obliterated, save the name of Doms Philip Staning in September. In 1572 occur such names as Uppingford, Rawle (frequently), Stote, Crode, Kent. In 1573 was buried a son of Henrye Blackford; in April one Coffin (Christian name gone) was buried. These names linger for the most part still among us, and we

1. D. Williams for several years held the curacy of Porlock with the rectory of Selworthy.

notice that the Staynings of Holnicote, the Blackfords, ancestors probably of the Blackford family who bought the Holnicote estate at the beginning of the 18th century, and the Coffins of Allerford, were at that time settled in this parish.

The entries for the rest of the year (1573) are very imperfect, but we find such familiar names as Crod, Briant, and Webber. The latter is described as of Withill—where is Withill? The entries in 1574 are few, and call for no particular mention. In June, 1575, one Christin (Christian) Kent buried his son John and his daughter Elizabeth, within a week of each other. In 1576 the name Kitnor occurs for the first time (a name, by the way, of British origin, and the same as Culbone), and the name of John Huish, described as of Porlock, seems to bring us back straightway into the 19th century. And so these few pages continue to give the record of names for the most part very familiar still to us—such as Horne, Rawle, Sporier, etc., until they close in November, 1579. The registers for the period between the years 1579 and 1673, as previously stated have disappeared. But in 1673 the burial registers recommence with the burial of Philip Hodges, and are quite perfect from that year up to the present date. William ffleete was succeeded in this benefice by Henry Byam, who held the living of Luccombe in conjunction with that of Selworthy. (*See* Chap. V.) He died June 16, 1669, and within six days, viz., on June 22, his successor, the Rev. John Wood, was instituted to the benefice of Luccombe, and on July 23 of the same year to the sister benefice of Selworthy. The worthy patrons,

Tho. Henly, Will Scott et Alex. Blackford, gen., seem to have lost but little time in filling up the benefices. These gentlemen were probably acting as guardians of John, second Lord Arundel, who was at that time a minor.

On March 23, 1674, Richard Blackford was buried. On February 5, 1682, Mrs. Ann Staynings. 1684, November 3, Mary Blackford. The year 1685 seems to have been a disastrous one amongst the Selworthy aristocracy, as on April 21, Mr. Charles Blackford was buried, and on May 21, Mrs. Susanna Staynings of Holnicote. On November 8, 1693, Mrs. Johan Steynings was buried, and on February 8, Walter, ye son of Walter Coffin. 1695, September 5, "Mrs. Christian Blackford of this parrish was buried." On January 9, 1696, Mr. Lewis Staynings, a brother of Charles Staynings, the last squire of Holnicote of that name. Lewis lived at Selworthy, as did a sister, Grace Oram, whose husband was a clergyman. Charles in his will provides for Lewis, by giving him a charge upon his Selworthy estate, and a life interest in his Over Stowey property, and also "the house he now lives in, called the West House, being part of my Mansion House in the p̃ish of Sellworthy." Lewis, however, pre-deceased his brother.

In 1701 we have the entry "Mr. Charles Staynings was buried ye 12th of December." He was the last of the ancient family whose name he bore, and which had resided at Holnicote from so long a period. The south aisle of the church, with its beautiful roof, was built by this family; and the interesting fifteenth century gateway at Holnicote was the entrance to their

Manor House. Mr. Staynings bequeathed his Holnicote property to his wife's nephew, Mr. Martin, of Oxton, in Devonshire. Mr. Martin resided for some time at Holnicote, but ultimately sold the estate to the Blackford family. In 1710 comes the entry, "Mrs. Mary Coffin, widow, was buried the 5th of September." Near the end of this first book of burial registers, we find an entry of the marriage of "Robert Gribbell and Cisillia Dinnis," and the book closes with the burial of Henry Widlake ye 29 of November. On the following blank page the Incumbent has written his name: "N. Brice, Curate" (*i.e.* Incumbent) "of Selworthy, 1732," and underneath, in another hand, his successor has added, "Left the cure March, 1775, and lives now at Aisholt, his native parish. March, 1777. D. Williams succeeded Mr. Brice in the cure March 25, 1775."

The burials in the second register book, according to Mr. Stephenson's list, begin with the burial of Sarah Batt, March 26. On March 10, 1723, was buried John Galard, rector. This gentleman had been presented to the benefice by John, first baron Arundel of Trerise, on the death of Mr. Solomon Cook, S.T.B. He was instituted on June 16, 1692, so that at his death he had held the living for thirty-three years. On June 23 of the next year, 1724, his widow, Susanna Galard, followed him to the grave. On March 31, 1725, Mr. Walter Coffin was buried, and on March 17, Mary Coffin, perhaps his wife. On Sept. 5, 1728, William Blackford, Esq., was buried, and on Nov. 12 another Mary Coffin. On April 6, 1731, William Blackford, Esq., son of the above William Blackford, was buried. Nov. 25, 1743, Richard Gould was buried, "died in ye snow on Porlock hills" says the register. In 1743, May 26, was buried Alice Clark; April 2, 1745, Abraham Clarke, and on July 4 of the same year, John Clarke, and on Sept. 21, Joseph Clark. Feb. 22, 1746, Mary Martyn was buried, probably a member of the Martyn family to whom Mr. Charles Steyning had bequeathed the Holnicote estate, and who at this date were residing there. August 18, 1748, was buried Mary Brice, the five-year-old daughter of the Rev. Nathaniel Blake Brice who was instituted to the benefice in 1730 and held it until 1775. From the year 1754 we find the ages of the subjects of the various entries occasionally added. The first entry to which this addition is made, is the entry of the burial of William Clarke ye 28th of March, 1754, aged 84. On ye 2nd Aug. was buried Robert Gribble, aged 94. On the 24th Aug., Joan Coffin, aged 93; on the 13th July, Joan Giles, aged 77; and on the 22nd Dec., Mary Ridler, aged 74. So folk lived as long at Selworthy one hundred and thirty years ago as they do now, notwithstanding the increased wisdom of the nineteenth century. In 1761 we find George Wood buried the 24th of May, Jenny Maria Wood buried the 31st May, Betty Wood the 2nd of August, James Wood the 13th Dec.—all of Minehead—a whole family killed off by some fatal ailment. Was the plague in Minehead as late as the year of grace 1761? These Woods were doubtless descendants of the John Wood who was rector of Selworthy, 1669—1687. On the 9th July, 1762, was buried Mary Moggridge. There are several entries in the registers concerning this family, who for a long period were landowners at Exford, and one of whom held at the same time the livings of Minehead and Porlock. They were an old Molland family, and had intermarried with the family of Courtenay of Molland, a branch of the Powderham family.[1] On the 13th Feb., 1768, was buried Mr. Benjamin Coffin. On the 20th March, 1770, Mr. Nathaniel Brice was buried, the youngest son of the rector, and on the 5th June, John Williams (gent.). The register closes with the burial of Joan Door (spinster), July 13, 1777.

There are but few entries of burials in the register book numbered 3 in Mr. Stephenson's list. They begin with the entry of the interment of Samuel Kent, April 4, 1778. April 25, Christian Greenslade, of Blackford, was buried. October 19, 1779, Mr. William Kent was buried. The prefix of "Mr." (about which our forefathers were very particular) marks him as a yeoman of position, probably a landowner. November 10, John Prescott "a farmer, aged 32," was buried. August 5, 1781, William Hole, "who died of the smallpox." On September 10, Joseph Cheek, "Sexton." In 1783, only two burials are recorded—a healthy year! In 1784, we have—January 20, Joan, Wife of Constance Sage. January 21, Anne, daughter of Constance Sage. January 28, Constance Sage (the husband and father). February 4, John Giles "a poor farmer." Then comes a member of a very ancient Somersetshire family—March 6, Anne the wife of Mr. Sydenham, (Minehead). July 11, Robert Slade, carpenter. September 4, Mrs. Grace Escott, a mem-

1. Vivian's *Visitations of Devon.*

ber of the family of Escott, of Escott, in Carhampton parish, now represented by the Rev. W. S. Escott of Hartrow Manor. January 13, Mr. Thomas Sydenham was interred beside his wife. Under the date May 6, 1787, is recorded the tragic end of Thomas Kent, "killed by a lime rock, which fell upon him unawares." May 8, Mrs. Mary Greenslade, of Blackford. December 29, Mr. Thomas White, "a farmer." March 16, 1788, was buried Betty Wood, widow, aged 88; and on October 4 of the same year, John Dunscombe "a famous huntsman in his time to Sir Thomas Acland." October 13, 1789, was interred Mrs. Alice Beague. The entries for the year 1791 close with the burial of Thomas Rue—the rector takes the trouble to note that he was "a young man." Evidently it was held a wondrous thing one hundred years ago, before we had telegrams and the penny post to bother us, that anyone should die young in healthy Selworthy! August 28, 1792, Mr. John Coffin, of Allerford, was buried. On December 29, William Slade a "poor labourer." In 1794, under May 29, is the entry "was buried, Sir Thomas Dyke Acland, at Broadclyst." On September 20, John Prichard, "basket maker," 78. January 1, 1797, Betty Davis "an ancient woman." The year 1800 begins with the burial of John, son of John and Sarah Gale (an infant). On May 17, Mr. Philip Tayler, 69, "a very good man." But on September 20, lest the Selworthy folk, we suppose, should rejoice too much in their virtue, we have the counter-balancing entry—Thomas H * * * *, "a worthless tailor"![1] On

1. "Worthless,' however, in this district sometimes bears the meaning of "penniless."

December 29, Betty Joyce, "a poor lame woman," was laid to rest; and on December 6, John Cooksley "a poor man," aged 49. And on September 8, the discursive, choleric, but warm-hearted rector, in whose bold hand-writing the previous entries are written, was laid himself in the quiet God's Acre above his house, after having held the benefice twenty-two years, and aged 72.

On May 28, 1790, William Slade, clerk of Selworthy parish upwards of fifty years, and upon the verge of eighty years of age, was buried after one day's illness (*sic*)—"a paralytic stroke on the brain, according to Mr. Roberts." "He was a strong, hail man, and followed the employment of gardiner to the day of his death. He lived at Holnicote in various capacities more than sixty years, and was an useful member of society throughout life. Nec meridies nec aurora unquam vident ejus ora."

On May 25, 1790, died Mr. John Beague, of Skilgate, in the seventy-fifth year of his age. Mr. Beague was buried at Dulverton on June 4, and was much lamented by all his friends and acquaintance throughout the land. "He was a native of Selworthy, and descended of an ancient family (as appears by the parish registers). As he was the last of his family there, the name is totally lost. I knew him well for five-and-twenty years. He was a fast friend, a chearful companion, very attentive to business, a good husband. a good father, and a very useful member of society. This is an abstract of his character, sketched out by D. Williams."

"Mr. John Coffin, of Allerford, died August 23, 1792,

in the 64th year of his age. He went off suddenly. The cause of his death is supposed to have been a kind of suffocation, or perhaps an apoplectic fit, for he went to bed as well as usually, very cool and sober; but next morning, about four o'clock, he was found speechless, and continued so till near eight, when he expired. He was a very honest, good-natured man, and did much good to the poor people of Allerford, as well as to others in his neighbourhood. He was buried at Selworthy in the family cave in the churchyard, the 28th of the same month, and is probably the last of his name who will be deposited there, as his only brother lives in Wales, and will probably be buried there in the grave of his father and mother. I shall lament him long, and always retain a mellancholy remembrance of him The day of his departure I will annually recollect with grief and sorrow of heart—quem semper honoratum, semper acerbum . . . habebo."

For the following careful transcript of the fragmentary Elizabethan register, the writer is indebted to Sir Wollaston Franks, of the British Museum.

Anno dni 1571.

Januarye.

Januarii die 24 Willm ffleete intravit in possessionem de Selworthy.

George Nicoll was buried ye iiijth Daye.

Julyan ye Daughter of Waltr. Baker was buryed ye xvth Daye.

Februarye.

John Horne was buried ye iiijth Daye.

Sr Richard Picke was buried ye vth Daye.

J(oa)n ye wife of John Cole was buried ye xxth Daye.

Marche.

. . . . . . Sporier was buried ye xxiijrd Daye.

(Tho)mas ye son of William Stodden was buried ye xxvijth Daye.

. . . . . of George Upham was buried ye xxxth Daye.

Aprill.

. . . . was buried ye xviijth Daye.

. . . .

. . . . . of Henry Rawle was buried ye vijth Daye.

. . . . buried the xvjth Daye.

September.

. . . . was buried ye xvijth Daye.

October.

. . . . . ell was buried ye viijth Daye.

. . . . . (H)arte was buried ye xijth Daye.

. . . . was buried ye xxviijth Daye.

. . . . . Peter Rawle was buried ye same Daye.

(No)vember.

. . . . was buried ye xth Daye.

. . . . . tr was buried ye xixth Daye.

(Dec)ember.

. . . . . . r of Mr. Phillip Staining was . . . . Daye.

Anno Dni 1572.

Januarye.

Thamsyn Uppington was buried ye xxviiijth Daye.

Februarye.

Marian ye wife of Thomas Rawle was buried ye viijth Daye.

Elizabeth ye wife of Willm Stote was buried ye xxijnd Daye.

Marche.

Samuell ye son of Robert Ewde was buried ye xxjst Daye.

Aprille.

Roger Langwell was buried ye xvjth Daye.

Maye.

Elizabethe ye wife of Walter Kent of T(ivington) was buried ye xxvijth Daye.

June.

John ye son of Henry Rawle was bu . . . .
Peter ye son of Waltr. Baker . . . .
Willm ye son of John Richards . . . .

July.

Michaell ye son of George Phillip was . . . .

Auguste.

Anne ye wife of John Rawle iunior was b . . . . . .
Peter ye son of George Uphome was . . . . . .
John ye son of Thomas Stere was bur . . . . . .

September.

Alice ye daughtr. of Robert Poore . . . .

October.

Joan ye daughtr. of George U(phome) . . . .
Richard Ewde was buried . . . . . .

December.

Joan the wife of Willm Tapscot was bur. the second Daye.
Cisley Coppe vid. was buried the xxth Daye.
Cisley Baker vid. was buried the xxviith Daye.
Lewis the son of John Rawle senior was buried the xxixth Daye.

Anno dni 1575.

June.

John ye son of Christian Kent vid. was bur. ye . . . . . . Daye.

Elizabethe ye daughtr. of Christian Kent was buried ye xiijth Daye.

Julye.

Marye ye daughtr. of Edward Quirke was . . . . . . ye ixth Daye.

Michaell ye son of Thomas Thorne was bu . . . . . .

Thomas Haine was buried ye xxvijth . . .

Auguste.

John ye son of Hughe Terell was buried . . . . . .

October.

Alice ye wife of John Homond was buried . . . . . .

Anno dni 1576.

Marche.

John Briant was buried ye vijth . . .

John ye son of William Horne was . . . .

Maye.

Richard Sporier was buri . . . .

June.

Phillip ye son of Edward Ewd . . . .

Auguste.

John Cole was buried ye . . . .

December.

Sidwell ye Daughtr. of John Kitner was buried ye xiijth Daye.

Anno dni 1577.

Marche.

Christin ye wife of Walter Baker was buried ye xxiijrd Daye.

John ye son of John Harisse of Porlock was buried ye xxvijth Daye.

Aprille.

Agnes ye wife of Peter Sporier was buried ye xxijnd Daye.

Maye.

. . . son of William Horne was buried ye xxth Daye.

June.

. . . . . e son of Waltr. Trotte was buried ye xvth Daye.

. . . . ye son of Edward Rowland was buried . . . th Daye.

. . . . . . ye Daughtr. of George Uphome was buried ye xxvijth Daye.

July.

. . . . (w)ife of John Wescot was buried ye . . . Daye.

. . . (Timber)scomb had ij children buried ye . . . Daye.

Auguste.

. . . . was buried ye vjth Daye.

. . . (d)aughtr. of Robert Rawle . . . ye xijth Daye

. . . . Willm Horne was buried . . . . Daye.

September.

Thomas Thorne was buried ye viijth Daye.

Anno dni 1578.

Maye.

Robert Rawle was buried ye xvth Daye.

July.

John ye son of John Kitner was buried ye xiiijth Daye.

September.

William Tapscot was buried ye xijth Daye.

October.

John ye son of Peter Rawle was buried ye xiijth . . .

Anno dni 1579.

June.

Susana ye Daughtr. of John Tayl . . . buried ye xiiijth Daye.

John Richard was buried ye xxijnd Daye.

Julye.

George ye son of Michaell Lewis was . . . .

Marian ffoster was buried ye xxixth . . . .

Grace ye daughtr. of Elizabeth . . . .

. . . . woman was buried ye xxijth . . .

September.

Grace ye wife of Thomas R . . . . ye third Daye.

November.

Edward ye son of John H . . . . ye xvth Daye.

The church chest is very ancient. It appears to have been hollowed out of a trunk of elm, and is banded with a multitude of iron bands. It is secured by the three locks prescribed by the law mentioned above, but the chest is evidently of an earlier date than its locks. It does not appear to have been opened until recently, for many years. On its being opened, a quantity of ancient papers relating to the parish, some of much interest, appeared to view, and in one corner was found the portion only, alas! and that in the last stage of decay, of the Elizabethan register inserted above. The chest also contains a number of deeds concerning property at Allerford, at one time belonging to the Church.

CHAPTER VII.

Parish Accounts.

THE churchwardens' accounts for the parish of Selworthy are contained in two folio volumes. The earlier of these volumes, a paper folio, 13in. by 9in., which is in a very dilapidated condition, only dates back to the year 1739; but recently the following fragment of an earlier book, containing the parish accounts for the year 1603, has been discovered.

Selworthy. ann. dom̃i. 1603.

The account of John Kittner and Edmund Pill the yonger for this year past wardens In maner and forme as foloweth. 1603.

Recets.

Impmes Receved of the olde wardens . . x*s.* viij*d.*

Item Receved of the sydde men at sundry times vj*li.* j*s.* vj*d.*

Item Receved of Gregory tayler his Rentte . . v*s.*

the some of our Recets . . . vj*li.* xvij*s.* ij*d.*

Payments.

Impmes payd for bearinge of accoppy of the Regester to Wells . . . . vj*d.*

It. payd for the marchelsy and Kinges [Bench] in may . . . . vijs. j*d.*

It. payd for our charges at the Visitation at donster . . . . xvj*d.*

payd for layne in [laying in] of our byll and for our boock . . . . xxij*d.*

It. payd to the glasers for worcke about the church . . . . xj*s.*

Itm. payd for the killing of a foxe . . . . . . xij*d.*

It. payd to Robert backer and george uphom for mending the church yeard walles . . . . vij*d.*

It. payd for six bushels of lime for the church . xxj*d.*

It. payd for iiij hundred of stonnes the sam time . iij*s.*

It. payd for carridg of the stones to thomas glas viij*d.*

It. payd for half a hundred of laftes . . . . . . vj*d.*

It. for halfe a peack of tyll pennes . . . . vj*d.*

It. payd for a thousande of laft nayles . . . . xx*d.*

It. payd to the Kings binch and marcheselsy in June . . . . vij*s.* j*d.*

It. payd for foure days worcke upon the church to the heller . . . . vj*s.* ij*d.*

It. payd to george backer for worcking aboute the church tow times . . . . iij*d.*

It. payd to John pore for a frame for the bear ij*s.* vj*d.*

It. payd to bridg watter at the Dismesion . . xviij*d.*

It. for our charges the same time . . . . . ij*s.* viij*d.*

It payd to the plomer for tow years for his dener and beade . . . . viij*s.* vj*d.*

It. payd at the visitation at Doster for our charges for making of our byll and deleuering of our byll . . . . ij*s.* ijd.

It. payd to the Kings binche and merchshelsy in octtober . . . . vij*s.* j*d.*
It. payd to george backer for tendinge the plomer iij*d.*
It. payd the xv of January to the Kings binch and mershalsy . . . . vij*s.* j*d.*

3*li.* 16*s.* 8*d.*

It. payd for three sackes of lyme . . . . . iij*s.* vj*d.*
Itm. payd to the healer for vij days and half at xx*d.* the day . . . . xij*s.* vj*d.*
for a hundred of laftes . . . . xiiij*d.*
It. payd for nayles for the laftes . . . . . . xvj*d.*
for a pecke of tyll pennes . . . . xij*d.*
It. payd for iij hundred and xx stonnes . . ij*s.* vij*d.*
It. payd to thomas glas for the carige of the stones . . . . xvj*d.*
It. payd for breade and winne for the communion for the hoil year . . . . xxviij*s.* iij*d.*
It. payd fo the parsh hous Rent . . . . j*d.*
It. payd for washing the church clothes . . . . vj*d.*
It. payd for the Cleaning of the church yeard . . ij*d.*
It. payd for kepinge of the Regester . . . . . xijd.
It. payd for keyinge of the bellss, and for oyll . xviij*d.*
It. payd for making of this byll . . . . ij*d.*
It. payd to Rychard Stoden for Recevng up of above for the p'he ues [parish use] the last yeare . . . . xviij*d.*

the some of Payments is . . vj*li.* xiij*s.* iij*d.*
Remayning in our hands . . . . . iij*s.* xj*d.*

Receved of the collection for the city of Geneva vij*s.* x*d.*

It. payd for v monethes . . . . . ii*s.* vj*d.*

It. payd for the caring to tanton . . vj*d.*
It. payd for a quetenc . . . . j*d.*
Payd iij*s.* j*d.*
Remayning iiij*s.* ix*d.*

Waywardens John Rychards the yonger Witti Tapscot.
George Sporyers Rent unpayd . . xij*d.*
Pts. *6li.* 11*s.* 9*d.*

Two bills paid by the overseers in 1736 for repairs to the Church House exist. They are the accounts of two tradesmen of Selworthy, Lewis Vicary and William Stenner. We see from these bills that planking ready for use was worth 2*d.* and 1*d.* per foot; the wages of a master workman are put at 1*s.* 2*d.* and 1*s.* 6*d.* respectively, and those of the assistants (in each case a son of the contractor) at 1*s.* per day. A window "lead" cost 1*s.*

Here is a list of some of the Ratepayers in Selworthy at this period, and of their payments:—

Allerforde.

	s.	d.
Samuel Stoate .	2	0
Peter Spurryer .	3	0
John Stutford . .	0	9
Wm. Stoate . .	2	0
Joan Hayward .	1	0
Wm. Slade. . .	0	6
Robt. Beague . .	2	6
John Beague . .	2	0
John Beague . .	0	8
Edwd. Tayler . .	0	8
Benj. Coffin (late Jones) . . .	0	4
George Hensley .	2	0
Benj. Coffin . .	3	2
Alice Amott . .	0	8
Late Robert Luckis	0	4
£1	2	8

Branding Street.

Thomas Greenslade	2	8
John Stoate . .	0	6

	s.	*d.*
Benj. Coffin . .	0	5
Wm. Stoate and Mary Quirks	0	7
John Beague . .	0	8
Samuel Stoate .	0	4
William Stoate .	2	6
Robt. Gribbell .	0	7
	8	3

West Lynch.

	s.	*d.*
John Clarke . .	8	0
John Clarke . .	2	0

	s.	*d.*
Robt. Bryant . .	1	4
William Clarke .	2	0
John Hensley for Coulands	2	8
	16	0
Richard Ferrill .	0	7
Ed. Hensley		
John Kent late Philip Spurrier		
Andrew Kitnor		
John Stutford . .	0	3

So that in these three hamlets alone there were at this time some thirty ratepayers.

The rate is confirmed by J. Trevelyan (bart., of Nettlecombe), Edwr. Dyke (Pixton).

In 1739 John Beague and Philip Tayler were overseers. Their total receipts were £63 9*s.* 9*d.*, and disbursements £61 14*s.* 5*d.* A sum of £1 10*s.* is entered as being expended for refreshment during this year at various meetings for the discussion of parish business. The other expenditure is mostly for the poor living in the Church House, and the maintenance of the building. The accounts, which for nearly fifty years are entered in this book, are for the most part well kept, and give us some interesting details as to local prices in this district. The book itself in 1739 cost 8*s.*, and was purchased of one Mrs. Wood. A pair of "stockins" for Wm. Edwards cost 1*s.* 1*d.*, but a pair for Joan Clements was obtained for 8*d.* A pair of shoes cost about 5*s.* for a man (Joseph Kent), and 2*s.* 6*d.* for a woman; and Mrs. Siderfin was paid, it is recorded, 8*s.* for a pig for the house. The general expenses of Joseph Kent, who alas! did not live long to enjoy his new shoes, amounted to 17*s.* 8*d.* The hire of a horse to carry "Mary Waltham to Minehead" was but 6*d.* In the "hard frost" that winter a sum of £1 0*s.* 6*d.* was distributed amongst the poor, and a new linhay for the Church House cost £5 0*s.* 2*d.* John Giles was paid 9*d.* for one dozen of buttons and thread for Wm. Staddon's coat; and for the burying of Mary Waltham 15*s.* were paid. The poor of the parish appear to have received from 1*s.* to 2*s.* per week each, besides clothing. A list of articles supplied to the Church House is given in very minute detail. From it we learn that wheat in this year of grace, 1739, was 3*s.* 7*d.* per bushel; peas 3*s.* 6*d.* per bushel; pork $2\frac{3}{4}$*d.* per lb.; a sheep's hanger and a leg of beef were obtainable for 1*s.* 4*d.*; while a shoulder of veal cost 1*s.* 6*d.* A payment of 5*s.* $8\frac{1}{2}$*d.* for "green beans" seems inexplicable. By November of this year wheat had risen to 4*s.* 3*d.* a bushel, and peas to 4*s.*; and for 48lb. of beef 8*s.* was paid, *i.e.* 2*d.* per lb. Two bushels of malt and grinding the same cost 5*s.* $5\frac{1}{2}$*d.*, and $\frac{1}{2}$lb of hops 6d. "$\frac{1}{4}$ hops" for small beer, 1*s.* $6\frac{1}{2}$*d.*; "trakle" to mix with it, 1*s.* 3*d.* 108lbs. of cheese cost 16*s.* 6*d.*, *i.e.* about $1\frac{3}{4}$*d.* per lb. Milk and butter are regularly entered, but unfortunately no quantity is ever mentioned. There are regular payments for "roots" (*i.e.* potatoes), and a peck of "turnaps" cost 8*d.* $\frac{1}{4}$cwt. of salt cost 2*s.* 1*d.*, two dozen of candles 2*s.* 9*d.*, and half dozen of spoons, 9*d.* There are also regular entries for oatmeal, as well as for apples and "trakle."

Meat for the pig through the year cost 1*s.* 3*d.*, and "the killing of him" 6*d.*; two pair of cards and a mawn caused an outlay of 4*s.*

In 1740 Mi. Snow and Wm. Horne were overseers. In this year considerable repairs were done to the workhouse, and from the list of them we gather that a carpenter received 10*s.* per week, and his assistant 4*s.*; that lime was 20*d.* a hogshead, and that 19ft. of inch board cost 2*s.* 4*d.* In November £2 3*s.* 4*d.* was paid to "Wm. Horne laiing in besnemton while his legs was in cure"; "besnemton" must be Bishopsnympton in North Devon, where, having adventured, poor Horne seems to have met with an accident. "Dr. Ball for siting ye boone of Mary Cook's leg and arme and his sollery for looking after ye poore this year £3 3*s.* 0*d.*" The doctor's customary yearly fee was £2 2*s.*, so an extra fee of £1 1*s.* was paid to him for setting the bones.

The overseers' receipts were from money out at interest, "due to ye parish £5 0*s.* 0*d.*," and "by six rates £50 12*s.* 6*d.*" In this year wheat had fallen to 3*s.* per bushel. The account is signed by:—

Nath. Brice, Curate.
Thos. Greenslade, } Churchwardens.
Tho. Trill, }
Thos. Greenslade, Senr.
John Stoate.
John Clarke, Junr.
Samuel Stoate.
George Lawfield.
Philip Taylor.

Syned and allowed by us,
J. Trevelyan.
Ph. Sydenham.

In 1741 there is an entry of many hundreds of brambles cut for one John Trelivin, and £1 was paid towards £500 that was raised on the county. 3½yds. of cloth cost 1*s.* 4½*d.* per yard, and "a wastcoat and britches for Wm. Edwards and making, 7*s.* 8*d.*" A whole suit for Wm. Staddon cost 15*s.* 3*d.* The following entries are in more than usual detail: pd. "for liquor when Mary Poor dyed and when she was buryed 1*s.* 6*d.*, for laying her out and going to Wootton to make the affidavit 2*s.* 6*d.*, for a shroud for her 5*s.* 2*d.*, for ringing the bell when she dyed and when she was buryed 1*s.* 6*d.*, for making the grave and carrying the beair 1*s.* 6*d.*, for the coffin 8*s.*"; "pd. for meat, soap, firing and candles when Sarah Staddon's clothes was washed and for making a change for Wm. Staddon 1*s.* 10*d.*"

1745. Benj. Coffin, Thom. Hemborrow, Overseers; Rob. Beague, Thom. Snow, Ch. wardens.

The rate as collected is now given in full:

Mr. Willis, Rectr.	18	0
Widow Horne .	1	8
Wid. Snow for Zeals	1	7
Mich. Snow for Broadmead .	1	4
Mich. Snow . .	0	4
John Beague, Tanner . . .	1	1
Robt. Griffith . .	1	4
Widow Escott .	1	7
Mary White . .	1	0
Mary White for Minners . .	1	4
John Knight for Maple ridges .	0	6
David Kent and Abram Phelps	1	0
Philip Tayler . .	2	0
West Myne . .	1	8
Lewis Tayler . .	1	0

Holnicote.

Sir Thos. Acland, Bart. . . .	18	0
Luke Halsey . .	0	7
Wm. Horn . .	1	7

John Cheeke . .	0	2
Wm. Horn . .	0	6

Tivington.

Thomas Greenslade	8	10
" "	0	10
Joan Kent, Wid. .	9	0
Wm. Kent . .	2	0
Benj. Alloway .	2	0
Benj. Coffin . .	3	10
George Lawfull .	2	5
Ven, or Occupier	1	6
Joan Blackford for Barley Ground	1	4
John Kent . . .	1	6
Mich. Snow "New Mead" . . .	0	7
Thomas Trill . .	3	0
" " . .	0	4
" " . . .	1	10
Austin Syderfin .	2	5
Mary Harrison, Wid. . . .	2	0
George Harrison .	2	2

Allerford.

Saml. Stoat . .	2	0
Peter Spurrier .	3	0
Joan Spurrier, Wid.	0	9
John Stoat . .	2	0
Rob. Beague . .	1	6
" " . . .	0	5½
George Hensley .	0	1½
Widw. Tayler . .	1	6
Philip Tayler . .	1	6
Lewis Tayler and David Giles .	1	6
John Devonshire	0	2
Wm. Horne . .	0	6
Wm. Horne for Martyns . .	0	10
John Stevens . .	0	4
Wid. Tayler for Mitchels . .	1	0
Simon Mogridge	0	2
John Beague for Stutfolds . .	0	6
Etheldred Ellis .	0	1
John Giles . .	0	4

West Lynch.

Wm. John and Wm. Clarke .	8	0
Isaac Clarke . .	2	0
Robert Bryant .	1	4
Willm. Clarke .	2	0
John Hensley and Isaac Clarke .	2	8
John Poole . .	1	0
Benj. Coffin for Slades . . .	0	6
Robt. Beague . .	2	6
John Beague (Raly)	0	8
Widw. Tayler .	0	8

Benj. Coffin for Jones	0	4
George Hensley	3	1
Benj. Coffin	3	2
Wid. Stenner	0	8
John Kent for Luckis	0	4

Branding Street.

Thomas Greenslade	2	8
John Stoat	0	6
Benj. Coffin	0	5
John Stoat	0	7
John Beague	0	8
Saml. Stoate	0	4
John Stoate	0	7
Benj. Coffin for Gribbles		

Overlands.

Richd. Tirrel	0	4
Widw. Hensley	0	1
John Kent	0	1
Phil. Spurrier	0	1
Andw. Kidner	0	1
Widw. Spurrier	0	3

This list is interesting as giving us a list of the principal inhabitants of Selworthy in 1745.

The accounts are confirmed by Sir J. Trevelyan and N. Poole.

In 1746 we find John Kent and Benjamin Coffin were overseers. Amongst their payments are "6*d.* for Hannah Stoat's child's grave," and "to the Constable ye County Stock Money 12*s.* 4½*d.*"

In 1748 the names of the ratepayers are again stated in full, and in a note subjoined we find the first mention of lord Arundel as a ratepayer as representing a portion of the estate of George Hensley.

In 1750, when Wm. Kent and Robert Beague are overseers, one of them enters "paid for ye expenses for myself and two horses to Sir John Trevelyan to take ye examination of Mary Hoe." "Spent at Luckham where we went to apprehend Thos. Williams." "Mr. Benjamin Coffin" was paid 5*s.* for apprehending T. Williams, and the churchwardens in their joy expended 1*s*. to celebrate the happy event. For a letter from "Ivilchester" "concerning the poor," the overseers paid 4*d*., and Saml. Bass received 3*s*. 6*d*. for the hire of his horse "for John Trelivyan to ride at Glastonbury."

In Jan., 1760, we have the following entry: "Gave two salers that came from French prison with a pass 6*d*." In each year there is a list of the poor receiving parish relief. They average from ten to twelve in number, and received from 1*s*. to 2*s*. a week on the average. The accounts for this year are signed by H. Fownes Luttrell.

In 1761 we have again an entry, "to four poor sailors yt came from French prison," and the same year, "gave three poor sailors yt came from French prison."

1762. "a man and a woman who had lost by fier," 2*s*.
Gave to sailors by pass . . . . 1*s*.
paid for laying forth John Rue and shrouding and syder bill . . . . 2*s*. 6*d*.
to four poor sailors yt came from French prison . . . . 1*s*.
to a woman and five children yt came from Fr. prison . . . . 1*s*.
gave a poor woman who had lost all she had by fire . . . . 1*s*.
gave three poor sailors yt came from French prison . . . . 1*s*. 6*d*.

The accounts for this year are confirmed by Tho. Dyke Acland.

In 1763 a list is given of forty recipients of a gift of 40*s*., from Mrs. Ilett Kent of the parish of Porlock, "to the poor of Selworthy parish which have no relief."

In 1765 we find, "to cash paid to a brief on account of a fire at Montreal, £1 1*s*.," and "to Joseph Kent his family having the Small pox, £1 1*s*."

In 1766 we find John Taylor's wife paid for "striking John Edwards (for the King's Evil) 10*s*. 6*d*."

In 1770 considerable repairs were executed on the Church House. Here is the cost of the material for the work:

1000 4ft. hart lafts	16	0
500 3ft. " "	5	6
3 hogshead of lime and carriage .	8	4

The work and timber supplied by John Darch.

The carpenter was paid £6 4*s*. 4*d*. for his labour, and he was also supplied with 1*s*. worth of ale. 10,000 of tyles cost 10*s*. per 1000; 2000 nailes 3*s*. 4*d*.; and a dozen and a half of creeses for the roof 2*s*. 3*d*. In 1782 we find £3 3*s*. given to "John Glass as being drawd for a Millitia man"; "pd for stretching forth of Joseph Cheek 2*s*."; and frequent entries are found of payments for "pairs of cards" for women, no doubt for spinning. The entry conjures up a pretty picture of the old pauper women sitting busily spinning outside the door of the quiet old Church House in summer, and by the great hearth of the "chamber" in winter.

Still living in the parish where they had been born and bred, the uneventful life of the pauper passed more cheerfully than it does now in the comfortable but prison-seeming District Workhouse. The uprooting of old associations and the rupture of life-long ties, must always, we fear, render the workhouse distasteful to the aged poor.

The book closes with an account of the Easter Vestry meeting for the year 1782.

On the last page is the agreement to pay Doctor Francis Bradley, Surgeon and Apothecary, for taking care of the poor of the Parish of Selworthy, in Physic and Surgery, two guineas annually.

The reader of these parish records is struck by the frequent reference to the outbreaks of small pox contained in them. It is worth noting here that tradition relates that the plague at its last appearance in England, was very fatal in Selworthy, and that seven bodies, no doubt all the members of the household, were brought forth at one time from the picturesque old house just above Tivington Farm, and drawn on a sledge all together (a gruesome company!) up the long hill to the churchyard.

GATEWAY TO STEYNING MANOR HOUSE.

Interior.

CHAPTER VIII.

Personal History.

WE do not know how or at what date the manor of Holnicote passed into the possession of the Steynings family, but this family appears to have held the estate for five generations before Philip Steynings, who died at Holnicote in 1589, aged nearly eighty years. In the parish of Stowey there is still an estate of the name of Steyning, and in this parish the Steyning family held property up to the time that they became extinct. It looks, therefore, as if this parish might have been the *cunabulum* of the family.

There is a pretentious brass to the memory of Philip Steynings in Selworthy Church. He married Alice, daughter of William Fry of Yarty, the head of a family of considerable consequence in East Devon. This lady died at the age of seventy-two, when on a visit to her cousin, Mrs. Worth, of Worth, near Tiverton, and was buried in Washfield Church. Here is her epitaph, written by her son-in-law, bishop Montgomery:

Alice daughter unto William Frye aud Philip Steyning's wife,
(Both squires) with her husband led a long and loving lyfe.

Nyne sons and daughters five she bore, and then as turtle true,
(He dying first) she lyved sole, and would not choose anew.
Birth, beauty, personage, good grace, court breedinge, gravity,
Chast love, trueth, virtue, constant faith, and sincere piety,
A lyfe made here beloved: and blest yea dead, tho' envye burst,
And malice self can speak but well, if they could speak the worst,
Aged Seaventie-two she yielded here her body to the dust,
Her soule into her Saviour's hands, in whom was all her trust;
By Whom in sorrow, sickness, health, lyfe, death she still was blest,
With Whom she now in heavenly joy hath everlasting rest.
Her birthplace Yarty was: her lyfe in Holnecott she led;
In Worth amongst her deerest friends she made her fatall bed.
Adieu; deere mother, we must part although we loved deerely
Yet spyte of death lyfe once agayne I hope shall join us neerely.
And for thy love, whilst thou didst live, I vow though dead thou lie,
Thy sonne Montgomerie's love to thee and thine shall never die.
Obiit 8th Aug., 1605, ætatis suæ 72.

Georgius Montgomerius gener posuit.

Of the large family of fourteen children which were born to Philip and Alice Steynings, Charles was the eldest. He married Margaret Pollard, of Kilve, but died young. His will is dated Aug. 25, 1591, and was proved Jan. 30, 1592, by his widow. He leaves to his wife his mansion house of Holneycote; to his three brothers, Henry, Hugh, and Alexander, £12 a year for three years. He leaves his "lands in Somerset to my daughter Johan, but if my wife has a son then 1000 marks to Johan." He leaves "my brother Robert Stevens, £5," and appoints "my uncle Lewes

Pollard, my uncle William Frye (of Membury), my father-in-law Mr. Richard Pollard, Overseers," of his will. To his three sisters he leaves 20 marks each. A son was born soon after his death who was named Charles after his father. His wife died at the age of seventy in 1631, having survived her husband forty years, and was buried in the Steynings vault in Selworthy Church.

The elder Charles' brothers and sisters seem for the most part to have survived him, but we do not know the history of all them. One of the brothers, Robert Steynings took holy orders and obtained the valuable living at Broadclyst in Devonshire, and lived a prosperous and easy life, going to London occasionally to look up his relations. He and his sister, we hear, with her husband John Willoughby, of Payhembury, near Honiton, went up to the coronation of James I.

Of the other brothers we know but little. Only two of the sisters married, Susan and Margaret. Margaret married in 1568 John Willoughby of La Hill, in the parish of Payhembury, co. Devon. The Willoughby family, a branch of the family now represented by Lord Willoughby de Broke, were originally of Wiltshire extraction. But *temp.* Henry VIII, Sir Robert Willoughby married Blanche, daughter and heiress of John Champernowne, the head of the ancient Devonshire family of that name, and came to live in Devonshire. Sir Robert's collateral descendant, Richard Willoughby, of Molland, married Agnes Culme, of Chamston, in that parish, and bought the estate of La Hill in 1602. Of their long family the above mentioned John was the eldest. By his marriage with Margaret Steynings he had one son, another John, who was born in 1571, and who died at the ripe age of 87, in 1658. This John Willoughby married (1) Elizabeth, daughter of John Bamfield of Poltimore; (2) Mary, daughter of John Davie of Creedy; (3) Jane, daughter of Sir Richard Strode of Newnham, knt. This last lady died on the 25th December, 1695, and lies buried under the altar in Seaton Church. John Willoughby had by his first wife a daughter and heiress, Mary, who married George Trevelyan of Nettlecombe, in 1655. Mrs. Trevelyan inherited the large collection of letters which her father had carefully preserved through the long period of fifty-six years, and which has supplied much of the information given in the following pages. The Editors of the Trevelyan Papers say of John Willoughby: "He was remarkable for his prudent management of his affairs, and his invariable good nature and consistent liberality to all who had any claim upon him. And thus he became the influential centre of a large family circle. For more than half a century, brothers, brothers-in-law, son, sons-in-law, nephews, grandsons, applied to him for help, and in return kept him posted in the news of the day."[1]

Susan, the elder daughter married the Rev. George Montgomery, who was a friend of Mr. Fleete, the rector of Selworthy, and it was, perhaps, through their friendship that he made his first acquaintance with the Steynings family.

This "courtier priest," the Trevelyan papers tell us, was the son of Adam Laird of Braidstone, a descend-

1. *Introd. Trevelyan Papers*, I. 32

ant of the earls of Eglinton. He was born at Braidstone in 1562, and was "for his worth and learning" in 1596, presented by queen Elizabeth to the living of Chedzoy, Somerset. He was in favour also at the court of James, for it seems that he had been in the habit of supplying his brother, the sixth Laird of Braidstone, who was established at the court of James VI, with information of much value from the court of Elizabeth. When that "bright occidental star" passed away, scolding in true Tudor fashion her minister, Cecil, almost with her last breath, and James I succeeded to the English throne, Dr. Montgomery was at once singled out for promotion. Besides giving him the deanery of Norwich, the king appointed him one of his chaplains, and in 1605 made him bishop of Derry. On his consecration to this diocese his former preferments were confirmed to him by the king, so that at the same time he was bishop of Derry, dean of Norwich, and vicar of Chedzoy. He seems also to have held another living *in commendam*. In 1605 the king made him a privy councillor, and sent him, on account of his ability for state affairs and his great skill in ecclesiastical matters, to Ireland, to acquaint him of the condition in which the church and state stood in that kingdom, and as a commissioner for settling the affairs of the clergy.

Dean Montgomery soon won the hearts of the Irish clergy, and was employed by the primate and bishops of Ireland to represent to the king the grievances of the clergy. In 1610 he was collated to Meath, which he held with Clogher till his death. He built an episcopal residence at Ardbraccen near Nairn, and repaired the church near it. He died at Westminster on Jan. 15, 1620, leaving a petition to the king in favour of his daughter, who had married into the Howth family, and from whom the present earl Howth is descended.

Many of the bishop's letters are in existence. Here is one to his old friend Mr. Fleete of Selworthy :—

"My occasion of absence kynd Mr. Fleete from home and my friends, have been as you rightly say, business which nowe are ended and I no more have to use that shifting excuse for a tyme. Wherfore that I may also leave you without anye, I will, when you looke not for mee, be with you and ease you of that veternum (lethargy) wherewith you seem to be much troubled, if God spare me and new occasions withdraw mee not." "In the meane tyme your mare shall have the best fare our moores are able to afford her, though it be not such as I wish." (He had been running a mare for Mr. Fleete on the Chedzoy moors). "And this late flood hath so overflowed that few places are as yet open for pasture. It is true that the king of Portugall is reported to be alive and the report published in print, but not beleeved by statesmen for anything I can heare. Other news I referre to our meeting, that we may have something to passe the time withal, only this in general. The Earle of Marre, late ambassador from Scotland is returned very well pleased with the usage and answeres he received of her Majestie and the Councell. God guydeth all and will make all serve for the best to His children : with whose good blessing I hartily commend yourself, your good bedfellowe, daughters, and whole charge, and with kyndest commendations unto you all from us all, wee wish you to fare well in the Lord. Chedseye this 7th day of June, 1601.

"Yours in assured love

"George Montgomerye.

"Alexander (the writer's brother) is lately returned from Ireland and reporteth that the rebellious Desmont is taken by the Whyte Knyght and delivered to the president of Monster,

Sr. George Carew, who was to send him over to the Queene. The Tyrone is in the North and his forces decaye daylie.

"To my right loving friend Mr. William Fleete at Selworthye speed these."

We do not know whether the promised visit to Selworthy ever came about, or Mr. Fleete cured of his ailment.

Montgomery's rapid preferment and favour at court did not alter his kindliness of heart. R. Steynings the vicar of Broadclyst, who was in London for the coronation of James I, writing in 1603, is astonished at the dean's popularity and delighted by his kindness to his relations.[1]

Here is a letter from him concerning their visit and other family matters :—

"R. Steynings to John Willoughby.

"My lovinge brother and sister I salute you both most hartelye. I retourned safelye long since, thanks be geven to God, from that faimous citye no newes stirring to make you partaker of, but that which I think is knowen to you alreadye. If you and my sister do meane to be at the coronation, I pray you to let me understaud thereof. We are nowe all for London. Mr. Read's house our inn, welcome to him any of the bloude of the Steynings; indeed I laye at his house some sixe dayes and had very good entertaynments for myselfe and my man. My brother Mountgomery, never so brave, Deane of Norwitch, in favor with prince and nobles; the olde proverbe 'honores mutant mores' taking no holde of him, he is still the same man, kynde, loving, and lowlye, readye prest for his friend as for him selfe neglect not the opportunitye. There be manye offices begged and granted worthy the havinge. I came a little too late to be Bishop of Bristowe. My beard would have borne it but there were other things wantynge, which made

1. *Trevelyan Papers*, vol. iii, p. 47.

me to drawe backe. What successe I had in my suytes or am like to have, you shall understand when we meete, both what my suytes are, and how I am likely to speede. Thus committing you with all yours to God's Most Merciful protection I take my leave.

"Broadclist, the 23d of June, 1603, your ever loving brother,

"R. Stey. (Steynings).

"Hester saluteth you both; we will be glad to see my sister and you here whensoever it shall please you to take the paynes to come, send us woorde, I pray, a little before, that we may be at home. After harvest, God willing, I will come and see my younge cousen.

"To his very loving brother, Mr. John Willoughby at Seaton, deliver these."

On June 24 of that year the dean himself writes to John Willoughby:—

"I desyred you to fynd out and advertyse some thing worth the asking, which you aunswer you can not doe for want of notice, and that I showed you was my want also: yet would you be aided by mee therein, it is true I have a collection of the most offices in England of the King's Guyft. But the king gives none except such as are merely void by death, or in the hands of those agaynst whom there is lawful exception. What these are is best knowen to yourself and such others as you in the country, where the offices are, not to us so far remote from them, and herein I desyred your advertysement."

James good naturedly seems to have kept on the officers of his own and also those of Elizabeth's household, until they could be provided for; any office therefore of value was speedily filled up. A difficulty, this letter tells us, arose in regard to the approaching coronation, by an outbreak of the plague.[1]

1. *Trevelyan Papers*, vol. iii, p. 48.

"The king this daye is removed to Windsore, from whence he rydeth to meet the Queene, and bringeth her and the Prince thither upon Wednesdaye, where they stay till the Coronation, viz. the 25th Julye, which yet holdeth yf the plague which increaseth apace in London do not let: 30 parishes are infected, there died this last week of the sicknesse 72."

At this time an exchange was on foot between dean Montgomery and Matthew Sutcliffe, dean of Exeter, the famous controversialist, who founded in 1616 Chelsea College for "learned divines" to be employed in controversial writing.

"I would," writes dean Montgomery, "you could persuade D. Sutcliffe as soon as you should persuade mee, then should I be your neerer neighbour."

At Exeter the dean would have been surrounded by his friends and relations. At Broadclyst was Robert Steynings, his brother-in-law; John Willoughby another brother-in-law lived at Payhembury near Honiton, or on his property at Seaton; and at Yarty near Axminster were his wife's cousins, the Fry family.

But dean Sutcliffe was not inclined to move out of sunny Devonshire, and the snug deanery which lies so cosily under the shadow of the cathedral; and the development of Montgomery's brilliant career was destined to take him much further afield. Meanwhile he is still seeking to get offices for his relations. A letter of his written in the September of this same year, 1603, shows the shameless way in which valuable posts were put up for sale:

"You have often loving brother byn desyrous to busye yourself in some office, and now is the office of Clerk of Assyse voyde by the death of Mr. Hancocke: you know in whose guyft it is, and by what means it is usually compassed."

This negotiation failed and another was entered into:

"George Montgomerye to John Willoughby.

"I receaved your note by my brother Alexr., and your letters by William Kirford, concerning the Escheatorship of Devon, which you would have to be procured for your uncle Andrew Willoughbye. I doubt when yourself and your unkle shall understand of the Course intended to be held for the wards, you will skarsely be willing to hazard any mony in procuring that office. It hath byn working long agoe and comissions are now com downe to take order with such gentlemen as hold any land of the King, in any tenure whereby there sonnes become wardes to the King, for a composition to be made of a certayne rate to be paid, that there children may be free and become wardes no more, which rate, if it amount to that summe which is now payed to the exchequor out of that office (as it is offered by the subjectes and more) then is the King pleased to ease his contrey of that thraldom unto the Court of Wards. Whereof so much hath byn complayned, which yf it fall out I see not wherin the escheator can benefit himself. And I think certaynly it will prove so, for that it hath byn earnestly urged of the contrey, and now the King hath consented and granted out warrants for the tryall of the matter. Yet will I wryte unto the Court within these two dayes for the staye of that place yf it be not already gone till I heare from you agayne. I have heard of the Escheator's dealing for Charles Steynings (the young owner of Holnicote, the grandson of old Philip Steynings and the son of Charles Steynings, the elder, and Margaret Pollard,) Wardship, and will talke with him when I can meet him, I think he can do him no hurt, much lesse my Mother. I am right glad of your resolution to be a house-keeper, but more of your providence that you be not overlayd with guests, which yet you performe with such a cover of prodigalitie, that he who knew you not would much be mistaken in you. But neyther shall your cheese, breade and cyder, cold intertaynement in a manor house of your sort, neyther your Mother's Misery and your beggerye, be such bugs as you would have them, nor skarre-crowes to dryve awaye travellers. Wee will make Peggye sing another note though you lowre at it."

In the December of this year he offers Mr. Willoughby the place of "a groome of the kings Privye Chamber," price £600 cash; the "fee" about £50 a year and board. Also of "a pensioner to the king," price £323 cash, and the fee £50 and an allowance of *2s. 6d.* per day for board when in office. There was also the place of "Usher quarter wayter in the Queen's presence" to be had, price £250; fee £40 a year, and "there table when they wayte, and when they wayte not there dyet at my Lord Chamberlane's table on the Queen's syde." "The groom's place is the best," the bishop considers, "if you like the condition."

Dr. Montgomery still remained in high favour at the court of king James. In January, 1604, he writes to Mr. Willoughby:

"to let you know that upon Fryday next after your departure, I receaved letters from His Majestie under his own hand and signet, by one of his ordinary messengers, willing mee presently upon recept thereof to come up and attend His Highnesses pleasure."

The king had sent for him to proceed to Ireland in the quality of privy councillor, to acquaint him with the condition of the church and state in that kingdom.

By the May of next year the dean had obtained episcopal rank, and we find Mrs. Montgomery writing thus to her brother-in-law:—

"Mrs. Montgomery to John Willoughby.

"Lovinge Brother Mr. Highgate ys nowe at Chedsye, and ys latelye com from Loundon, and he assureth me that my

Lord Bushope wilbe at home before Wensdaye night. The Kinge hath bestowed one him three Fresh Bushipricks: the names of them I can not remember, they are so strange, except one, which ys Derye. I pray God yt may make us all merye."

In April, 1605, the bishop goes again to Ireland on the king's business. He therefore leaves his wyfe at "Charles'" (Charles Steynings' at Holnicote) until he can come over and fetch her, but if he cannot come his cousin Ric. Cullom is to convey her to Dublin. He invites Nicholas Willoughby to join him in London and ride with him to West Chester, to embark thence for Ireland:

"if he cannot, he maye passe in a bark of Milford, which now lieth at Bridgwater, wherein I transport some of my stuff to Duplyn."

How strange this tiresome and lengthy method of travelling seems to us in the nineteenth century!

In August of 1606 the bishop and his wife seemed to have at last finally move from Chedzoy, but not without hopes of returning soon again to England, by the exchange of his Irish sees for an English one. On the 21 Aug., 1606, Mrs. Montgomery writes to Mrs. Willoughby at Payhembury:—

"We had thought to have time gone long since, but Mr. Montgomerye hath had so manye businesses to be despatched in London, and the Kinge of Denmarkes beenge ther hath also hinddered him, thus he could get no fitte oppertunitye to take his leve of the Kinge before he was gone. The Kinge of Denmarke is nowe departed towards his own countrye againe and Mr. Montgomerye did yesterday take his leve of his Majestie, of home he had many gracious words and fair promises . . . . I hope we shall not long staye in Ireland, but once he must needs goo."

Mrs. Montgomery had been shopping in London for her sister-in-law. The cost of linen fabrics at that period is noticeable!

"I sent you downe by Mr. Chose an ell of lawne and cambrike which cost xxs. I receved fortye shillings of my cosen William Willoughbye for to bestowe it in holande lawne and cambrike: as for your holand, I bought none because I could not get anye good of that price which my brother Willoughbye wold have had . . . . There ys no news to wryte unto you but that the plage begeneth to encrease in London: ther dyed this wicke fourscore and five."

The next day the bishop writes to John Willoughby, to take his farewell of you and "my loving sister." The king, he says,

"hath most gratiously and contentedly dispatched mee with hopefull promises for my good. Upon Mondaye next, by God's help, wee set forward for London to West Chester, from whence to embark to Ireland."

On the morning of his departure he had an opportunity of despatching another line of farewell to Mr. Willoughby:—

"Having so fit an opportunity by Mr. Spurwaye I have taken occasion to salute you and bid you farewell, being this daye readye to take horse for West Chestre. My wyfe, your brothers, cosens and others of my company are I thank God in healthe, and feare no robbing by the waye to West Chestre." He mentions his cousin, Nicolas Frye, of Yarty, and ends, "I wrote unto you lately and therefore now I only kisse your hands and wish unto you, my loving sister, my kynd cozen B. B., and all your frends at Peheınbry, Leygh, and Worth all harty contentment here and happiness hereafter."

William, a brother of John Willoughby, who accompanied the bishop, soon got tired of Ireland, and finds he has "great business to be done at home"; and in the October of the same year Mrs. Montgomery writes from Derry to Mr. John Willoughby :—

"Loveing brother and sister having the opertunitye of this bearer my cosen William Willoughbye who is mynding to returne for Englande, I thought good to wryte these fewe lynes unto you. Signifyinge therebye that we are in good health and that we have, thanks be unto God, well and safely passed the daungers of the sease, so also the long myles bye lande, yet God blessed us with as fyne weather as we could wish for both by lande and sea, which made our journye and vyadge the more pleasanter. We are settled in the Derye in a verye pretye litell house byldyd after the Indglesh (English) fashone, but somewhat whith the lest for companye. We have our fatte beefes and fatte sheepe brought in by our tennants as far as we can use them, and we want no good companye as my cosen William can show you, to helpe eate it up. I fynde Derye a better plase than we thought we should, for there we find manye of our countrye folkes both gentlemen and gentlewomen and as brave as they goo in ther apparel in Indgland. I thanke God I like yet (Ireland) indifferante well this fare (far). The most that I do mislyke ys that the Iresh doth often troubell our house, and manye times they doth lend to us a louse which makes me many times remember my daughter Jane, which told me that if I went into Irlande I should be full of lyce."

A sample of the "countrye flixe and threed" is sent with the letter.

"The flixe ys vi*d.* the pound and the threed xii*d*. Although it loukes of colare greene yet ys never the worse for that, but they say that yet wilbe the whitter."

The letter is signed S. Montgomerye, and dated viiith Oct. (1606). In the postscript we hear of two members of the Stevens family, probably of Stowey, near Bridgwater.

"Mr. Montgomery," his wife tells us, "hath manye thousande

acres of as good land as anye in Ingland: yf yet were pepeled yet were worth manye hundred pounds by the year: he hath great sute made unto him bye dyvers for it."

On the 29th November, 1608, the bishop writes to Mr. John Willoughby "from my chamber at Mr. Mr. Cooper's over against the Commons." The king seemed unable to do without his help, and now he is sent for to act as:

"a Commissioner for the plotting and devyding of the contreye (Ireland) which I feare will keep mee heere this Christmas agaynst my will; and agaynst my will it shall be indeed yf I eat not som of my cosen's Beaumont's Christmas pyes and so tell her I praye you." (Mrs. Beaumont lived at Gittesham near Honiton.) "I hope," the good bishop goes on, "my sister (Mrs. Willoughby) and she have receaved the water (*i.e.* strong water) I sent them in a little runlet of a bottle, a quart for a peece."

This was evidently a sample of Irish whisky. The bishop seems to have kept about him a considerable number of young men of birth, mostly apparently relations. This letter mentions Alexander Steynings, son of old Philip Steynings of Holnicote, who had at this moment gone across to Ireland to bring Mrs. Montgomery to England, and Philip, as well as the above mentioned William, and Nicolas Willoughby. Some of these young men seem to have been more than the bishop could manage:

"I was loath my cosen Philip (who had accompanied him to London) should staye here longe and therefore took order for some odde items he owed here and hasted him away for feare of trouble: for he walked openly against my will. He hath taken tyme to be advysed by his friends what course to followe, but let them set him in a course by times, before opportunity to doe him good be past."

Life, even for bishops and their retinues, seems to have been rough in Ireland in the reign of James I. Nicholas Willoughby writes in October, 1606, to John Willoughby:

"The life which we lived in England is much altered, for when we were in England when we had traveld hard all day, at night we should have good lodging and good meat and drincke which is a comfort to anie man: and here we shall have barley bread and oaten cakes baked upon a brandice and boniclabbor for our drinke, which is sweete milke and sower mixt together, and excellent feather beds, everie feather a yard longe: but God be thanked meat enough of all sorts, beafe mutton porke and cockrels and all sorts of fish and fowle indifferente cheape: but the extremitie that we indue is but when we travell, but then we are in great danger of cutting our throats, for you shall have in some places forty rogues together hunting the woods and caves underground. This is the hardness we indue. Now for the countre, if ther were good husbands upon it, it would be almost as good as England: but the people be so beastlie that they are better like beasts than Christians. Here is land enough, but here wants stocke to stocke it; for I cannot blame them that are loathe to live here, for he shall live as it were amongst beastes, and if he lives out in the land, he shall be in danger of his life; but all my Lord's land for the most part is excellent good for fish and fowle; if one had but the tenth part of it in England, he might live more like a prince than a subject; so I for my owne part doe wish all my friends, if they have anie living in England, never to sell it, thinking to mend his pennons in Ireland."

The prices of agricultural produce were of a kind to astonish us even in these days of agricultural depression.

"If a man," Nicholas Willoughby goes on, "had monie lyinge by him he might doe himself some good, as in buying salmon and herrings, for you shall have it verie good and cheape: and you shall buy a fatte cowe for xxs. which is worth in England much more, if the price of beafe continue as it was when I was there: and you shall have a fatte pigge for 4s. but I speake of the best sort: or in buying tallow you shall have it for 1d. a pound, and sometimes whithin; or in buying hydes: and send those things into England, if one chance of a trustie friend to order those things for him, one might doe himself some good, and for to returne barley and wheate into the Dirrey, it is there well sold 2d. one wine qt. . . . . ."

As a postscript Mr. Willoughby adds:—

"My paper is bad
My hand is worse
God send me some monie
To put in my purse."

Bishop Montgomery is still busy during this time helping his relations:

"I am lyke," he writes to Mr. John Willoughby, "to make you one of the surveyors of the Princes Lands in Devon and Cornwall, which is a place of credit, though no greate benefit, onlye it may be a step and entrance to some better place hereafter: it will be no charge unto you, for your charges are borne when you goe about the service, and you are thereby acquainted with the state of things to doe yourself or your frend pleasure thereby, as occasion shall be offered."

He speaks again of his employment in:

"settling down and planting of the King's Lands in the North of Ireland."

In July, 1608, the bishop was again in England, as the king desired to consult him concerning the "erection of byshopricks in the north."

"The whole winter will be required," he says, "for the work, and it will be neere All Hallowtide before our survey is ended."

He is busy, too, at this time, providing a curate for the living of Chedzoy which he still held with his Irish bishopric.

Bishop Montgomery returned to Ireland, and we hear no more of him until on the 16th February, 1614, he writes from Dublin the following letter, endorsed

"To my right loving brothers and sisters and cousins, Mr. Robert Steynings, Mr. John Willoughby, Mr. Philip Elley, Mrs. Margaret Willoughby, Mrs. Ann Steynings, and to my right loving cousin Mrs. Agnes Willoughby these and to any and everyone of them,"

telling them of the death of his wife.

On the 20th August, 1618, the bishop writes to John Willoughby from the episcopal residence he had recently built near Navan, announcing the approaching marriage of his daughter.

"I have matched," he writes, "your cosen my daughter unto a noble house, the best of the Pale of Ireland."

He then asks John Willoughby's help for his brother, Nicholas Willoughby, who was on his way to England to obtain funds wherewith to buy land in Ireland.

"Good brother use him kindly, and let him return cheerfully and well pleased, and you and your children may happily find in this kingdom a new colony of your own kindred in all the four branches and families your children are nearest unto: of Steynings, Willoughbyes, Culms and Fryes: and unto every one of them I have given a friendly footing for a ground and beginning."

This is the last letter which has been preserved from the bishop. On the 15th of January, 1620, he died at Westminster, and his body was taken back to Ardbraccan, to be laid beside his wife in the church of Ardbraccan, which he had restored and beautified.

Of the rest of old Philip Steynings' family, Charles the eldest son married one of the ancient family of Pollard of Kilve, but did not long survive his father. The infant unborn at his death proved to be a son, who was called Charles, after his father. Bishop Montgomery writes concerning the child and his mother in May, 1604:

> "if you will adventure upon his wardship in the King's sight, and try the tytle and traverse Mr. Arundell's office, I will procure the wardship to you at as easie a rate as any man in England shall: my sister (Charles Steynings' mother) is desirous of it, but will hazard no money, and I am loath to adventure much without a sound ground."

This second Charles Steynings married Cicell, the heiress of the Lucar family, the owners of the manor of Blackford, which closely adjoins Holnicote, and on which the Steynings family must long have looked with a covetous eye. The old house has long since been removed, but its dovecot still remains.

Charles Steynings' life must have been a troubled one, for he was the owner of Holnicote during the civil wars. The valley was strongly royalist, greatly, no doubt, owing to the influence of that prominent ecclesiastic, the Rev. Henry Byam, who held at the time the two sister livings of Selworthy and Luccombe. Some fighting seems to have taken place about Selworthy in those days, if cannon balls found in the churchyard and a little further eastward are any proof. Minehead was for the most part parliamentarian, and the worthy Puritans of that ancient seaport doubtless looked with no kindly eye upon the royalist valley.

The whole district must have been in those troubled times in a state of strange confusion. Mr. Luttrell held Dunster for the parliament, but his relations and near neighbours, the Wyndhams of Orchard Wyndham, and the Trevelyans of Nettlecombe, were for the king. At Bagborough, Mr. Popham was marshalling the trainbands against the royalists, while his neighbour, Sir John Stawell of Cothelstone, "a man of great possessions in those parts," was a supporter of the throne. Every man's hand was against every man's. A notable family were then living at Kentsford, the old Wyndham house which lies near the railway, just below St. Decuman's Church. Sir Thomas Wyndham of Kentsford, kt., had married Christabella, the heiress of Hugh Pyne of Cathanger, Somersetshire, a picturesque old house well worth a visit. They had two sons, both of whom turned out bold and brilliant soldiers, and did much for the royal cause. Colonel Edmund, the eldest son, who was high sheriff of the county at the time of the outbreak of the civil war, was made by the king governor of Bridgwater. Clarendon describes him as "being a gentleman of fortune near the place, and of a good personal courage." Colonel Edmund's wife had been nurse to the prince of Wales, and retained a strong hold on his affections. Her influence over him, however, seems to have been used in the most unfortunate manner. "She had many private designs of benefit and advantage to herself and her children, and the qualifying of her husband to do all acts of power in control upon his neighbours, and laboured to procure grants, or promises of reversion of lands, from the prince." One of these grants we find was of the foreshore and marshes at Seaton, the property of the above mentioned John Willoughby, Charles Steynings' uncle. Mr. Willoughby was, however, evidently able to maintain his title to his property, even in the face of the royal gift, as the property is still in the hands of his representative, Sir Walter J. Trevelyan. Mrs. Wyndham was "a woman of no good breeding and of a country pride: 'Nihil muliebre praeter corpus gerens,'" Clarendon tells us, and she "valued herself much upon the power and familiarity which her neighbours might see she had with the prince of Wales: and therefore upon all occasions in company and when the concourse of the people was the greatest could use great boldness towards him: and which was worse than all this, she affected in all companies where she let her self out to any freedom, a very negligent and disdainful mention of the person of the king; the knowledge of which humour of hers was one reason that made his majesty unwilling his son should go further West than Bristol," and the lords of the council took care that the young prince should be removed from her company. Mrs. Wyndham seems always to have retained her influence on Charles II. Pepys tells us under date December 3, 1665: "Dined with Captain Cocke and Colonel Wyndham, a worthy gentleman whose wife was nurse to the present king, and one that while she lived governed him and everything else . . . . . the old king putting mighty weight and trust upon her."

Colonel Francis Wyndham was at the time of the outbreak of the civil war residing at Sandhill, an old house near Washford, now in the possession of the Luttrell family. He assisted considerably with his brother in the early success of the marquis of Hertford and prince Maurice in their march westward in June "Taunton, Bridgwater, and Dunster Castle so much stronger than both the other, fell before them." The marquis made colonel Francis governor of Dunster, and he held that castle for the king during the civil war, and had the honour of lodging the king himself in that stronghold during his visit to the west. "At the end of the war, when all of the places were surrendered in that county, he also surrendered that upon fair conditions, and made his peace, and afterwards married a wife with a competent fortune, and lived quietly without any suspicion of having lessened his affection towards the king."[1]

His wife brought to him Trent Grange near Sherborne. Here he was living the life of a quiet country gentleman, his heart no doubt afire at the news which had reached him of the landing of the prince, with whom he and his brother had so many ties, and then of the fatal battle of Worcester, when one day he received a visit from a stranger who declared himself to be lord Wilmot, and who told him that the king was in concealment at the house of a Mr. Norton not far away, and anxious to speak with him. A meeting was arranged in a neighbouring town, and the king was conveyed by colonel Wyndham to Trent, where he lay concealed, until colonel Wyndham at length was able to arrange for a ship to take the king across to France from Lyme. It is a matter of history how after a perilous ride to Lyme, this scheme fell through on account of the suspicions of the captain's wife, who

1. *Hist. of the Rebellion*, book xii, l. 42.

commanded at home if her husband did on the sea. With difficulty Charles regained Trent, whence he at length made good his escape into Normandy.

Charles Steynings was still a young man when the wave of civil war broke over the land, and its eddies reached even to our secluded valley. He must have been troubled what to do. Should he side with Mr. Luttrell and the Clubmen of Dunster and Minehead, or should he attach himself to the royalists, and throw in his lot with the Wyndhams and the Trevelyans? Much influenced, no doubt by Henry Byam, Charles Steynings seems ere long to have made up his mind, for in 1643 we find him writing to George Trevelyan of Nettlecombe:

"Noble Sir, I heere present you with a man and horse for his Majesties service, sooner I conveniently could not, neither yet is my rider soe well accommodated with military necessaries as it is fit hee should bee which I will furnish him with all, as soon as possibly I can procure it: in the interim I hope you will excuse the defects. The horse is not so readdy nor hath beene soe well ridden as I could wish for the service, but yf you please to send it with your approbation, I will endeavour to gett another in exchange of this, which perchance may bee more serviceable and lesse troublesome, for I doubt this horse (by means of his mettle and defect of discipline) will ride very hott amongst a troope, and soe not please so well as a cooler horse: but this I leave to your choyce and dispose: as hee is, I commend him to your command. Even soe, with my humble and best respects to your selfe and worthy consort I rest,

"Yours unfeynedly to serve you,

"Cha. Staynings.

"Holneycott.

"To my much honoured freind and Kinsman George Trevelyan Esqre. at Nettlecombe, present these."

Mr. Trevelyan was at this time straining every nerve to raise a regiment of twelve hundred men under a commission sent him by Charles I. We should like to have had preserved for us the name of the Selworthy man who went out for the king. In this parish the same names can be traced back to "the spacious times of queen Elizabeth," or as far as our parochial records go back, and no doubt the collateral descendants of this bold trooper still remain amongst us.

Mr. Trevelyan seems to have been successful in his efforts to raise his regiment, for on June 30 of this year, 1643, we find the famous royalist general Sir Ralph Hopton writing to him from Frome, congratulating him on his having levied "a good part of his troope," and sending him an officer to drill them. "For your better assistance I have here sent you an able souldier to serve you as a lieutenant which I heare you want; he is a man that understands horse well, and hath commanded before in good service," writes Sir Ralph.

We know nothing of Charles Steynings' history through the next few years, but we know that it was a troubled time enough for our valley. In the late autumn of 1648 we find Mr. Steynings tired out by the local troubles, and half ruined by the exactions of the parliamentarian forces, anxious to leave Holnicote and settle in Exeter. He writes to his uncle, John Willoughby, who had been busy procuring a house for him in Exeter:

"The winter is so suddenly taken upon us by means whereof I cannot with conveniency remove and carry my household stuff, nor make any provision for wood and other necessaries, and being yet uncertain of a house too, I must . . . . content myself to winter in my own house; but God willing at the spring of the year, I will remove either to Exon or elsewhere out of our country; in the interim (if it please God) I will give you a visit, but cannot as yet for I am far back in sowing, and of late our poor parish have been troubled and infested with billetting and quartering of soldiers, one whole month together 3 men and horse falling out to my share, and yet we are like to have them again when it comes to our turn, for they intend to take up their quarters this winter upon five parishes only within our hundred, viz.: Mynehead, Wootton, Timberscombe, Luccombe, and Selworthy, so that our poor country is like to be exhausted and indeed undone, remedy or relief or ease in this pressure and burden we are like to have none. They are in number some 7 or 8 and 40, and most horsemen. Dragoons at least 40, and they will not only have hay but oats too for their horses, so that we shall hardly "eat hay with our horse" as the old saying is ere winter overpass. This is a part of Sir Hardresse Waller his brigade under the command of one Captain Fulcher. I could enlarge myself upon this subject as showing you their abuses in their quarters, but time nor paper will not permit me . . . . ."

This quartering of the dragoons took place as Mr. Steynings feared. At the end of January of the next year he writes again to his uncle from Holneycott:

"Lewes Steynings has a desire to present you with a few chestnuts which he got out of a ship that was bulged in on the sands near the quay at Mynehead: she was wholly laden with French wines and chestnuts, of which she had abundance, in so much that the country folk fetched away divers horse-loadings for many days together, to feed their hogs withal.

"We are all in health, I thank God heere, but the soldiers will have a care to keep us from wealth, having a charge of £15 per week imposed on our little hundred toward the quartering of a hundred soldiers of Colonel Popham his company, relating to the castle at Dunster: and not long before we had in our parish, for a month's space, 40 dragoons and upwards of Sir Hardross Waller his brigade under the command of one Captain Fulcher."

We hear no more of Mr. Steynings, and we hope when the war was ended, he was able to return to Holnicote and live peaceably for the rest of his days on his property. At all events, he did not suffer so much for the royal cause as his "much honoured friend and kinsman," George Trevelyan. Colonel Trevelyan was in a sad condition indeed when the parliament gained the upper hand. He had foes on every side, and at Nettlecombe rectory was roundhead Mr. Gay, a bitter enemy of the royalist cause, who especially was determined to give him no peace. Gay is said to have led on in person the attack on the court house, which ended in the destruction of the barton and outbuildings. But for the powerful protection of his uncle, Mr. Luttrell, who returned to Dunster Castle after it had been given up to admiral Blake in April, 1646, things "would have gone badly indeed with Colonel Trevelyan." Mr. Luttrell writes himself, somewhat sternly, on the 5th May of that year, "I have hitherto preserved your estate from plundringe in hope that you will be yeeldable unto such conformity as all other of your neighbours have been."

George Trevelyan was fined the large sum in those days of £1,560 for bearing arms against the parliament. The fine fell hardly on him, as he had already raised every shilling he could on the remnants of the once extensive Raleigh estate in Glamorganshire for "the present relief of his majesties armies," and the parliamentary forces had robbed him of all his farm stuff and horses. But there was no mercy for so determined a malignant, and as no horses could be obtained, his wife, Margaret Trevelyan, travelled to London in a coach drawn by six oxen, to pay the fine at Goldsmiths' Hall. Mrs. Trevelyan got safely to London, but caught the small pox on her way home and died at Hounslow, where her monument is still to be seen.

From the letters from which so much of these notes has been compiled, we get an interesting list of the arms which a horse soldier had to have in those days, such as Mr. Steynings would have supplied the Selworthy man with who went out with George Trevelyan. It is comprised in an order to Mr. John Willoughby to provide a "lyghte horse." [1]

> "Whereas," writes Mr. Prydeaux, "the Lord Lieutenant hath received direction from the Lordes of the Counsell for the increase of horse for his Majestys service, his lordship have thought fit to set you to one light horse, to be verye sufficient: the rider to be armed with his curate,[2] headpiece, powderans, vanbrace,[3] and cusses,[4] also his sworde and Frenche pistoll rather with a fier lock than snaphance,[5] and a bigge saddle with bitte and good furniture."

Accoutrements of all kinds became exceedingly dear just before the Civil War broke out, when men saw

1. *Trevelyan Papers*, iii, p. 194.

2. Curate, a curet breastplate. Later used for a whole suit of armour.

3. Vambrace, or vanbrace, from the French *avantbras*, armour for protection of arms.

4. Cuisses, armour for the thighs.

5. The lock of the pistol.

that trouble was at hand. John Turberville of Gauldon in the parish of Tolland, whose ancient house is still to be seen, and who married Mr. Steynings' first cousin, Bridget Willoughby, in 1639, writes to his father-in-law, John Willoughby, from Clerkenwell, in September, 1640:

"Your buff coat I have looked after and the price; they are exceeding dear, not a good one to be gotten under £10, a very poor one for 4, 5 or 6 pounds: but for your belt you may have a substantial one reasonable."[1]

Charles Steynings' wife died in 1646, leaving a large family of young children behind her, the care of which must have added much to Charles Steynings' difficulties, during the troubled times in which his lot was cast. The two elder sons, Philip and Antony died young, but Charles, Lewis (the young man who sent his uncle John Willoughby the chestnuts, the spoil of the French boat that went ashore at Minehead), Ames, Robert, and six daughters must have been living at the time of their mother's death. The inscriptions on the brasses in Selworthy Church to this lady and her two young sons are given in Chap. IV. Another member of the Steynings family much in evidence during the Civil War, was John Steynings, a grandson of Philip Steynings of Holnicote. He joined the parliamentarian forces, and thus we have the curious spectacle of the elder brother a devoted royalist, while the younger brother is in arms against the king; and the uncle is evidently sore troubled as to which side to take. At first Mr. Willoughby evidently hesitated, and was rebuked by Sir Samuel Rolle and the Devonshire committee for

1. *Trevelyan Papers*, iii, p. 194.

his backwardness in serving the parliament. The success of Sir R. Hopton and the king's forces in Cornwall seems to some extent to have influenced him, and he lent £100 for support of His Majesty's officers to "withstand the present invasion and rebellion." John Steynings, however, does not hesitate to send him some colours taken by him from the royalists at the battle of Marlborough, and in 1645 John Willoughby pleads his readiness to take the National Covenant and oath of the 5th April, and his having lent the parliament "£140 besides horses and arms."

John Steynings had early chosen the army for his profession, and he took part in the expedition to the Netherlands in 1639, but the issue of the expedition, as far as he was concerned, was an unfortunate one. He writes to John Willoughby.[1]

"Noble and ever much respected Uncle . . . . Divers letters have I written unto you since my departure from you, two out of Duncarke, but I never had answer to them. For as I was going over from the Netherlands in a Flushing ship I was taken and divers passengers besides; and they stripped us out of all that we had (therefore sweet Sir let me desire you to commiserate my case) and therefore I were in prison eleven days and then we were sent for England again. And so being very sick when I came at Gravesend I took means under Captain Sidham (Sydenham) for his serjeant was there taking up of men: and if it be that you send me any relief, I would desire you that you could be pleased to send it unto Mr. John Turberville (his cousin and a lawyer in London) at the Inner Temple . . . . ."

This is a dismal picture enough of the young soldier brought up amidst comfort and plenty, "stripped out

1. *Trevelyan Papers*, iii, p. 191.

of all he possessed," by French privateers, and finding his way back to Gravesend sick and penniless, to enlist, for the sake of a livelihood, as a private, to sail again for the war.

The letter is dated from Broedawe (Breda), August, 1639, and it is endorsed by Mr. Willoughby, August, 1639. "John Staynings letter whereupon I sent him in money 40/-" We do not know how John Steynings fared in the campaign in the Netherlands, but we find him in 1642 attached to the parliamentarian army which in the March of that year was besieging Plymouth.

The glimpse we have of this young man, born of an ancient family and wealthy parents, and yet very imperfectly educated and glad to enlist as a private soldier, is a striking commentary upon the advance that has been made in the wellbeing of the commonwealth in the last two hundred years.

Another of the Steynings family was the comfortably settled rector of Broadclyst, who married John Willoughby's sister. One of his sons, Amias, entered the army, and served like his cousin, John Steynings, as a private soldier. He went on the expedition to the Netherlands under the command of the Marquis of Hamilton, an expedition which was secretly supported by Charles I, but for fear of the emperor, was declared to be independent of his authority. On the 26th April, 1631, we find him writing to Mr. John Willoughby from "Gerckcum under Serjeant Major Morris."

"I give God praise that I am safely landed: It pleased God that we did lie 16 days upon the water, but I give God praise that we have overcome it. We were 4 hours chased by a Dunkeark (privateer) but it pleased God we lost him in the evening . . . . . I hope your worship will be pleased to send me over some cloth or a suit of apparell yearly . . . It is hard living upon the States means—it is but four shillings in eight days."[1]

A passage, evidently of danger, of sixteen days to Holland, sounds odd enough to our nineteenth century ears; and sixpence a day does not seem high pay for a young man "gently born and bred." In the July of the same year, Amias writes, "From our leaguer at Masestréet in Lukeland" (Maestricht in Luychland, the Bishopric of Liege or Luck), at great length to his uncle, reciting some of the miseries they had suffered on the campaign.

"We have passed through a great many miseries both by sea and land, since we left England and are now in great want of victuals all things are at such a dearth in our leaguer (the lives of the besiegers) that the States means is not able to find us half the week. Had I not brought with me some money for the which I was glad to pawne my trunk with my apparel I had not written unto you at this time; it was never known to the oldest that now lives in our army, such lamentable dearth for all things; many a gentleman which never took spade in their hands are now constrained to work in the trenches, and venture their lives in the mouth of the cannon, only for means to keep them from starving, and besides have spent all that ever they could make and many of them have lost their lives. We do undermine day and night to work under the walls, and we are come within a stones cast of them. We lie day and night in our arms and can hardly have two hours rest in four and twenty. If the King of Spain do lose this town—then may the King of Sweden easily come into Flanders with his

1. *Trevelyan Papers*, iii, 181.

army. Good Uncle it is a great deal of misery that a soldier doth endure besides dangers every minute of his life."

Amias had his son with him who was also called Amias; and both of them appear to have pawned their clothes so as to have a little money in their pockets when they started on their expedition. The elder Amias begs Mr. Willoughby to send them four or five pounds to redeem their clothes "which we shall lose if you send not unto us, and then we are quite undone."

"It hath been a hard journey and a most miserable leaguer. It would but greve you to express our miseries—the hard ground must content us for lodging before we return to garrison, and our diet will be but miserable; for all which we thank God and for my part I do endure it with patience, and poor Ames (his son) too with my persuasions.—We shall lose our trunks and clothes which are better worth than ten pounds and our credits too if you send not unto us, for our clothes which we now weare will be all worn before we come to garrison, for we lie day and night in them and many times in dirt and mire."

Ames Steynings also enquires about the portion of the tithes of the parish of Broadclyst, which were due to his father's estate. His father must therefore have been dead at this period. We do not know what part Ames Steynings' father and son took in the Civil War or whether indeed they left their bones in the "leaguer" at Maestricht.

The last act of Mr. John Willoughby's life was to obtain a "pass" to visit his relations at Gaulden, in the parish of Tolland, and at Selworthy. A marriage certificate attested by his son-in-law, John Turberville of Gaulden, still exists among the Luccombe church papers. He died in 1658 leaving an only son, John, whose only child, Mary, as before stated (p. 132), married in 1655 George Trevelyan of Nettlecombe, the son of the George Trevelyan who had suffered so terribly on account of his loyalty to the Stuart family.

Mr. Charles Steynings was succeeded by his third son, Charles, who married Susanna, daughter of Sir Nicholas Martyn and of Elizabeth his wife. By her will dated December, 1663, dame Elizabeth "late wife and relict of Sir Nicholas Martyn of the same knight" leaves "to my couzin Thomas Gorges of Heavytree in ye countye aforesaid, Esqre., one hundred pounds of currant money of England, under the trust and use followinge, that is to say to buy with the said one hundred pounds two jewells with what convenience may be and then to deliver or cause to be delivered unto my daughter Susanna Steynings for her use during life, and after her death to her eldest son or daughter, and in case she dyes without any issue they the sayd jewells to be delivered unto my grandchild Nicholas Martyn of Heavytree, aforesd. Esqr."

Mrs. Steynings died at Holnicote on the 8th May, 1685, and Charles Steynings himself on the 4th of December, 1700, aged seventy-eight. He lies buried in the Steynings aisle in Selworthy Church.

A copy of Mr. Steynings' will is to be found in the Appendix By it he bequeathed the Holnicote estate to his wife's nephew, William Martyn of Oxton, co. Devon. Mr. Martyn, after living at Holnicote for some years, sold the estate to William Blackford, son of Richard Blackford of Dunster.

One of the old gateways remains of the earliest house at Holnicote. The house, which must have borne a great resemblance to Bratton Court near Minehead, evidently formed with its outbuildings a square round a court yard ; the outer walls of the buildings, on three sides at all events, forming a strong defence. Many old farm houses on the hill country are still to be seen built in this fashion, no doubt for safety in the insecure times of two or three hundred years ago. The grand old jambs of the great gateway at Holnicote still remain, and portions of the oak doors; over the gateway, as at Bratton, is the porter's room. This earlier house, which was of late fifteenth century date, was pulled down to make room for a large square house of the Queen Anne or Early Georgian type, which adjoined the present stables. This second house was burnt down in 1794, and in course of time a long low house, in the cottage style, was built on the site of the present house. This house, says the author of *A Tour in Search of Genealogy*, writing in 1811, "is perfectly the cottage without, having a thatched roof; woodbines, jasmines, and roses clothe the walls, producing the most pleasing effect: but within we meet with every fashionable accommodation that high life can require, or that taste can suggest; nor is there good collection of books wanting. The drawing room is elegantly furnished by the most charming specimens of Mrs. Fortescue's pencil." At dinner on the evening of his arrival, he tells us there were present, "a gentleman and lady and their daughter, relations of the family: the gentleman all mildness, good humour and benevolence:

and his lady with a mind in perfect unison with his and an angelic face, the fit show glass of the precious gem the casket contained. The daughter, without possessing a very extraordinary show of beauty, had such a countenance and manner as rather excited respect than love at first sight; but a longer acquaintance took full possession of the heart." There was also present a "young man of fashion who was hurrying to town with the fall of the leaf . . . . . Of my host and his lady I have not said much; but if dignity without pride, the greatest affability and good temper, a desire to oblige, and a considerable knowledge of the world be ingredients to form a pleasing character, Mr. Fortescue has the claim for admiration, and his lady was formed to make such a man happy. . . . She is likewise the physician of the poor of the neighbourhood."

The third house was burnt down almost entirely in 1851, and large additions were made to what remained of it by the present baronet in 1873.

BLACKFORD FAMILY.

Of this family, which owned Holnicote for two generations, little more is known than is stated above in the history of that manor. The name is a not uncommon one still in North Devon, and there was a family of this name living at Holt, in the parish of Luccombe, in the seventeenth and eighteenth centuries. A branch of the family also lived at one time at Holt, in the parish of Selworthy, and intermarried with the Siderfin family of Knoll. They appear to have been yeomen. The connection of the name with the district appears to make the suggestion possible, that Richard Blackford, a master in chancery, having made his fortune in London, retired into his own district before his death. There are tombstones in Luccombe churchyard to the Blackford family, and one of the oldest tombstones in Selworthy churchyard is to a member of that family, Joan Blackford. The date is obliterated, but the stone belongs apparently to about the beginning or middle of the seventeenth century. Alex. Blackford, gent., was one of the two trustees who presented the Rev. John Wood to the benefice of Selworthy in 1669, and there are several entries concerning this family in the Selworthy Registers during the seventeenth and eighteenth centuries. A certain Richard Blackford who witnessed two leases of the property then held by feoffees for the church, in 1661 and 1663, may well have been the father of the Richard Blackford mentioned above.

William Blackford married Elizabeth Dyke of Pixton, and died in 1728, leaving a son called William, also of Holnicote. This second William died on March 20th, 1730, leaving an only daughter, Henrietta, on whose death in her seventh year the Holnicote estate reverted to her great aunt Elizabeth Blackford, daughter of Richard Blackford of Dunster, her heir at law, and the wife of Edward Dyke of Pixton in the parish of Dulverton. Thomas Dyke of Tetton, nephew and heir to Edward Dyke, had one only daughter and heiress, Elizabeth, who married Sir Thomas Acland, seventh baronet, of Killerton.

The will of Richard Blackford, of Dunster, Somerset, one of the king's Masters Extraordinary in Chancery, is dated Jan. 8, 1688, and was proved by his widow Elizabeth, 4 April, 1689, in the Probate Court of Canterbury, entry 48. He bequeaths "To my daughter Dyke, wife of Edw. Dyke, the fee simple of the messuage called Foxcombe, in Hawkridge. To my daughter Sidwell the interest and fee of the messuage called Culverwell in the parish of Bicknoller, but William Blackford to have power to pay his sisters £100 each, and take the land." Mentions besides his sister, Mary Coffin, cousin Robert Siderfin, his sister Hawkins and her son. Gives 10*s.* towards repairs to each of the parish churches of Dunster, Selworthy, and Luccombe.

The will of Elizabeth Blackford, dated 23 October, 1693, was proved in the Probate Court of Canterbury, 23 May, 1699, by her two daughters Elizabeth Dyke and Sidwell Dyke, the residuary legatees. She mentions her late husband's two sisters, her kinsfolk Mr. John Quirke and his wife, Mr. Walter Coffin (then residing at Allerford) and his wife, my cousin Mr. Robert Siderfin and his wife, and Joan Atkins, Mr. Edward Haberfield.

Mr. Charles Blackford of Selworthy, who was buried 21 April, 1682, must have been a near relation, and Mrs. Christian Blackford of Selworthy, who was buried 5 Sept., 1695, was a sister of Richard Blackford.

To the latter Richard Blackford bequeaths in his will "a broad piece of gold of two and twenty shillings coyne."

The will of William Blackford, of Holnicote Court, Somerset, grandson of the above, dated March 11, 1730, was proved March 3, 1731, by the executors.

To the poor of Selworthy, Dunster, Bossington, and West Luckham he bequeaths £20. He mentions also "my brother-in-law Edward Leeds of the Inner Temple, London." "George Sawbridge Little of Bridge Row, London, Merchant, James Sampson Counsellor at law, Gregory Gardner of Kings Brompton, Somerset, Esq., and Richard Cridland of Comb Flory, Gent., attorney at law," are left as Tres: of "all my lands, Manors, etc., for the use of my daughter, Henrietta Blackford. Her guardianship to my sister Leeds."

For the rest of the history of this family *see* Blackford pedigree.

Part of the estates of the Blackford family was the manor of Mallingden in the parish of Cliff near Rochester. It is stated in Hasted's *Kent* that the court baron is held under a tree, there being no manor house remaining.[1]

DYKE OF KINGSTON.

At the west end of the south aisle of Kingston Church, co. Somerset, there is a brass to a certain Thomas Dyke and Anna his wife. The inscription engraved on it runs as follows:

"Here lye buried the bodyes of Thomas Dyke and Anna his wife. She died 15th day of May, 1630. Ætatis suæ 32. He died 26th day of May, anno dni 1672. Ætatis suæ 81.

"Farewell fond world I found thee vaine at best
In Abraham's bosome I find sweetest rest.
Here lyes just, pious, prudence, which is more:
Here lyes the father of the orphan poore.
King, country, church, the poore, all these have lost:
Good subject, servant, son those father most.

"Abi viator et vale donec resurgamus."

1. Hasted's *Kent*, vol. i, p. 533.

On the brass is a shield charged with three cinquefoils. Crest: an arm with hand gloved and holding a mace.

This Thomas Dyke represented a branch of the Dyke family of Dulverton, for some time settled at Kingston. He was born about the year 1591, and died on the 26th May, 1672. We do not know from what family his wife Anna sprung. She was born in 1598, and died in 1630, forty-two years before her husband, and was buried in Kingston Church. One son, born in 1613, was left to carry on the many virtues of Thomas Dyke as borne witness to by his monument, who was also called Thomas. Thomas proved his father's will, dated March 10, 1671, in the Archdeaconry Court of Taunton on 24 June, 1672. By it the elder Thomas leaves to his son and Elizabeth his wife £10 apiece for a ring; lands in Broomfield parish to his son; to his niece Jane Pearse and her husband, and to "my cousin" Margaret Dyke of Dulverton, and "my cousin" William Dyke and his mother-in-law 20*s.*; to Thomas Dyke, son of John Dyke, late of Dulverton, £1000; to Wm. Dyke, Edward Dyke, Grace Dyke, Eliz. Dyke, children of the said John Dyke, deceased, £500 apiece; to all the children of my uncles Wm. Dyke and Richard Dyke, 20*s.*; to Richard Dyke of Kingston £5. His daughter-in-law to undertake care of his funeral; to be buried in Kingston Church. His son Thomas to be executor and residuary legatee.

Thomas, although well to do, did not settle down idly as a country gentleman, but studied for the medical profession, and took the degree of M.D. He married (1) Elizabeth, the sister and eventually the co-heiress of Edward Pepys, esq. After her death he married (2) a certain Joanna Deane, who may have been living as a servant in his house, and by whom he had had a son, who in 1689 had already arrived at man's estate. Joan, and her son Thomas Deane, who took the name of Dyke on his father's marriage with his mother, proved the second Thomas Dyke's will on 7 Feb., 1689. By this will Thomas Dyke conveys the manor of Ashway in the parish of Dulverton to Thomas Deane als Dyke, of the Inner Temple, gent. Should the said Thomas Deane als Dyke die without issue, the estate to go to Thomas Dyke, son of John Dyke of Pixton, on his paying to Thomas Dyke, Lawrence Dyke, William Dyke, Elizabeth Dyke and John, children of William Dyke, late of Ashill in Somerset, gent., deceased, to each of them £100. Lands in Broomfield to pass with manor of Ashway. Thomas Deane to take name of Dyke. Moieties of rectories of Kingsbrompton and Winsford to go for maintenance of poor scholars at St. Mary's Hall, Oxford. Joanna and Thomas Deane residuary legatees.

A brass to Thomas Deane's (2) memory is to be seen under the one that commemorates his father and mother in Kingston Church. It bears the following inscription:

"Hic depositæ sunt mortales exuviæ quōdam Thomæ Dyke in Medicinis Doctoris, exuviæ quidem meræ, et non magis illius partes quam vestes, aliaque corporalia tegumenta. Ille enim integer (id est spiritus ejus) nihil in Terris relinquens fugit hinc 22nd die Decembris 1689, totusque excessit rediens ad Deum qui dedit illum nasciturum 5th die Aprilis, 1613.

"Who ere thou art that here dost passe
Learne this thou mayst of me
As thou art now soe once I was
As I am soe shalt thou be.

"Vade, vale, resi pisce.

"Portus mortis, porta vitæ."

On the brass is the same shield as on his father's.

Thomas Deane, now Thomas Dyke the third, died s.p. in 1730. His will which bears date 4 June, 1717, was proved by his cousin yeoman Geo. Deane on the 24th Oct., 1730. Thomas Dyke is now described as of Tetton, co. Somerset, esq. His plate to his wife, afterwards to Thomas Dyke of Jews (in Wiveliscombe parish), and if dead to Edward Dyke of Pixton. His lands in Taunton Deane to his wife for life, then to said Thomas Dyke of Jews and his heirs male; remainder to Edward Dyke of Pixton. To Thomas Dyke of Lydeard Punchardon his house; my servant Elizabeth Dyke, £100 and £10 for money; Mary Dyke, formerly of Jews, £1000 and £20 for money; George Deane £4000; Edward Dyke, his wife and children, George Deane, Mary Dyke, his said brother Thomas. Mr. Blackford and his son, Sir Thomas Wroth, a ring of £1 1*s.*; Edward Dyke of London, George Deane and Thomas Dyke of Lydeard Punchardon £500 to buy an advowson for John Dyke of Lydeard Punchardon if qualified to hold a living; advowson to go to Thomas Dyke of Jews and his heirs. Remainder to Elizabeth Dyke of Pixton in fee. No executor appointed. Administration granted to George Deane, next of kin, 24 Oct., 1730.

George Deane, who is described as of Pyrland

House in the parish of St. James, Taunton, was the nephew of Thomas Dyke's (3) mother. He married a daughter of old John Dyke of Pixton, who died before her husband. George Deane died in the winter of 1741, and his will was proved by his only child and residuary legatee Elizabeth Deane, in the Probate Court of Canterbury on 1st Feb., 1742.

To my brother-in-law and niece Dyke, to my nephew Hole, and to each of my trustees £10; to my housekeeper Mary Bartlett an amount of £100 per year; to my godchild Henrietta Johnson £5000; lands in Lydeard St. Lawrence, Aish Priors, lands and hereditaments in South Molton, North Molton, Maryansleigh, Rose Ash, Nymet Episcopi, in Uffculme and Dunkeswell, and elsewhere in Devon, and elsewhere, to my daughter Elizabeth Deane and her heirs; if she die without issue, to the said Mary Bartlett, with remainder to heirs of the body of my late sister Nott, and for want of such heirs, to my own rightful heirs. George Speke of Dillington and Francis Robinson of Willby, Trēs. The executors renounced administration, and the will proved by daughter 1 Feb., 1742.

Elizabeth Deane did not live long to enjoy the large large fortune she had inherited from her father. Her will is dated 13 Nov., 1742, and was proved by her executor and residuary legatee, Elizabeth Dyke, at that time "living with my said uncle Edward Dyke," at Pixton, on 11 Aug., 1744. Elizabeth Dyke was the daughter of Thomas Dyke of Tetton in the parish of Kingston.

Dyke of Dulverton.

According to a tradition held by their descendants

the Browne family of New Zealand, the Dyke family were originally land agents settled at Dulverton and Kingsbrompton. But however this may be, we find them already in the seventeenth century people of considerable importance.

The will of a William Dyke of Kents, in Kingsbrompton, gent., dated 10 Feb., 1665, was proved 30 Nov., 1667, in the Probate Court of Canterbury, by his widow Amy Dyke and his son William Dyke. He mentions "my son William Dyke, my aunt Mary Bean, my wife Amy Dyke, my brother John Dyke, my brother-in-law Gregory Gardner, my sisters Jone Pearse, Jane Gardner, and Margaret Dyke; my cousin Mrs. Elizabeth Dyke, my sisters Mrs. Wood, Mary Davidge and Joane Everard; my godson William, son of John Dyke; my cousin Edward Dyke, my brother-in-law Tristram Wood, and Dr. Dyke guardian of my son.

The family appears also to have been settled at Pixton in the parish of Dulverton, for some generations before John Dyke of Pixton, esq., who died intestate in 1699, and to whose effects administration was granted 7 Feb., 1700. His wife Margaret survived him and died in 1703. Her will was proved in the Archidiaconal Court at Taunton by Edward Dyke of Pixton, her eldest and only surviving son, 1 March, 1704. She bequeaths her farm of Heale in Kingsbrompton parish to her son Edward Dyke, on condition of his paying £300 to "my other son Thomas Dyke." "£200 to my daughter Elizabeth, wife of William Blackford, gent.; to Elizabeth Dyke the wife of my son Edward Dyke, and Sidwell, wife of my son

Thomas Dyke, £10; to John Dyke and Margaret Dyke, children of my said son Edward, £200; to Thomas Dyke, Elizabeth Dyke, Mary Dyke, and Ursula Dyke, children of my said son Thomas, £10 apiece; to William, Elizabeth and Mary, children of the said William Blackford, £10 apiece." Codicil mentions death of her son Thomas.

The will of the above mentioned Edward Dyke (1) is dated —— 1728. By it he appoints his wife Elizabeth his sole executrix and residuary legatee. She however died without proving the will; and on 26 June, 1740, administration with will annexed was granted to Edward Dyke her son, by the Probate Court of Canterbury (Brown 167). "Estates in Bampton to son John, with remainder to son Edward; daughter-in-law Mary Dyke, £20; granddaughter-in-law Elizabeth Dyke £20; my daughter Grace £5000; my son Edward, manor and barton of Pixton and all other estates, subject to his mother's life interest in them."

This Elizabeth Dyke was a daughter of Mr. Richard Blackford of Dunster, a Master in Chancery. She survived her husband and died in Feb., 1736. Her will was proved by the above named son, Edward Dyke (2) of Pixton, Jan. 27, 1736. In this will she bequeaths her estate of Hunscombe to her son Edward, subject to the following payment: "to my daughter Grace £1000; £20 to John Dyke." Grace Dyke (afterwards Grace Smyth) residuary legatee. Codicil 25 Jan., 1735. Edward Smyth £20, Francis Smyth £1000, Elizabeth Smyth and Lavinia Smyth £100, Grace Smyth £50 in lieu of plate, Elizabeth Deane wife of George Deane £5 for a ring.

Edward Dyke (2) of Pixton and of Tetton married Margaret, daughter of Sir John Trevelyan of Nettlecombe, bart., and widow of Alex. Luttrell of Dunster Castle. This lady died at Mrs. Vanderwall's at Greenwich, 20 June, 1764, and was buried at Dunster on the following 4th July. Edward Dyke died s.p. at Tetton in the parish of Kingston, on the 14th Aug., 1746, and was buried at Dulverton the 21st of that month. By his will dated 29 Sept., 1744, he bequeaths estates in Bampton and elsewhere to his nephew Edward Smyth, directing him to take the name and arms of Dyke; and the rest of his property he bequeaths to his niece, Elizabeth Dyke of Tetton, the daughter of Thomas Dyke of Tetton who had died in the previous year, whom he appoints his sole executor. He directs that Elizabeth's husband shall take the name of Dyke. £100 to his daughter-in-law Margaret Luttrell. Tres.: Sir John Trevelyan of Nettlecombe, Geo. Trevelyan of Lea Hill, Cannon Southey of Fitzhead, Richard Cridland of Coombe Florey.

Elizabeth Dyke who had married Sir Thomas Acland the seventh bart. of Killerton in the previous year, proved her uncle's will in the Probate Court of Canterbury, 4 Oct., 1746.

Lady Acland thus became a great heiress. Her uncle, John, who is described as of Holnicote Court, esq., died *s.p.* in the spring, 1732, and the Holnicote estate passed to her brother Edward, who proved his brother John's will 24th May, 1732. And so, on the death of Edward Dyke (2), the estates both of Holnicote and Pixton passed to her. Already she had come into possession of the Pyrland estates by the bequest of her first cousin, Elizabeth Deane, and of Tetton on the death of her father.

In a deed poll existing at Killerton, Lady Acland conveys to certain Trustees her "manors and hereditaments situate in the several parishes of Selworthy, Luckham, Minehead, Porlock, Dulverton, Brompton Regis, Exford, Dunster, Carhampton, Timberscombe, otherwise Emberscombe, St. Decumans, Old Cleeve, Crowcombe, Bicknoller, Cutcombe, Bossington, Stock Pero, Brushford, Winsford, Hawkridge, Withy-combe, East Anstey, Oakeford, and Bampton in Somerset and Devon, part of which manors and heredits. were late the lands and inħance of William Blackford, Esq., decd, since that of Henrietta Blackford his only child and heir at law, also deceased, and other portions of such manors and lands were the lands of Byam Wood, Esq. and Mary Wood, spinster."[1]

Seldom have two successive heads of houses married so well as the sixth Acland, bart. and his son, the elder obtaining by his marriage the great estates of the Wroth family, the younger the above princely inheritance of Elizabeth Dyke.

Pyrland House was bought in 1756 by Sir William Yea, the first bart. of the name who had married Julia, eldest daughter of Sir George Trevelyan, bart., of Nettlecombe. The property was copyhold, but was enfranchised by Sir William, who rebuilt the house there in 1758.

1. B. and M. Wood's property was bought by Edw. Dyke.

ACLAND FAMILY.

"Akeland," says Sir William Pole, "has given name unto a race that have many descents dwelled there. The first that I find was called Baldwyn de Accelana, (2) Baldwyn, (3) William, which, by Sarah, daughter of John de la Pille, of Pille had issue, who had issue Baldwyn anno. 14 king Edward II."

Hugh de Accalen was living at Accalen or Akeland co. Devon, in 1155. He died about the year 1191, and was succeeded by his son the first Baldwin de Accellana of Sir William Pole, whose son Baldwyn de Accalen, *temp.* Henry III, was the father of William de Accalen, who *temp.* Edward I married Sarah, the daughter and heiress of John de la Pille. Baldwyn de Accalen who was living in the ninth year of Edward II had two sons, John and Richard. Richard died without issue in 1347; but John, who married Agnes, daughter and heiress of Richard de Leigh, of Leigh Barton, in Loxbeare, in Devon, had one son, by whom he was succeeded in 1365, John de Accalen, of Accalen. This John, Sir W. Pole tells us, was a famous soldier, and acquired a great reputation in the stormy reigns of Edward III and Richard II. We find Sir John (9 Richard II) conveying all his estates in Aclane, Gratton, Barnstaple, Little Bray and South Molton, to Thomas Affeton, John Stafford, and John Collin, to raise money for his redemption in case he should be taken prisoner, without sale of his lands. This fact is interesting as showing how gentlemen in those days provided for these contingencies.[1] This

1. Acland family papers, quoted by Polwhele. Ed. 1797.

John de Accalen married Alice, the daughter and heiress of William Hawkridge, of Hawkridge, in the parish of Chittlehampton. They had issue, John, who died without issue, 4 Henry IV, and Baldwyn, who married Joan, the daughter and heiress of William Riverton.

Baldwyn Akelane died in 1410, and was succeeded by his son, Robert Akelane, who married Cicely, daughter and co-heiress of Roger Hakeworth. Robert died in 1445, and was succeeded by his son, Baldwyn Akelane, who married Joan, daughter and co-heiress of Sir John Prideaux, of Addiston, and widow of William Drewe. Baldwyn was succeeded in 1490 by his son John Akelane, who married Elizabeth, daughter and heiress of John Fortescue, of Sprideston. Their son John married (1) Elizabeth, daughter of Thomas Hexte, of Kingston, in Devon, and (2) Mary, daughter of John Francis, and widow of John Cruwys, of Cruwys Morchard, in the same county. By his second wife he had no issue, but by the first he had (with other offspring) a son, John Akeland, who married Elizabeth, daughter of the before-mentioned John Cruwys, the first husband of his father's second wife, by his first wife, Elizabeth, daughter of Thomas Whitle. This last named John Akeland left issue by Elizabeth his wife, John (heir to his great grandfather) as hereafter mentioned; Antony (of Hawkridge), and Ellen or Helena, who married Robert Chichester, of Hall, co. Devon.

John Akeland, who, as before mentioned, married Elizabeth Fortescue, outlived both his son and his grandson, and on his death the representation of the family devolved upon his eldest great grandson John; whilst the estate of Hawkridge, in Chittlehampton fell to the portion of his second great grandson, Antony, who married Agnes, daughter of John Courtenay, of Molland, co. Devon, a branch of the Courtenays of Powderham. From Chittlehampton his descendant, Richard Acland, is said to have removed to Fremington, having purchased in 1672 that manor and barton. His son Richard Acland left two co-heiresses, (1) Frances, who married, in 1765, Hugh Fortescue, rector of Filleigh, and Susanna, who married Dr. Barbor, of Barnstaple, in May, 1748.[1]

John Acklande, as mentioned above, succeeded his great grandfather. He married Margaret, daughter and co-heiress of Hugh Radcliff, of Stepney, by whom he had issue: (1) Hugh his successor; (2) John Ackland, of Culm John, who succeeded to the estates in Middlesex. This John was knighted at the Tower, on March 15th, 1603, on the accession of James I, and was a man of much prominence at this time. He was for a considerable period M.P. for Devonshire, and was sheriff of Devon in 1608. Sir John purchased the estate of Columb or Culm John, an estate which as early as 1233, had been held for at least three generations by the Culme family, a branch of which ancient family was seated *temp.* Elizabeth, at Molland. One of this family was Dean of St. Patrick's, in 1647; and his letters to his cousin, John Willoughby, at that time from Ireland are interesting.[2] From the Culme family the estate passed to Courtenay, earl of Devon.

1. *Somerset and Dorset Notes and Queries*, vol. iv., p. 378.
2. *Trevelyan Papers*, v. iii, pp. 265, 266.

After the attainder of the marquis of Exeter it was transferred to the Bassett family. From them it passed to the Rousewell family, from whom it was purchased by the above-mentioned Sir John Acland, who built a house there on the foundation begun by the earl of Devon, and a chapel for the use of his family and tenants. Sir John was a great benefactor to the charities of Exeter, and to the University of Oxford. He married (1) Elizabeth, daughter of George Rolle, of Stevenston, and (2) Margaret, daughter of William Portman, of Orchard Portman.

Sir John died at Culm John in 1613, without children, leaving a considerable estate to his brother, Sir Hugh Ackland. The elaborate monument to his memory described below is to be seen at the end of the north aisle in Broadclyst Church:

"On a tomb about 5 feet high from the ground lies his portraiture in full proportion cut out of stone, all in armour except head and hand. In his hand he holds a book. His two wives are represented kneeling each before a desk, the one at the head the other at the foot with their faces towards him, all within two pillars near 20 feet in height, large and finely wrought, on the top of which are placed several figures that greatly adorn the whole. On the 1st pillar is the motto 'Mors janua vitæ,' on the second pillar 'Mors mihi lucrum.' In the middle of the monument above the effigies is a blank table of marble, left, as it is supposed for an epitaph, which hath not hitherto been supplied; before the arch that covers the figure of St. John, are in one place 'Caro mea requiescat in spe'; in another, 'Post tenebras spero lucem.' Over the monument is a large achievement with many quarterings."[1]

Sir John's brother, Hugh Akeland of Akeland, was sheriff of Devon, 8 and 9 James I. He married

1. Polwhele's *History of Devon*, vol. ii, p. 136.

Margaret, daughter of Thomas Monke of Powderidge, co. Devon, and great aunt of Monke, earl of Albemarle. He survived his brother and succeeded to his large estates, and no doubt erected the costly monument to Sir John's memory mentioned above. He was succeeded by his son, Sir Arthur Akelande, who married Eleanor, daughter and heiress of Robert Mallett of Wooley, a manor situated in the parish of Beaford. This manor passed by successive heiresses to the families of Hacche, Mallet, and Acland. Sir Arthur was knighted in 1603 and died in 1610. His son and heir, John Acklande, was nineteen years of age at the death of his father in 1610, and in 1617 he married Elizabeth, daughter of Sir Thomas Vincent, bart. This John Acklande was a noted royalist, and and at the beginning of the civil war he garrisoned the house at Culm John which his great uncle had built, and held it for the king. At one time, Clarendon tells us, Culm John was the only stronghold that the king could reckon on in Devonshire, to check the movements of lord Stamford, who was lying with his army at Exeter, or of any further parliamentary forces that might arrive either by land or by sea. But col. Acland had to fly from Culm John, and we find Fairfax taking possession of the house as his head-quarters, while the main body of his forces lay at Silverton. It is recorded that Fairfax, with his usual moderation and liberality, treated lady Acland and her household with the greatest consideration and kindness. Perhaps the family connection with general Monke helped to insure her safety; but nevertheless the house at Culm John was afterwards plundered, and Sir John himself had a fine of £1800 imposed on him, which amount was afterwards increased to £4,000. This fine was subsequently reduced to the original sum by the intervention of some of his friends. Sir John was sheriff of Devonshire in 1641. By his wife, the above named Elizabeth Vincent, of Stoke d'Abernon, he had issue, Sir Francis, his successor; (2) John; (3) Hugh; and two daughters—Eleanor, who married Sir John Davie of Creedy, and Susannah, who married (1) Edward Helsall, equerry to queen Catherine; (2) John Carleton, esq., equerry to Charles I and II. Sir John died August 24th, 1647, and was buried in the church of Stoke d'Abernon. Sir John was created a baronet for his services to the crown in 1644, but the letters patent were destroyed in the civil war, when no doubt little at Culm John, of any value, escaped the clutches of the parliamentarian garrison. They were renewed to his son, Sir Hugh, in 1677, with precedence from the former date.

Sir Francis Acland, the second baronet, died unmarried in 1649, and was succeeded by his brother, Sir John Acland.

Sir John, third baronet, married Margaret, daughter of Dennis Rolle, of Stevenstone, by whom he had a son, Arthur, his successor, and a daughter, who married John, Lord Arundel of Trerice. Through this marriage and the settlements connected with it, the Arundel estates in Devon and Somersetshire ultimately devolved upon the Acland family. Sir John died before he came of age in 1645. Sir Arthur also died before he came of age, and the title and the estates reverted to his uncle, Sir Hugh. Sir Hugh Acland, fifth baronet (third son of Sir John, the first baronet) was M.P. for Barnstaple in 1678, and for Tiverton in 1655. He married Ann, daughter of Sir Thomas Daniel of Berwick Hall, co. York, and widow of Sir Thomas Chamberlain of Oxfordshire, by whom he had issue a family of six sons and two daughters. Of these children, John the eldest son settled at Wooley and died on October 28th, 1702, before his father, being then M.P. for Callington, in Cornwall. He left issue by Elizabeth his wife, daughter of Richard Acland of Fremington, four sons. One of their sons, John, was rector of Broadclyst, and we find the following curious note in connection with that parish during his incumbency ; "Some years since (c. 1750) Clyst Gerard Chapel was converted into a barn by one James Baker, who is said to have been in good circumstances before this act of profaneness, but never thrived afterwards. He had his leg shot off ; he quitted his native country ; and he died abroad in poverty."[1]

Sir Hugh Acland, the eldest son and sixth baronet was M.P. for Barnstaple in 1713. He married Cecily, the daughter and co-heiress of Sir Thomas Wroth of Petherton Park, co. Somerset, by whom he had issue : (1) Sir Thomas his successor ; (2) John, who died an infant ; (3) Arthur, who settled at Fairfield, and married Elizabeth, daughter of William Oxenham, of Devon, by whom he had three sons, Hugh, John, Peregrine, and several daughters.

Note on the family of Wroth.

Sir Thomas Wroth was the lineal descendant of Sir

1. Old MSS., quoted by Polwhele.

Hugh de Placet, brother of John, earl of Warwick *temp.* Henry III, who married the heiress of John de Wroth, of Wrotten, co. Kent. Sir Hugh was sheriff of that county, and also of Devon, warden also of the Stannaries and lord of the manor of Newton Forester, which he held in right of his wife, by grand serjeanty, together with the office of keeping the park of North Petherton and other royal forests within the county of Somerset. His descendants took the name of Wroth. Their representative, Sir Thomas Wroth, was twice M.P. for Wells, during the reign of William III, and through the whole reign of queen Anne. On Sir Thomas' death in 1720, his estates came to his eldest daughter, Cecily, Lady Acland.

Sir Thomas Acland, the seventh baronet, married Elizabeth, daughter and heiress of Thomas Dyke of Tetton, co. Somerset, and also heiress of her uncle, Edward Dyke of Pixton. By this marriage the Pixton and Holnicote estates came into the Acland family. Sir Thomas had issue: John, who died in his father's lifetime, 1778, having married lady Christian Harriet Caroline Fox-Strangways, daughter of Stephen, first earl of Ilchester, by whom he left issue: Sir John Dyke Acland, who succeeded his grandfather as eighth baronet, and died *s.p.* 1785, and one daughter, Elizabeth Kitty, who married Henry George, second earl of Carnarvon in 1796, taking with her the Pixton estate as her dower. According to the Selworthy registers the seventh baronet's eldest son "John Dyke Acland Esqr., was born Jan. 21, 1747," and his second son, Thomas, on the tenth of April, 1752, at Holnicote.[1]

1. See Chapter VI.

Lady Acland died at Holnicote on the 30th June, 1753. Her husband survived her and died February 24, 1785. He was succeeded by his grandson, Sir John, the eighth baronet, who died *s.p.* April 15th of the same year, and was succeeded by his uncle, Sir Thomas Dyke, the ninth baronet, who married July 4, 1785, Harriet, only daughter of Sir Richard Hoare, bart. He left behind him four children, and his widow married in the May of the next year, captain M. Fortescue, a retired officer in the navy, and a brother of the first earl Fortescue. Sir Thomas appears to have been a great sportsman, as the very remarkable lines to his memory transcribed above[1] appear to show. He and his father were masters of the staghounds and did much in their time to keep that noble sport alive. The heads of the Acland family had held the lease of the royal forest of Exmoor for some time, and continued to hold it until the sale of the forest.

Sir Thomas Dyke Acland, the tenth baronet, was born March 29, 1787, and was high sheriff of Devon in 1809. He married, April 7, 1808, Lydia Elizabeth, the only daughter of Henry Hoare, esq., of Mitcham, co. Surrey, by whom he had issue: right hon. Sir Thomas Dyke, eleventh baronet, his successor, born May 25, 1809, succeeded his father in 1871; Arthur Henry Dyke, born 1811, died 1857, who took the name of Troyte on succeeding to the Huntsham Court estate; Charles Baldwyn Dyke, born Nov. 1, died May 10, 1837, *vide* Chapter IV, p. 57; Sir Henry Wentworth Dyke, bart., F.R.S., etc., born 1813; Rev. Peter Leopold Dyke, born 1819, prebendary and sub-

1. Selworthy Registers, Chap. VI, p. 98.

dean of Exeter Cathedral; John Barton Arundel, born 1823, who settled in New Zealand, and is a member of the Legislative Council; Dudley Reginald Dyke, died 17th July, 1837, æt. 10; two daughters, Agnes Lucy, who married in 1848 Arthur Mills, esq., of Bude; Lydia Dorothea Harriet.

A monument was erected by public subscription to Sir Thomas Acland, during his lifetime, at Exeter. The inscription on it runs as follows:

"As a tribute of private worth and public integrity and a testimony of admiration of a generous heart and open hand, which has been ever ready to protect the weak, to relieve the needy, and to succour the oppressed of whatsoever party, race, or creed."

We must not conclude this short sketch of a family whose connection with the parish has been so singular a benefit to it, without returning for a moment to that illustrious Selworthy man and brave soldier, John Dyke Acland, eldest son of the seventh baronet, and his heroic wife. He was born, as we have seen, at Selworthy, in 1747, and married in 1770, lady Christian Harriet Caroline Fox-Strangways, sister of Stephen, first earl of Ilchester. Mr. Acland entered the army, and became major of the 20th Foot. He was colonel of the Devonshire Militia, and served at one time as M.P. for Callington, but on the outbreak of the American War his regiment was ordered on active service. Lady Harriet accompanied her husband, and shared with him all the terrible hardships and privations, which attended that disastrous expedition. Major Acland was soon struck down by the terrible sickness which attacked the English army, and which was more to

THE LADY HARRIET ACLAND

From a contemporary engraving in the possession of Mrs. S. W[illegible].

be feared than their French foes No better accommodation could be obtained for the sick man than a miserable log hut destitute of every comfort. To this wretched shelter lady Harriet had her husband conveyed; and here they abode, suffering terrible privations, until she had nursed him back to health.

Again in 1777, lady Harriet probably saved her husband's life. Colonel Acland in that year was engaged in the disastrous battle of Ticonderoga, and dangerously wounded. Lady Harriet had not been allowed to accompany him in this hazardous enterprise; but on hearing the disastrous news, she hurried across the lake of Champlain in an open boat, at the risk of her life from wind and wave, and of capture by the enemy, once more to devote herself to nursing him. Her good care of her husband was once more successful, and he rejoined his regiment and returned to the front, still accompanied by his wife.

The position of major Acland's regiment at this time, was a peculiarly trying and dangerous one. He was in command of the Grenadiers, who formed the advanced guard of general Fraser's battalion, and so energetic were the enemy, and so great was the danger of a surprise, that for a long period a hurried sleep in their clothes, was all the rest either officers or soldiers could dare to take. To the constant danger of attack and the bitter cold, was added the want of the commonest necessaries. And soon another trial befell colonel Acland and his wife; for one night the tent in which they were sleeping caught fire, and they barely escaped with their lives and the loss of nearly all their clothing.

Greater sufferings, however, were still in store for poor lady Harriet. As the army advanced the Grenadiers were liable to attack at every moment, and major Acland directed his wife to stay behind with the baggage, with three other ladies who were with the army, the baroness Ruysdael, and the wives of two other officers, Mrs. Hamage, and Mrs. Reynell. At last the expected storm broke; and at the commencement of the engagement lady Harriet with the three other ladies, took refuge in a small uninhabited log hut, where they listened with horror to the unceasing rattle of the musketry and the roar of the cannon. But they were not long left alone in the hut, as it was soon taken possession of by the surgeons as a refuge for the wounded. We can well imagine the agony which these poor ladies endured through these long hours, surrounded by every form of suffering and anguish, and expecting every moment to see their husbands brought in wounded, or to hear that they were dead. And indeed the sad news soon reached Mrs. Ramage that her husband had been killed, and a little later Mrs. Reynell was told that lieutenant Reynell had been dangerously wounded. A period of longer suspense was the lot of lady Harriet, for not until the end of that terrible day, was she able to ascertain major Acland's fate. Then, as it was growing dark, she heard at last that he had been seriously wounded and taken prisoner.

Straightway lady Harriet's extraordinary heroism again asserted itself. Worn out as she must have been with the long suffering of that terrible day, she conceived the bold scheme of endeavouring to enter the enemy's camp in search of her husband, and gaining permission to nurse him. The night was closing in, and there was not a moment to lose. With the assistance of the chaplain to the Grenadiers, Mr. Brudenell, lady Harriet found a small boat, and accompanied by him, she dropped down the river to the French outposts. When challenged by the sentry, Mr. Brudenell held up a white handkerchief on a stick to show their peaceful intentions, and endeavoured to get the sentinel to understand the object of their journey. But he refused to convey any message to his commanding officer, and threatened to fire upon the boat if they moved. So a fresh horror was added to poor lady Harriet's many troubles. Surrounded by a foe, infuriated by the heavy fighting of the previous day, without a single wrap to protect her from the biting cold of that bitter spring night, and without food, through the long dark hours, she and her companion remained in the boat, in imminent danger of being at any moment fired upon from the bank. With the morning her immediate troubles were however over, and she was received by the enemy's general, with all the respect due to such heroic conduct.[1]

Once more lady Harriet nursed her husband back to health, and they soon were able to return to the old homes at Pixton and at Holnicote. In the spring of 1778 a son was born to them ; but the joy of the quiet home life was doomed soon to come to an end. In an unpublished MS. of Mr. P. Rogers Webber's, we find under the date "Nov. 11, 1778, Col. Acland fought a

1. *Polwhele's Devonshire, etc.*

duel on Bampton Down with Capt. Lloyd of the 20th Regt. of which he" (colonel Acland) "was Major. Died the 15th. Buried at Columb John the 18th." The family tradition is that colonel Acland contracted a chill during this encounter, which proved fatal. He was buried at Broadclyst, and not at Culm John; at least that is the tradition in the family.

Killerton, the present Devonshire home of the Acland family, originally belonged to a family of the name of Killerton, from whom it passed by an heiress to Sir John de Vege. After passing through the hands of several owners, the estate was purchased in the reign of Elizabeth, by Edward Drewe, serjeant-at-law, who built himself a house on the site of the present mansion. His son sold the estate to Sir Arthur Acland, father of Sir John Acland, the noted royalist. The present house was built in 1788. The manor of Broadclyst was purchased by the last baronet, about the beginning of the century. The owner of this important manor at one time possessed *jura regalia*, the right of life and death.

The Acland arms were of old, 3 oak leaves. At present the family bears the following coat: Chequy argent and sable a fesse gules; and for a crest, a man's hand couped at the wrist, in a glove, lying fesseways, therein a falcon perched, all proper.

Arundell Family.

Playfair states that Roger de Arundell came over with the Conqueror, and that he was possessed of twenty-eight manors in Somersetshire, in the reign of that monarch. On the other hand, the Cornish historian, Gilbert, tells us that although the name of the family appears on the corrupted Roll of Battle Abbey, it appears more likely to have been derived from the town and castle of Arundell, in Sussex, which were held before the Conquest by the thane Ederic, who was then dispossessed. Sir John Arundell, the last owner of the ancient Cornish home of the family, stated to Mr. Gilbert that he could never understand that there was any such local place in France, as Arundell. But whatever doubt may exist with regard to their first origin, it is clear that for many centuries the Arundell family was one of the foremost, and the most widely ramified families in Cornwall. Polwhele tells us that in the seventeenth century, there were no less than ten families of the name existing in his native county. For the following short account of the family the writer is indebted to many sources, notably to colonel Vivian's *Visitations of Cornwall*, Polwhele's and Gilbert's *Histories of Cornwall*, kind assistance given by Mr. A. J. Jewers, etc.

Maude, the heiress of Lansladron, married John Goviley, of Goviley. They had a daughter and heiress, Rose, who married Trerise, of Trerise. Their grand daughter, and ultimate heiress, Jane, married Ralph Arundell, the second son of Ralph Arundell, of Caerhayes, a descendant of Sir Oliver de Arundell, of Carshayes, who was living *temp.* Henry III; and this Ralph Arundell had one son, Nicholas Arundell, of Trerice, who married Elizabeth, daughter and heiress of Martin Pellor, of Pellor, co. Cornwall. In the east window of the north aisle of Selworthy church is a coat of arms Quarterly 1 and 4 arg. three chevrons sable (the colours curiously enough are wrong and should be reversed) 2 and 3 az. three pellets or (Pellor) Imp.—1 gone 2 and 3 vert, St. Andrew's cross gules between four eagles displayed gules (Leigh) 4 arg. three buckles? Leigh Barton, near Tiverton, passed to the Arundell family by a marriage of an Arundell with the heiress of that estate, and it is still the property of Sir Thomas Acland.

Sir John Arundell, the son of Ralph and Elizabeth, married Jane, daughter and heiress of John Durant. At that time, Sir John's cousin, Sir John Arundell of Lanherne, and the head of the family, was the largest landowner and most important man in Cornwall. He was also vice-admiral of Cornwall, and held the rank of general in the French wars. We find John, earl of Huntingdon, who states himself to be lieutenant-general to John, duke of Bedford, constable and admiral of England, writing to Sir John for the release of a ship, which he had arrested by virtue of his office.[1] Holinshed tells us that Sir John and the lord Camois and Sir George Seemor having had the government of Gascony entrusted to them, they "manned towns, gathered people, and comforted the fainting hearts of the Gascoigners." This Sir John, in 1379, repulsed an attack of the French, on the coast of Devonshire, and sailed for Brittany with a considerable force to aid the brave resistance the Bretons were making against the attempts of Charles V of France[2] to annex that duchy to his crown.

The expedition, however, was unfortunate. The

1. Carew, fol. 146.
2. Baker's *Chronicle*, p. 137.

squadron was overtaken by a violent storm and dispersed, and some of the ships were driven upon the coast of Ireland, some on that of Wales, some on the Cornish cliffs; and Sir John and 1,000 men of his little army perished. It is related, to show the magnificence of the nobles of that day, that Sir John Arundell was reputed to have had in his "furniture," fifty-two new suits of apparel of cloth-of-gold and tissue, which were all lost in the sea.

But to return to Sir John Arundell of Trerice. By the above mentioned lady he had an eldest son, Nicholas, who married Joan, daughter and heiress of Edward St. John, of Luccombe. By this marriage the manors and advowsons of Luccombe and Selworthy came into the Arundell family, with whom they remained until the family became extinct, and the Arundell estates devolved on the late Sir Thomas Acland. Johanna survived her husband, and died 5th July, 1463. The writer is inclined to think that the church of All Saints was built, or rather re-built, by this lady and her husband.

The date of the older part of the church agrees with this theory, which is also supported by the repetition of the emblems of St. John the Evangelist and of the head of St. John the Baptist, on the roof of the nave and chancel. Immediately over the altar too are the head and shoulders of a man wearing a helmet of the character of this period, which looks as if it might represent the founder of the church, or the person in memory of whom it was founded, or rather rebuilt.

Sir John Arundell, his eldest son, succeeded Nicholas Arundell. He married a daughter of Sir Hugh

Courtenay, kt., by which lady he had two sons who died young. He married secondly, Anna, daughter of Sir Walter Moyle of Eastwell, by whom he had issue Robert Arundell who succeeded him. His death in the year 1471, fulfilled, very curiously, a prophecy which had been uttered concerning him. Sir John had left the ancient house of the Arundells, Efford near Bude, and gone to reside at Trerice, because of a prophecy which declared that he "should die on the sand." Now in 1471 the earl of Oxford, a zealous Lancastrian, suddenly seized St. Michael's Mount by a clever stratagem. Sailing with a small body of troops from Milford Haven, he anchored under St. Michael's Mount. Disguised as pilgrims, and in friars' apparel, under which each had lodged a small sword and a dagger, he and his company went ashore. They pretended that they had come on a long pilgrimage from the remotest parts of the kingdom, to perform a penance laid on them by their father confessors, and to pay their vows at the altar of St. Michael, and they were admitted within the walls by the unsuspicious monks. But no sooner were they within the gates, than they seized the mount in the name of king Henry. The earl then renewed the fortifications and prepared to stand a siege. King Edward IV on hearing of the capture of this stronghold, sent word to John Arundell, then sheriff of Cornwall, to gather a force and march to the relief of the inhabitants of the mount. Sir John hastened to gather his troops together and invest the place. But his forces were repulsed by a vigorous sortie, and Sir John himself was slain "on the sand" between the mount and the mainland. He lies buried in the chapel of the castle.

Robert Arundell, his son and successor, married Ellen, daughter of John Southwood, and had one son who died without issue in Dec. 1491, and was succeeded by his uncle, Sir John Arundell. In the contest between Richard III and the earl of Richmond, the gentlemen of Cornwall and Devon were for the most part hostile to Richard. The king however, with the activity natural to his character, came down to Exeter, and tried by all the means in his power to conciliate the affections of his people. But suspecting disloyalty, from his own observation of the movements of the nobility, and struck by a circumstance which he considered ominous, he left the city with a melancholy presentiment of his fate.[1]

> "Richmond! When last I was at Exeter,
> The mayor in courtesy show'd me the castle,
> And call'd it Rougemont: at which name I started,
> Because a bard of Ireland told me once,
> I should not live long after I saw Richmond."[2]

The result of the king's investigations was that he sent down lord Scroope with a commission to hold a Sessions. This nobleman established his court at Torrington, and at this court a large number of the gentry of Cornwall, amongst whom we find Thomas Arundell, kt., John Arundell, dean of Exeter, were indicted of high treason, "all which fled and shifted for themselves, some into Britaine (Brittany) and some elsewhere. Saving Sir Thomas Sentliger and one Sir John Kame who were brought to Excester and there at the Carfox beheaded."[3]

1. Polwhele, p. 43.
2. *Richard III*, Act iv, scene ii.
3. Hooker.

December 5, 1485, 1 Henry VII, the king named John Arundell, dean of St. Peter's in Exeter, and one of his privy council together with Sir Richard Edgecumbe "to meet and treat with all captains, lieutenants, officers, persons paying tribute or inhabitants in the town of Callis, tower of Resetant, tower and castle of Guynes, castle of Hammes and marches thereof relating to all nations that concerned the crown of England in said places, and to admit all persons therein to their allegiance."[1]

Robert's successor, Sir John Arundell, was a very leading man in Cornwall in his time. He was sheriff of Cornwall, and also vice-admiral of the West to Henry VII and Henry VIII, and we find the queen in 1488 advertising "John Arundell of Trerice Esqre. that she was brought to bed of a prince."[2] In the second year of Henry VIII, Sir Piers Edgecombe, with Robert Willoughby de Broke, kt., John Arundell, kt., and Richard Carew, kt., were empowered to array and review all men at arms, archers and others who were to accompany Sir Thomas Darcey, kt., captain of the castle of Berwick, in his expedition against the Moors and other infidels, and to certify to the king and to his council the number of men at arms, archers, and others under Sir Thomas's command. In 1520 the king wrote to Sir John Arundell of Trerice, that he should expect his attendance at Canterbury about the "entertaynment of the emperor," whose landing was immediately expected.

Two years later we find that "John Arundell of

1. Rymer's *Foedera*, vol. 12, p. 279.

2. Carew, p. 146.

Trerice, esq., tooke prisoner Duncane Campbell a Scott" in a fight at sea. On this, Thomas, duke of Norfolk, "to whom he then belonged," writes to him:

"Right well beloved in our hearty wise we commend us unto you telling you wit, that by your servant this bearer wee have receyved your letters dated at Truro the 5th. dy of April, by which we perceyve the goodly valiant and jeopardous enterprise it hath pleased God of late to send you, by the taking of Duncane Camel and other Scots on the sea: of which enterprise we have made relation unto the king's Highnesse who is not a little joyous and glad to heare of the same your so doing, we doe not only thanke you in one most effectuall wise but also promise you, that during our life, wee will be glad to advance you to any preferment we can. And over this you shall understand our said Sovereigne Lord's pleasure is, that you shall come and repaire to his Highnesse with diligence in your own person, bringing with you the same captive and the master of the Scottish ship: at which time you shall not only be sure of his special thanks by his mouth and to know his pleasure therein but also of us to further any your reasonable pursuits unto his highness, or any other during our life, to the best of our power accordingly. Written at Lambeth the 11th dy of Aprille aforesaid," Endorsed "to our right well beloved John Arundell of Trerice."[1]

In 1544 the king wrote to Sir John Arundel of Trerice touching his discharge from the admiralty of the fleet lately committed unto him, and directing that he should deliver the ship in which he sailed unto Sir Nicholas Poyntz. "The same yeare the king wrote to him againe that he should attende him in his warres against France, with his servants, tenants and others within his roomes and offices, especially horsemen."

1. Carew, f. 146b.

"Again the king writes to his servant John Arundell of Trerice, Esq., willing him not to repaire with his men and to waite in the rereward of his army, as hee had commanded him; but to keepe them in readinesse for some other service." A little later he writes again "to Sir John Arundel of Trerice, Esq., praying and desiring him to the court the quindene of St. Hilarie next wheresoever the king shall then bee within the realme."

A little later we find the king was himself in Cornwall, having gone down to see to the fortifications of the castles of Mawes and Pendennis. Henry made Talverne, the principal house of the Arundel family, his residence during his sojourn. It was then the property of Sir John Arundel, the "kind and valiant" Sir John, as Carew calls him.

The great Cornish insurrection *temp.* Edward VI, was, it was said, first stirred up by one Kilter of St. Keverne, who murdered Mr. Body, the king's commissioner, as he sat at Helston on the matter of the proposed reforms. Mr. Body was endeavouring to carry out the injunctions of Edward, and seeing to the destruction of the images in Helston Church, when a priest, accompanied by Kilter, came behind him and stabbed him to death. Kilter was sent to London and executed, but the revolt continued to grow apace.

Next year the revolt became general, and Humphrey Arundell, at that time owner and governor of the priory or abbey of St. Michael's, which had been dissolved and given to the king (33 Henry VIII, 1533) agreed to become its leader with an army of 6000 men. On his leaving the mount the inhabitants garrisoned it against him, but he despatched a party of horse and foot against it from his camp at Bodmin and soon reduced it. This success increased the popularity of his cause, which was looked upon as the cause of religion. The pyx was pourtrayed on his banner; and the holy vessel itself, containing the host, together with crosses and candlesticks, and with the banners of the patron saints of the leaders waving above it, was brought into the field in a carriage, like as the ark in the time of Eli went out to war. The people were told that these sacred emblems which always accompanied the camp, would defend them from "devils and adverse power." Encouraged by the religious character of the campaign, as the Yorkshire men were at the Battle of the Standard, the rebel army grew stronger and stronger, and Job Militon, then sheriff of Cornwall, though backed by a strong force, durst not attack or encounter it. The leaders, confident in the popularity of their cause, proceeded to draw up a petition to the king. It was long before its terms could be agreed upon; but at last the well-known seven articles were sent up to the court. To each of these articles the king replied, offering a general pardon to all who would lay down their arms. His overtures however were rejected, and the scarcity of funds and provisions necessitated the taking of some decisive step. The rebel army marched into Devonshire, Sir Peter Carew, the High Sheriff, falling back before it, and called upon Exeter to surrender. But the bishop and the mayor and the stewards, among whom was a relative of the rebel general, one Geoffery Arundell, defied them. Arundell then laid formal siege to the city "boasting that his men would shortly measure all the silks and sattins in it by the length of their bows." The attacking party pushed up to the very gates of the city, which Arundell ordered his men to fire. The gates quickly kindled and fell in, but not before the citizens had had time to throw up a barricade which the enemy were unable to storm. Attempts to undermine the walls and to scale them were defeated by the watchfulness of the citizens, and the only hope left to the besiegers was to starve the defenders out.

Lord Russell however, a soldier of much experience, was now on his way to relieve the city. At Honiton he was reinforced by a strong body of troops under lord Grey, and the united army marched upon the rebels and offered battle on August 6, 1549. The Cornishmen fought boldly, but were at length obliged to retire, and the siege was thus relieved after a duration of nearly five weeks. The inhabitants had shown through the whole time the most undaunted courage, although provisions had run so short that they had been obliged to eat "horses, moulded cloth, and bread made of bran." After the raising of the siege Arundell rallied his dispirited troops and made a desperate stand. His men fought with the courage of despair, but they were utterly routed and the greater number of them were slain on the spot. Arundell himself and some of his chief officers were taken prisoners and sent up to London, where they were tried and executed.

A certain Sir A. Kingston, who had married a Courtenay heiress and lived at Cathays, near Honiton, was appointed by the king to restore order, and appears to have acted with a cruelty worthy of Judge Jefferies. It is recorded that amongst his many victims was the mayor of St. Columb, whom he hung on the sign of the principal inn. The mayor's wife had been advised to plead for his pardon ; but it is related that she was so long putting on her new French hood, then the latest fashion, that her husband was hung before her arrival.[1]

We are also told that Kingston wrote to one Boyer, the mayor of Bodmin, who had been forced to take part in the rebellion, telling him he would dine with him at his house on a day appointed. The mayor prepared a great feast, to which Kingston duly came with a great company, and was received with much ceremony. A little before dinner he called the mayor aside, and whispered in his ear that an execution must be done that day in the town, and therefore required that a pair of gallows should be made and erected against the time dinner were ended. The mayor was diligent to fulfil his command; and no sooner was dinner ended than Kingston asked if the work was finished. The mayor answered all is ready. "I pray you," said Kingston, "bring me to the place;" and "therewith took him friendly by the hand, and beholding the gallows he asked the mayor whether he thought them strong enough." "Yes," said the mayor, "doubtless they are." "Well," said the provost, "get you up speedily, for they are prepared for you." "I hope," answered the mayor, "you do not mean as you speak." "In faith," saith the provost, "there is no

1. Hals MSS.

remedy, for you have been a burly rebel;" "and so he presently hung him up.[1]"

"Letters exist directed to Sir John Arundell, of Trerice, from the King's Counsell: by some of which it appeareth that hee was Vice Admirall of the King's shippes in the West Seas, and by others, that hee had the goods and lands of certain rebels given him for his good services."[2]

Cornwall was no more than a spectator of the stormy times of Mary. "It is a happy circumstance," says the author of *Magna Britannia*, "when good people are out of harms way." But through this reign the Arundell family appears still to the fore. When Philip of Spain was coming to England the queen wrote to Sir John Arundell, of Trerice, "praying and requiring him that hee with his friends and neighbours should see the Prince of Spain most honourably entertained if he fortuned to land in Cornwall." She wrote to him (being then sheriff of Cornwall), "touching the election of knights of the Shire and burgesses for the Parliament." And on another occasion, with a double dealing worthy of herself, we find the peerless Gloriana desiring him privately (contrary to the public directions to the justices) to gather together a force "for the defence and quieting of the country," and "to certifye what force of horse and foot he could arme."[3]

It is curious that in the time of the Armada no record appears to exist of the part taken by the

1. Baker's *Chron.*, p. 305.
2. Carew, f. 147, 6.
3. Carew, f. 147, 6.

Arundell family. Their name does not appear amongst the lists of the justices of the peace for Cornwall at that time, nor, as far as the writer can find, amongst the officers appointed to levy forces.

Devonshire was then divided into three divisions. In the east, Sir William Courtenay and Sir Robert Denys were colonels; and amongst the captains we find captains Gifford, Waldron and Acland. The only adventure connected with the Arundell family at this time is not a very creditable one. Two Dutch ships of the Hanseatic towns, always free traders, were driven during the Spanish war into Falmouth harbour. Dame Jane Killigrew, widow of Sir John Killigrew, boarded the two ships with a party of ruffians, murdered the Spanish traders, and carried off a large amount of treasure. The whole party were found guilty at the assizes at Launceston, of wilful murder, and were condemned to death. But Sir Thomas Arundel and his son-in-law, Sir Nicholas Hals (had they, we are inclined to wonder, a share in the profits?) obtained a reprieve for lady Killigrew. All the rest were executed, lamenting as they went to the gallows that "they had not the company of that old Jezebel Kiligrew at that place," and praying that "some judgment might fall upon her and her property, and on those who had obtained so unrighteous an interference with justice." "It is observed," says Hals, "that her grandson spent the whole paternal estate of his ancestors; as did Sir Thomas Arundel, kt., son of Sir John Arundel aforesaid, and John Hals, Esq., son of Sir Nicholas Hals in their own times."[1] The reign of James I saw the ruin of the

1. Hals MSS.

head of the house of Arundell. A curious story was set afloat, and believed, that an island to which the name of Old Brazil was given, was floating somewhere in the American ocean. Of this island, Sir Thomas Arundell was constituted by the king sole proprietor; and in his vain search for it, Sir Thomas dissipated the great fortune which had descended to him from a long series of ancestors.

The above Sir John Arundell, of Trerice, married Jane, daughter of Sir Thomas Grenville, who married (2) Sir John Chamond; and lies buried in Stratton church, according to the directions contained in her will, between her two husbands. By this lady, who died in July, 1512, Sir John Arundell had a son, Sir John Arundell, kt., of Trerice, who was a lad of seventeen at the time of his father's death, in 1512. He had been early attached to the person of Henry VIII, and young as he was he was knighted by that monarch for his bravery, in 1513, at the battle of Guinegate, or "the battle of the Spurs," as it was jestingly called from the panic-stricken flight of the enemy's cavalry. Sir John, who died in November, 1561, like more than one of his predecessors, was vice-admiral of the west, and was also twice sheriff of Cornwall. He married Julia, daughter of John Ericey, by whom he had a son, Sir John Arundel, of Trerice, who married Gertrude, daughter of Sir John Dennys, of Holcombe. This Sir John was sheriff of Cornwall, in 1574. He died 15th Sept., 1580, and was succeeded by his son, John Arundel, of Trerice, the famous soldier, who was better known by his nick-names of "Jack of Tilbury," or "Jack for the king." By his wife, Mary, daughter of George Carey, of Clovelly, esquire, this John Arundell had two sons, John, who died an infant, and Richard, who was M.P. for Lostwithiel *temp.* Charles I. When Sir Nicholas Slanning, of Beckley, the governor of Pendennis castle, was slain at the battle of Bristol, July 6th, 1643, Charles I made John Arundell, then an old man, but full of vigour and resource, his successor. At Pendennis, in 1644, Arundell had the honour of receiving queen Henrietta Maria, and in 1645, prince Charles.[1] It is curious to note that one of the queen's travelling trunks bearing her cipher and crown, stolen or lost during her flight, is still preserved in an old country house in Devonshire.

At first a British, and then a Roman fortification, Pendennis Castle, as we saw, had been fortified in a plain fashion by Henry VIII. Elizabeth much improved the fortifications, and threw into the castle a garrison of one hundred men and a large quantity of guns and ammunition. Soon after John Arundell had taken over the command of the fortress, it was besieged by colonel Fortescue on behalf of the Parliament. The attack was pushed on with the utmost ardour; but just as vigorous was the defence. For six months the siege continued. No supplies could reach the garrison, hemmed in by the enemy's troops on land and guarded by their ships at sea, and the garrison and the grey old governor, and even the ladies of his household, were compelled to eat horse flesh. Still there was no word of surrender. But at length it was apparent that the famine-stricken soldiers

1. Lyson's *Mag. Brit.*, p. 85.

could no longer hold the walls. The castle had already held out longer than any royalist castle, save Raglan in Wales. "Pendennis," says lord Clarendon, "refused all summons, admitting no treaty till they had not victual for twenty-four hours, when they carried on their treaty with such firmness, that their situations were never suspected, and they obtained as good terms as any garrison in England." So in August, 1646, just six months after the siege had begun, the gallant old gentleman, with his emaciated garrison, marched out with flags flying and mounted arms.

Meanwhile brave old colonel John's son had been distinguishing himself in the Civil Wars. We find him gallantly fighting in many of the battles of that stormy period; and at the Restoration on March 23, 1664, he was created baron Arundel of Trerice by Charles II, in recognition of his father's and his own services to the Royalist cause.

By his wife, the daughter of Sir James Bagge of Saltram, co. Devon, and widow of the Sir Nicholas Slanning mentioned above, lord Arundell had issue, John, second baron Arundel of Trerice, who married (1) Margaret, daughter and heiress of Sir John Acland, kt., of Columb John, co. Devon, who lies buried in Newlyn Church. From this connection and from the various settlements and arrangements growing out of it, the great estate of Trerice, which included the manors of Luccombe and Selworthy, ultimately passed to the late Sir Thomas Acland. Lord Arundell married (2) Barbara, daughter of Sir Henry Slingsby of Scriven, co. York, the widow and sole executor of the will of Sir Henry Mauleverer. They had issue, John, third baron Arundel of Trerice, who married Elizabeth, daughter of Dr. Bean, bishop of Llandaff, who died in 1706. Their son John, fourth baron Arundell died s.p. in 1768. This nobleman married Elizabeth, daughter of Sir William Wentworth and sister of Thomas earl of Strafford. He was succeeded by his nephew William Wentworth. (*See* Chapter II.) The last lord Arundell presented the silver flagon to Selworthy Church which is still in use. The flagon bears his arms: quarterly 1 and 4, sable, 6 swallows close 3, 2 and 1 arg.; 2 and 3 arg. 3 chevronels sa. Supporters, two panthers regardant or, spotted various colours, with fire issuing from their mouths and ears.

Raleigh Family.

The Raleigh family, who held for a considerable period the manor of Allerford, and property besides in Porlock, were descended from the family of Raleigh of Raleigh, co. Devon. *Temp.* Henry II, Collinson tells us, John, son of Gilbert, marshal of England, granted the manor of Nettlecombe to Hugh de Raleigh of Raleigh, co. Devon, and to his heirs, to be held by the tenure of finding one soldier for two whole months in time of war, and forty days in time of peace. This deed was attested under the great seal of Henry II, and confirmed by Reginald earl of Cornwall. John's two sons, Gilbert and Walter, were parties to the deed. In consideration of it Hugh de Raleigh gave to John a sorrel nag and eighty silver marks; to John's wife an ounce of gold; to his son, Gilbert, a horse and two dogs; to his son, John, one talent; and to his other son, Walter, another talent of gold.[1]

Hugh de Raleigh was sheriff of Devonshire 7—14 Henry II. He was succeeded in his estates by his son, Warine de Raleigh, who was succeeded by his son, Ralph de Raleigh. In the disputes between king John and the barons, Ralph sided with the barons, and in 17 John his estates were confiscated, and granted by the king to William de Briewer. De Briewer for a consideration of twenty marks, conveyed his interest in the property to Ralph's brother, Warine; and soon after William Marshall earl of Pembroke confirmed the estates to Warine and his descendants on the service of a whole knight's fee. Warine was succeeded by his son, Warine, who held Nettlecombe in 1242. In 1242 the above Warine, with the consent of his wife Margaret, enfeoffed their second son, Simon, of this manor, to be held by him and his wife, Ela de Reigni, by a yearly rent of three shillings and fourpence and the services due to Reginald de Mohun. This Margaret gave by deed to Hawise the wife of her elder son, Sir Warine, a ring of St. Lazarus, which once was the property of queen Berengaria, and a silver vessel containing a piece of the Holy Cross, and she prays that these sacred relics may prove as blessed to the lady Hawise as she had proved them to be in her own case.

In the reign of Henry III, Sir Wymond de Raleigh the lineal ancestor of Sir Walter Raleigh of Elizabethan fame, went out from Nettlecombe and settled at Smallridge in the parish of Axminster. Here this

1. Collinson, v, iii, p. 536.

branch of the family lived until the reign of Henry VIII, and were "knights and men of very great respect." "One of this family," Risdon, the Devonshire antiquary records for us, "being taken prisoner in France, at his return built a chapel here to the memory of St. Leonard, because he was delivered on St. Leonard's day, and in the same he hung up his target, which, with the records of the foundation, was given by the priest of Axminster to the late Sir Walter Raleigh, kt." The tradition is that de Raleigh effected his escape in an open boat without oar or rudder, and drifting across the channel into the mouth of the Axe, was carried up the river by the tide, until his boat was stranded beneath his home, and that on the spot where he landed he built the above mentioned chapel. Does this signal escape and the connection of the Raleigh family with our parish, account for the dedication of the chapel at Tivington? At all events the parish of Selworthy can claim an interest in the brilliant statesman and soldier of Elizabeth's reign, whose chief misfortune lay in the fact that he was born two hundred years too soon.

Warine de Raleigh, fourth of that name, left a son, Reginald, who died s.p., and was succeeded by his uncle, Sir Simon, who lived in South Wales, where he had obtained a great estate through his marriage with the above Ela, daughter and heiress of the great baron Sir Milo de Reigni. He was succeeded by his son, Simon, who also lived at Wrentchester Castle in South Wales.

This second Sir Simon was knighted 30 Edward I, and had the custody of the county of Glamorgan. He married Joan, daughter and heiress of Lawrence le Tort, of Old Knoll in the parish of Carhampton, by whom he had two sons, John and Simon. His wife Joan survived him, and retired to her manor house at Rowdon in Stogumber parish, in which she founded a chantry. John succeeded to the Somersetshire estates of the Raleigh family, but the second son, Simon, inherited the greater portion of the South Wales property, and also the property of his grandfather, Laurence le Tort, including Old Knoll, Cutcombe (hence Cutcombe Raleigh), Upton Tort, etc.

In 10 Edward II, we find the two brothers active in the rebellion of Thomas earl of Lancaster. They were fined respectively £100 and £40; but this fine was remitted in the first parliament Edward III.

John Raleigh married Margaret, daughter and coheiress of Sir Richard Bret, kt. He was succeeded by his son, John de Raleigh, who on the death of his uncle Simon, united once more the Somersetshire and South Wales estates of his family. He married Ismayn, daughter of John Hanham, of Hanham, co. Gloucester, and had issue two sons, John and Simon, and two daughters, Maude and Joan. John died *s.p.*, and his brother Simon inherited the family estates.

Simon de Raleigh was a great soldier. In 10 Richard II we find him with the duke of Lancaster's army in Spain, and in 17 Richard II he was fighting side by side with Sir Matthew Gournay and Sir Richard Arthur, in Guienne. In temporary disgrace, when his friend and commander, Hereford was banished, he must have rejoiced when, accompanied by another West-countryman, archbishop Arundell, Lancaster, as he had then become, landed at Ravensburne.

And no doubt Sir Simon brought no small contingent of stalwart West-country labourers and yeomen to swell the great force of sixty thousand men, at the head of which Henry marched triumphantly to London, to claim the crown. Sir Simon was much in favour with Henry, who knew how to value a soldier of so much experience and courage; and no doubt he held command amongst the hastily levied forces with which Henry crushed the northern rebellion at the battle of Shrewsbury. He survived Henry IV, and we find him fighting side by side with his old master's son at the battle of Agincourt.

At length, battered and growing old, Sir Simon returned home to Nettlecombe, to pass the rest of his days in peace. His first wife, Ismayn, died soon after his return, and he married again, Joan, daughter of Oliver Huish, of Donniford. By neither wife did he have any issue; and so, subject to the provision for the maintenance of a chantry in the chapel of St. John the Baptist, at Nettlecombe, which he had caused to be founded in remembrance of the many miraculous escapes that had been vouchsafed to him, and in order that prayers might daily be said in it for the rest of his soul, and that of his wife, and his cousin, Sir John de Raleigh, he left all his estates to his sister Joan, who had married John Whalesborough of Whalesborough, co. Cornwall. We do not know when Allerford, and the estates which the Raleigh family held in Porlock, passed away from this family. It must have been before the building of the present Church, otherwise, no doubt, they would have assisted in the re-building of it, and their coat of arms would have appeared amongst those in the chancel. As a family they were great benefactors to the cause of religion, and their coat of arms is to be seen at Cleeve abbey, Leighland chapel, etc.

A member of the Raleigh family, Dr. Walter Raleigh, the second son of Sir Carew Raleigh of Fardell, co. Devon, and nephew of the famous Sir Walter Raleigh, succeeded bishop Montgomery, whose history is related above, in the benefice of Chedzoy. Dr. Raleigh held with Chedzoy the livings of Street, Wilton St. Mary, and Elingdon, and also Wroughton, co. Wilts. He was a chaplain in ordinary to Charles I, and was in 1641 appointed to the deanery of Wells. When the Civil War broke out he fled to Bridgwater, and on the fall of that stronghold he was taken prisoner, and imprisoned in his deanery house at Wells. Here he was murdered on the 10th Oct., 1646. The late dean of Wells used to show the room in which the murder was committed. Dean Raleigh was engaged in writing a letter to his wife, which the Puritan soldier who kept guard on the room demanded to see. The dean refused to show the letter, and the soldier at once ran him through with his sword.

Lucar Family.

Little is known of the Lucar family, but we find the following notices of them :—

Sir John Gille, M.P. for Minehead, 1625, *o.s.p.*, married Jane, daughter of Hugh Trevelyan, of Yarnscombe, and relict of Cyprian Lucar.

Roger Greenwood, of North Perrott, Som., gent., by his will, dated October 27th, 1613, leaves to his kinsman, Emmanuel Lucar, "my silver bason and Ewer." This was E. Lucar, of Maidenbrook, Somerset, who had married Wilmot, daughter of Henry Greenwood, of Torrington, co. Devon. Roger Greenwood mentions also Mark Lucar, son of above Emmanuel; and "his cousin Joan Lucar."

The will of Antony Lucar, of Blackford, Som., gent., dated April 2nd, 1625, was proved May 3rd, 1625. He desires "to be buried in S. Botolph, nr. Billingsgate London with my father and grandfather." He mentions "My mother Lady Joan Gill wife of Sir John Gill, my manor of Blackford, my sister Cicell Staynings wife of Charles Staynings Esq: my daughter Ann Lucar. My cousin Emmanuel Lucar of Maidenbrooke."

George Hobbes, of Stogursey, Somerset, gent., by his will dated October 11th, 1649, proved April 11th, 1650, by Dorothy the relict, bequeaths to John Lucar 40*s.*, Mark Lucar £5, Gabriel Lucar 40*s.*, to his cousin Charles Luttrell £5, to George Lucar "my kinsman and servant" £10.[1]

In the Visitations of Somerset we find from a document there quoted, that Emanuel Lucar of London (but apparently of a Bridgwater family), by his wife Elizabeth, had issue "Mary the elder, Emmanuell, Henrye, and Jane." "After the decease of his said wife the said Emmanuell married Joanne, daughter of Thomas Trumbull of London, the 15th of May, 1541, and had issue by the said Joanne, Cyprian Lucar the elder and Luke the younger, Marke, Martha, John, Matthew, and Mary; our said father Emmanuell died

1. This will is given at greater length in Brown's *Somerset Wills*, iii, 97.

the 28th of March, 1574. It is to be supposed that William Lucar, foster of the forest of Exmore at the overthrowe of the said kinge Henry the sixth, fled into Ireland, of whom descended and came the Lucars of Waterford."

"Richard Lucar took part with Henry VI against Edward IV, and was with the said Henry overthrown at Barnett fielde, anno domini 1471."

Did William Lucar the ranger of Exmoor, *temp.* Henry VI, or the hapless Richard Lucar, slain on Barnet field, own Blackford? and what relation were these two worthies to the Emanuell Lucar living in London in the sixteenth century? We only know for certain that Cyprian Lucar, Emanuell's son, owned Blackford, and married the above named Jane Trevelyan, and that his daughter Cecily, on the death of her brother Antony, succeeded to the estate.

De Ling, Franks, and Clarke Families.

An estate of much antiquity in the parish of Selworthy, although probably never a manor, is *East Lynch.* It seems to have been for a considerable period the possession of a family called De Ling or De Linch.

One of the steps of the staircase of the church tower is formed of an ancient tombstone. On it is an incised and floriated cross, and on one of the bevelled edges the following inscription: "Le corz de Ricard. de Ling." The tower is understood to be of a not later date than the end of the thirteenth or beginning of the fourteenth century. The tombstone would appear therefore to be of a very early date.

In the Assize Rolls, co. Somerset, 8 Edward 1, No. 579, we find:

Hundrēd de Karhemptoñ.
" Hugo de Luccomƀ. Ricũs de Lynz.
Galfrũs de Lucomƀ, Wiłłi Evãrd.
Willĩ Musseuls. Roƀs de Estcote.
Ricus de Avele Jũr hundred . Cōtemptu in mĩa

At the Exmoor Forest pleas, held at Ilchester on "the morrow of the Ascension," 1270, we find the following presentment: "Hugh de Luccombe is a wrong doer as to the venison of the Lord King in the aforesaid forest, who came and was kept in prison. And the same Hugh was attached at another time by Richard de Cloutsham, 2*s*., Richard de Lynch alibi. . ." This is perhaps the same Richard as is mentioned above, and it may be his tombstone that is still to be seen in the church tower.[1]

The estate during the Middle Ages belonged to the ancient West Country family of Franks, which is at present represented by Sir A. W. Franks, K.C.B., F.R.S., etc., of the British Museum. We subjoin a pedigree of this ancient family, for which we are indebted to Sir A. W. Franks. An ancient building to the north of the new farmhouse has a very ecclesiastical appearance, and a vessel resembling a holy water stoup was found near it some years ago. A picturesque Elizabethan house until recently occupied the site of the present house.

West Lynch is an ancient house. It appears in the reign of Elizabeth to have been the property of the

1. Rawle's *Forest of Exmoor*, p. 57.

Horne family. For more than one hundred years it has been in the family of Clarke.

Rawle Family.

The above family, as the earliest church registers show, lived in the parish of Selworthy for many generations, and descendants of the family still exist in the district. The history of the family has been fully treated in the recent sumptuous volume of Mr. E. J. Rawle.

For the annexed very complete series of extracts from the Somerset Subsidy Rolls I am indebted to Mr. Chadwyck Healey, Q.C. They are of much interest, as giving us the names of the families resident in our parish at the early periods to which they refer, and also some idea of the population of the parish at those times. It would appear from these records that the population of Selworthy in the Middle Ages was considerably larger than it is at present. The first list is of those who subscribed to the subsidy granted to Edward III in 1327. This was the year of the expedition against the Scotch, in which Edward was outwitted in so signal a manner by the superior skill and activity of his foes.

Extract from Subsidy Roll, co. Somerset, 1 Edw. iij (1327) $\frac{169}{5}$.

This is the collection of the twentieth granted to the king in the first year of his reign.

Hundred of Karhampton.

Alreford.

From John de Hiwyssh . . . . iij*s.*

From Alice la Gist	xij*d.*
From Walter Bryendebrok	vij*d.*
From Thomas Crosman	vij*d.*
From John Tethingman	viij*d.*
From Walter Herigand	vij*d.*
From Adam Uppehull	viij*d.*
From John Uppehull	ix*d.*
From Mathew Hamelyn	vij*d.*
From William de Campilden	viij*d.*
From John Muryweder	vij*d.*

Total of the 20th from the vill aforesaid
proved 9*s.* 8*d.*

(There are collections from Luccombe 10 entries, and from Bossington 8 entries, in this roll.)

Subsidy Roll 7 Edw. iij (1334) $\frac{169}{4}$.

The heading of this roll is lost, but it is described in the collection of tenths and fifteenths. The date is fixed by the acknowledgment on the roll of its receipt on May 3, 7 Edw. iij.

Alreford.

Robert de Hiwisch	ij*s.* vj*d.*
Alic̃ le Gist	ij*s.*
Robert Everard	ij*s.*
Thomas Crosman	xviij*d.*
William Campeldene	ij*s.*
John Randulf	xviij*d.*
Adam Uppehull	xij*d.*
William Wibham	xvj*d.*
Robert le Hor̃	xij*d.*
John le Ballard	xij*d.*

John le Ware	xviij*d.*
Walter Hergand	xviij*d.*
John Uppehull	x*d.*

Total xix*s.* viij*d.* proved.

Subsidy Roll, 38 Hen. viij $\frac{170}{230}$.

This is stated to be "a contribucion freely granted to the king by his subjects both of the clergy and laity."

Tithing of Allerford.

From George Harryson	16*s.* 8*d.*
From John Glasse	£1 5*s.* 0*d.*
From Henry Horne	£1
From Robert Phyllyppe	£1 0*s.* 10*d.*
From John Rowe	16*s.* 8*d.*
From John Langwyll	15*s.* 0*d.*
From William Peersse	12*s.* 6*d.*
From John Crotte	12*s.* 6*d.*

Extract:—Subsidy Roll, 36 Hen. viij $\frac{170}{213}$.

Account of the "names and surnames of every person inhabiting within the said county that have liberally granted and advanced to the Kinges Matie by the waye of Benevolence any some of money as also the severall and particular somes of money by them granted."

Deceñ de Allerforde.

John Glosse	viij*li.*
John Rowe	xl*s.*
John Langhill	xl*s.*

George Haryson	iiij*li.*
John Horne	xl*s.*
Willm̃ Presse	xxij*s.* vj*d.*
Cycell Rall	xl*s.*
Robert Phelipp	liij*s.* iiij*d.*
John Hunt	xl*s.*
Willm̃ Long	vj*s.* viij*d.*

(No mention of Selworthy in this roll.)

Extract: Subsidy Roll, 1 Edw. vj 170/284.

This is "the certyfycat made the 5th daye of Marche yn the fyrste yere of the rayne of Edw. VI, of the last payment of the subsydye" granted to the king.

Deceñ de Allerford.

Georgius Harryson	in bon.	xx*li*	sub.	xxvj*s.* viij*d.*
Robtus Phylypp .	"	xxv*li*	"	xxx*s.* iiij*d.*
Henricus Horne .	"	xxiiij*li*	"	xx*s.* ......
Willms Pearse . .	"	xij*li*	"	xij*s.*
Johnes Gloss . .	"	xvj*li*	"	xvj*s.*
Johnes Rowe . .	"	xij*li*	"	xij*s.*
Johnes Huntt . .	"	xij*li*	"	xij*s.*
Johnes Langwyll .	"	v*li*	"	......
Johnes Hammant .	"	v*li*	"	......
Johnes Trott . .	"	viij*li*	"	......
Rogus Horne . .	"	v*li*	"	......
Johnes Trowte . .	"	vj*li*	su..................	
Michaell Tayloure.	"	v*li*	s.....................	
Willms Rychard .	"	v*li*	....	
Ricus Horne . .	"	xij*li*	....	
Johnes Horne, jun.	"	v*li*	....	

Robtūs Rawle . .	„	v*li*	....
Ricūs Stodden . .	„	v*li*	....
Willm̃s Stodden .	„	v*li*	....
Johnēs Gloss, jun. .	„	v*li*	....
Willm̃s Long . .	„	xiij*li*	sub..................
Elizabeth Horne .	„	xij*li*	....
Cecilia Rawle . .	„	xij*li*	....
Ricūs William . .	„	xj*li*	....

Smā hujus deceñ xij*li*. ij*s*. viij*d*.

These extracts are of singular value as giving us the names of the principal inhabitants of the northern side of our parish during the Tudor times. There were evidently a good number of men of considerable substance living in the parish at that period. It is interesting to note how many of the names entered above are still to be found amongst us.

Extract:—Subsidy Roll, 2 and 3 Edw. vj $\frac{170}{244}$.

This is the certificate "of the third paiment of a relief for goodes" granted by parliament in the 2 and 3 Edw. vj.

Deceñ de Allerford.

Johnes Hunt wever valet . . .	in bonis	x*li*.	Reliviñ	x*s*.
Alicia Rawle, vidua	„	x*li*.	„	x*s*.
Anastacia Troute, vidua . . .	„	x*li*.	„	x*s*.
Cecilia Rawle, vid.	„	xij*li*.	„	xij*s*.
Willm̃s Pears, tanner	„	x*li*.	„	x*s*.
Juliana Philyppe, vidua . . .	„	xvj*li*.	„	xvjs.

Georgius Harryson, husbond . .	„	xxv*li.*	„	xxv*s.*
Johnẽs Glosse, tanner . . .	„	xxiiij*li.*	„	xxvj*s.*
Henȓ Horne, smyth	„	xxiiij*li.*	„	xxiiij*s.*
Johnẽs Langwill, smyth . . .	„	xiij*li.*	„	xiij*s.*

Smā vij*li.* xiiij*s.*

Extract: Subsidy Roll, 23 Elizth. [illegible].

Return of the "fyrst payment of the subsydie of the laytie" granted at Westminster in the 23rd Elizabeth.

(*Part* of Allerford entry torn off).

			Sub.
John Wescote . . .	in bon.	iiij*li.*	vj*s.* viij*d.*
William Gardener . .	„	iij*li.*	v*s.*
Robert Horne aꝉs spurrier	„	v*li.*	viij*s.* iiij*d.*
William Stedden, senr. .	„	iiij*li.*	vj*s.* viij*d.*
William Harte . . .	„	iij*li.*	v*s.*
Gregorye Douche . .	„	iij*li.*	v*s.*
Henry Rawle	„	iij*li.*	v*s.*
John Stodden	„	iij*li.*	v*s.*
Julian Horne aꝉs spurrier, vid.	in terr.	xx*s.*	ij*s.* viij*d.*
Alice Peares, vid. . .	in bon.	iij*li.*	v*s.*
John Hammote . . .	„	iij*li.*	v*s.*
John Sulley	„	iij*li.*	v*s.*
William Dennes . . .	„	iij*li.*	v*s.*
Lewes Tayler	„	iij*li.*	v*s.*

Robert Gilles	„	iij*li.*	v*s.*
John Holle	„	iiij*li.*	vj*s.* viij*d.*
Nicholas Jacobbe als Snowe	„	iij*li.*	v*s.*
Elizabeth Bushope, vid.	„	iij*li.*	v*s.*
Nicholas Yewde . . .	in terr.	xx*s.*	ij*s.* viij*d.*
Alice Yewde, vid. . .	„	xx*s.*	ij*s.* viij*d.*
William Stodden, junr.	„	xx*s.*	ij*s.* viij*d.*
Christian Stodden . .	„	xx*s.*	ij*s.* viij*d.*
John Badcocke . . .	„	xx*s.*	ij*s.* viij*d.*
Hugh Parramore . . .	„	xx*s.*	ij*s.* viij*d.*
Edward Pyle	in bon.	iij*li.*	v*s.*
George Upham . . .	in terr.	xx*s.*	ij*s.* viij*d.*
George Philpes . . .	in bon.	viij*li.*	xiij*s.* iiij*d.*
John Frayse	„	vj*li.*	x*s.*
William Stote	„	iiij*li.*	vj*s.* viij*d.*

Sm. xij*li.* viij*d.*

Extract :—Subsidy Roll, 39 Elizth. $\frac{171}{321}$.

Return of the second subsidy granted to the queen in the 39th year of her reign by the laity.

Deceñ de Allerford.

			Sub.
Willm̃ Stoden, junr . .	in terr̃.	xx*s.*	iiij*s.*
Robte Hensley . . .	in bonis	iij*li.*	viij*s.*
Henr̃ Ralle	in terr̃.	xx*s.*	iiij*s.*
Xpĩan Tayller, vid. . .	„	xx*s.*	iiij*s.*
Thoms Glasse . . .	„	xx*s.*	iiij*s.*
Walter Snowe als Jacobe	in bonis	iij*li.*	viij*s.*
Willm̃ Bonishopp . .	„	iij*li.*	viij*s.*
Peter Ewed	in terr̃.	xx*s.*	iiij*s.*

Alice Ewed	"	xx*s*.	iiij*s*.
Edward Ewed.	"	xx*s*.	iiij*s*.
Willm̃ Stoden al̃s Sealye	in bonis	iij*li*.	viij*s*.
George Hensley . . .	in terr̃.	xx*s*.	iiij*s*.
John Badcock . . .	"	xx*s*.	iiij*s*.
George Upham . . .	"	xx*s*.	iiij*s*.
Gregorye Tailer . . .	in bonis	iij*li*.	viij*s*.
Richard Stodden . . .	"	iij*li*.	viij*s*.
John Widlake	in terr̃.	xx*s*.	iiij*s*.
George Phillippes . .	"	xx*s*.	iiij*s*.
Richard Phillippes . .	"	xx*s*.	iiij*s*.
Willm Stoyte	in bonis	iiij*li*.	x*s*. viij*d*.
John Emmes	"	iij*li*.	viij*s*.
Thomsyn Glasse, vid. .	in terr̃.	xx*s*.	iiij*s*.
Jone Lyell, vid. . . .	in bonis	iij*li*.	viij*s*.
Jone Hart, vid. . . .	in terr̃.	xx*s*.	iiij*s*.
John Frasse	in bonis	iij*li*.	viij*s*.
Willm̃ Dem̃ys	"	iij*li*.	viij*s*.
John Shapland . . .	"	iiij*li*.	x*s*. viij*d*.
Julian Spurrier, vid. .	in terr̃.	xx*s*.	iiij*s*.
John Westcott. . . .	in bonis	iij*li*.	viij*s*.
Edward Pill	"	iiij*li*.	x*s*. viij*d*.
William Harison . . .	in terr̃.	vj*li*.	xxiiij*s*.
Walter Spurrier . . .	in bonis	iiij*li*.	x*s*. viij*d*.
Willm̃ Stoden	"	iiij*li*.	x*s*. viij*d*.

Smã xj*li*. ix*s*. iiij*d*.

Subsidy Roll, 3 Chas. j $\frac{172}{577}$.

Allerford.

Richard Worth, gent. .	in terr̃.	viij*li*.	xxxij*s*.
Henry Dennes . . .	"	j*li*.	iiij*s*.
Walter Yewde	"	j*li*.	iiij*s*.

William Spurrier . . .	„	j*li.*	iiij*s.*
William Stodden ał̄s Sulley	„	j*li.*	iiij*s.*
John Eame, jun.	„	j*li.*	iiij*s.*
Cyprian Kent	„	j*li.*	iiij*s.*
George Webber	„	j*li.*	iiij*s.*
John Sulley	„	j*li.*	iiij*s.*
Edward Yewde	„	j*li.*	iiij*s.*
Robert Bowring	„	j*li.*	iiij*s.*
Charles Horne	„	j*li.*	iiij*s.*
John Shapland	in boñ.	iij*li.*	viij*s.*
Margaret Snow	„	iij*li.*	viij*s.*
Robert Taylor	in terr̃.	ij*li.*	viij*s.*
Walter Spurrier	in boñ.	iij*li.*	viij*s.*
Robert Huish	in terr̃.	iij*li.*	xij*s.*
John Andrewes	„	j*li.*	iiij*s.*
Sidwill Stodden	„	ij*li.*	viij*s.*
William Stodden ał̄s Blackford	„	ij*li.*	viij*s.*
John Phillps, sen. . . .	„	iij*li.*	xij*s.*
Johane Slocombe . . .	„	j*li.*	iiij*s.*
Robert Hensley	in boñ.	iij*li.*	viij*s.*
John Edbrooke	„	iij*li.*	viij*s.*
John Phillps, jun. . . .	in terr̃.	j*li.*	iiij*s.*
John Kent	„	j*li.*	iiij*s.*
John Dyer	„	j*li.*	iiij*s.*
John Eame, sen. . . .	„	j*li.*	iiij*s.*
John Stete	in boñ.	iij*li.*	viij*s.*
James Reede	„	iij*li.*	viij*s.*
Ratóls { William Stodden	in boñ.	iij*li.*	viij*s.*
Ratóls { Robert Phillps .	in terr̃.	j*li.*	iiij*s.*
Ratóls { William Eame .	„	j*li.*	iiij*s.*

Sum̄e xj*li.*

Subsidy Roll, 4 Chas. j $\frac{172}{387}$.

Allerford.

Richard Worth, gent. . . .	in terr̃.	viij*li.*	iij*li.* iiij*s.*
Henry Dennis	in boñ.	iij*li.*	xvj*s.*
William Spurrier	in terr̃.	xx*s.*	viij*s.*
William Stodden ats Sulley	„	xx*s.*	viij*s.*
William Erne	„	xx*s.*	viij*s.*
Alexander Badcock . .	„	xx*s.*	viij*s.*
Sidwell Kitner, vid. . .	„	xx*s.*	viij*s.*
George Webber	„	xx*s.*	viij*s.*
Robert Phelps	„	xx*s.*	viij*s.*
John Sulley	„	xx*s.*	viij*s.*
Edward Yewde	„	xl*s.*	xvj*s.*
Charles Horne	„	xx*s.*	viij*s.*
John Shapland	in boñ.	iij*li.*	xvj*s.*
Margarett Snowe, vid. . .	„	iij*li.*	xvj*s.*
Robert Taylor	in terr̃.	xl*s.*	xvj*s.*
Walter Spurrier	in bon.	iij*li.*	xvj*s.*
Robert Huishe	in terr.	iiij*li.*	xxxij*s.*
John Androwes	„	xx*s.*	viij*s.*
Sidwell Stodden, vid. . .	„	xl*s.*	xvj*s.*
William Stodden ats Blackford	„	xl*s.*	xvj*s.*
John Phelps, sen.	„	iij*li.*	xxiiij*s.*
Johane Slocombe, vid. . .	„	xx*s.*	viij*s.*
John Blackford ats Stodden	in boñ.	iij*li.*	xvj*s.*
Robert Hensley	„	iij*li.*	xvj*s.*
John Eame	in terr̃.	xx*s.*	viij*s.*
John Stote	in boñ.	iij*li.*	xvj*s.*
James Read	„	iij*li.*	xvj*s.*

	William Stodden . . .	"	iij*li.*	xvj*s.*
Rato's	John Edbrooke .	"	iij*li.*	xvj*s.*
	John Phelps, jun.	in terr̃.	xx*s.*	viij*s.*
	John Dyer . .	"	xx*s.*	viij*s.*

Summa xxij*li.* xvj*s.*

Subsidy Roll, 16 Chas. j $\frac{173}{347}$.

Return of the "two first of the foure entire subsidies" granted by parliament in the 16 Car. I (John St. Albin and Charles Staynings, Esqs., were the Assessors in this case, and James Cade of Halsway, Stogumber, gent., was the High Collector).

Allerford.

Henry Byam, clarke .	in terr.	ij*li.*	viij*s.*	viij*s.*
Mrs. Mary Worth widowe . . .	"	x*li.*	ij*li.*	ij*li.*
George Joyce . . .	"	iiij*li.*	xvj*s.*	xvj*s.*
Richard Blackmoore .	in bon.	iij*li.*	viij*s.*	viij*s.*
Isott Shapland . .	in terr.	j*li.*	iiij*s.*	iiij*s.*
William Eame . . .	"	j*li.*	iiij*s.*	iiij*s.*
John Eame	"	j*li.*	iiij*s.*	iiij*s.*
Richard Matthew . .	"	j*li.*	iiij*s.*	iiij*s.*
Robert Hewish . .	"	iiij*li.*	xvj*s.*	xvj*s.*
William Stocke . .	"	j*li.*	iiij*s.*	iiij*s.*
John Kent	"	j*li.*	iiij*s.*	iiij*s.*
Walter Spurrier . .	in bon.	iij*li.*	viij*s.*	viij*s.*
Walter Yewde . . .	in terr.	j*li.*	iiij*s.*	iiij*s.*
Elinor Stodden . .	in bon.	iij*li.*	viij*s.*	viij*s.*
Henry Spurrier . .	in terr.	j*li.*	iiij*s.*	iiij*s.*
Johane Philps, wid. .	"	ij*li.*	viij*s.*	viij*s.*

George Hensley . .	"	j*li.*	iiij*s.*	iiij*s.*
John Stodden . . .	"	j*li.*	iiij*s.*	iiij*s.*
Mary Edbrooke . .	in bon.	iij*li.*	viij*s.*	viij*s.*
Elizth Stote . . .	"	iij*li.*	viij*s.*	viij*s.*
Sidwell Blackford .	in terr.	iij*li.*	xij*s.*	xij*s.*
Edward Pyle . . .	in bon.	iij*li.*	viij*s.*	viij*s.*
Robert Phillps . . .	in terr.	j*li.*	iiij*s.*	iiij*s.*
John Phillps . . .	"	j*li.*	iiij*s.*	iiij*s.*
Henry Dennies . .	"	j*li.*	iiij*s.*	iiij*s.*
John Amdrewes . .	"	j*li.*	iiij*s.*	iiij*s.*
Charles Horne . . .	"	j*li.*	iiij*s.*	iiij*s.*
Assessors.				
James Reade . . .	in bon.	iij*li.*	viij*s.*	viij*s.*
Henry Hensley . .	"	iij*li.*	viij*s.*	viij*s.*
Nicholas Snowe . .	"	iij*li.*	viij*s.*	viij*s.*
Ciprian Kent . . .	in terr.	j*li.*	iiij*s.*	iiij*s.*

Suma xxiij*li.* xij*s.*

("Charles Staynings Esquire" figures in the tithing of Bossington

"in terr. viij*li.* xxxij*s.* xxxij*s.*")

In the second actual year of the reign of Charles II, but which was called the thirteenth, a so-called "Benevolence" was granted to the king by the parliament. We find the following payments made to it from the tythings of Blackford and Allerford:

Blackford Tything.

John Trull, one shilling	*li.*00	01	00
Joseph Kent, one shilling	00	01	00
Henry Clement, one shilling . . .	00	01	[illegible]
William Elstone, one shilling . . .	00	01	00

Eliz. Blackmore, one shilling	00	01	00
Joane Coffin, widow, one shilling . .	00	01	00
Joane Elstone, widow, one shilling. .	00	01	00
Joane Bryant, widow, sixpence . . .	00	00	06

Allerford Tything.

Walter Coffin, seaven shillings and six-pence	*li.*00	07	06
Henry Hensley, three shillings . . .	00	03	00
Walter Yond, two shillings	00	02	00
John Beage, one shilling	00	01	00
George Hensley, one shilling. . . .	00	01	00
John Stoate, three shillings	00	03	00
Edward Pyle, two shillings	00	02	00
John Cotes, sixpence	00	00	06
John Reade, one shilling	00	01	00
Edith Huish, three shillings and six-pence	00	03	06
Nicholas Snowe, ...	00	01	06
John Eame, senr., one shilling . . .	00	01	00
Richd. Marchant, one shilling and six-pence	00	01	06
Alexander Blackford, two shillings and sixpence	00	02	06

Somerset Archæological and Natural History Society's Proceedings, vol. xxxv, pp 76, 79, 80.

CHAPTER IX.

Folklore.

OUR forefathers, Mr. Brand tells us, divided witches into three classes. First came the black witch, which could hurt but not help, then the white witch which could help but not hurt; and besides these there was the gray witch which could both hurt and help.[1] A woman becomes a witch, we are told, in this way: she is tempted by a man in black to sign a contract to become his, body and soul: on the conclusion of the agreement he gives her a piece of money and causes her to write her name or make a mark on a slip of parchment with her own blood. On departing he gives her an imp or familiar. This familiar is in the shape of a cat, mole, or other animal, and day by day she feeds it with her own blood.[2] At various times the witches met together at a witches' Sabbath, where they anointed themselves with magical ointments, and then rode about in the air on broomsticks and spits. They feasted too and danced while the devil himself played for them on the pipes. They then proceeded to the graveyards and

1. Brand's *Antiquities*, vol. iii p. 1.
2. Grose, quoted by Brand.

took from corpses their finger joints, with which to work spells; and the devil, before the assembly broke up, distributed to them fruits and various small articles suitable as presents. These gifts, when given to any one against whom the witch had a spite, wrought them terrible injury. And our forefathers would not have accepted even an apple from any one suspected of witchcraft. Preventives against witchcraft were many. The suspected one was weighed against the church bible, or, as the writer has known happen in North Devon, "scratched above the breath"[1] till the blood came. This was supposed to be an excellent remedy when cattle are overlooked.

Any poor old woman who was half-witted or had any physical deformity or was of peculiar appearance, was set down as a witch; and from that time her life was not safe, and she was likely at any moment to be dragged out of her home to be subjected to the most terrible tortures and indignities, unless she had powerful friends to defend her. That learned scholar and "defender of the faith," bishop Jewel, in a sermon preached before queen Elizabeth, actually asserted that witches and sorcerers had of late years much increased within the realm. "Your grace's subjects pine away even unto the death, their colour fadeth, their flesh rotteth, their speech is benumbed, their senses are bereft; I pray God they never practice further than upon the subject."[2] This sermon is supposed to have been the cause of the introduction into parliament, at its next

1. The wound was considered more efficacious if inflicted above the mouth.

2. Strype's *Annals of the Reformation*, vol. i, p. 8.

session, of a bill dealing with witchcraft. This was in 1558, and in 1559 the hint given by Jewel seems to have taken root even in the masculine mind of Elizabeth, and a Mrs. Dier was apprehended under the recently-passed statute, for bewitching the queen.

That extraordinary mixture of learning, dense stupidity, and vice, James I, was, as we may well imagine, a great believer in witchcraft. He wrote a treatise on Demonology, which was, we are told, "ornamented with much learning." In this learned work he gives the following wise account of the trying of a witch by "fleeting on the water." It appears, says this wise ruler of England, "that God hath appointed for a supernatural syne of the monstrous impieties of witches that the water shall refuse to receive them into her bosom that have shaken off from them the sacred water of baptism and wilfully refused the benefits thereof."

James believed that witchcraft was the cause of his being nearly drowned on his return from Denmark, and of the loss of a ship laden with presents for his bride, in a storm off Leith. The prime instigator in this attempt on the royal life, was supposed to be a certain Dr. Fian, who was called the Devil's Registrar, and was well known to have preached frequently to congregations of witches, and especially to those who so nearly destroyed the prospects of the Stuart dynasty. In consequence of the above storm a supposed witch was subjected to most terrible tortures "until she confessed all," and Dr. Fian was consigned by the king's order to the "horrible torment of the boot," and then strangled and burnt on the Castle

Hill, Edinburgh, in January, 1591. "They cannot even shed tears," says the above royal author, "although women in general are like the crocodile, ready to weep on every light occasion."

By statute 1 James I, c. xii, it was ordered that all persons inviting any evil spirits, or consulting, covenanting with, entertaining, employing, etc., any evil spirit: or taking up dead bodies from their graves used in any witchcraft or sorcery, charm or enchantment, or killing or otherwise hurting any other person by such infernal acts, should be guilty of felony, without benefit of clergy, and suffer death. And if any person should attempt by sorcery to recover lost treasure or stolen goods or hurt any man or beast by sorcery, etc., the offender was to suffer the punishment of the pillory for the first offence, and death for the second.

During the seventeenth century, executions for witchcraft were frequent throughout Europe, as they were found to be an useful means of getting rid of people who were in the way. It was under an accusation of witchcraft that cardinal Richelieu condemned to the stake the famous Urban Grandier, whose only fault was that he had satirized and laughed at the all-powerful minister. And the clever wife of marshal d'Ancre was condemned also to be beheaded about the same time for having bewitched the queen. "What was the sorcery you used to bewitch her majesty?" demanded the judge. "None" was the scornful reply, "save the ascendancy a strong mind has over a weak one." Here is the bill for burning a Scotsman and his wife at Kirkcaldy in 1633, who were accused of witchcraft, which is preserved for us by Mr. Brand.

For ten tons of coal to burn them .	£3	6	8	Scot.
For a tar barrel	0	14	0	
For Towes	0	6	0	
For harden to be jumps to them . .	0	3	10	
For making of them	0	0	8	

An ancient story comes from Scotland which shows the similarity of most stories of witchcraft. A farmer was much troubled at night by the constant presence of a multitude of cats who much disturbed his rest. At last he struck at one with his sword and cut off its leg. When he took the limb up, he found it to his astonishment to be a human member, and next morning he discovered that an old woman in the neighbour had lost a leg suddenly. This story has many akin to it in the West of England. To most people, too, is familiar the story of the hare which no shot gun can injure, until at last the gun is charged with silver coins cut into small pieces. This story has many homes, but the outline is always the same :—the puzzled farmer unable to shoot the hare which creeps nightly by his house; suspicion aroused at length; counsel sought of the white witch, and the unusual charge for the gun prepared; the lying in wait once more; the limping off of the wounded creature; the discovery next day of some old woman in the neighbourhood laid up with an injured limb.

King James I, we are told, condescended to send for a man who was supposed to play for the orgies of witches, and bade him play before the majesty of England the tunes which inspired those servants of Satan to their unlawful and secret deeds. Nor did the stern, practical religion of the Commonwealth, or the great revival of learning in the end of the seventeenth and the beginning of the eighteenth century, shake the strength of this universal belief which has lingered down to our own days. Even John Wesley declared that "to give up belief in witchcraft was to give up the Bible."

At the beginning of the seventeenth century arose the class of professional witchfinders who were supposed to have special gifts for discovering such folk as had sold themselves to the devil. Amongst the most celebrated of these witchfinders was the notorious Mathew Hopkins, who has worthily found a place in the recent history of "the Twelve Worst Men." It is said that he caused to be hanged in one year sixty reputed witches in his own county of Essex alone. One of his favourite methods of trying a witch was trial by water. The thumbs and great toes were tied together and a cord tied round the waist of the victim, the ends of which were held by two men who were thus able to lower her into the water or raise her. When one thinks of the wholesale murders this fiend in human shape perpetrated, it is almost with satisfaction one reads that at last Hopkins was put to the water trial himself as a wizard, and condemned and executed. Few men have better deserved their fate!

Still among the wild coombes of North Devon and West Somerset the old beliefs handed down from time immemorial linger on, and no doubt maintain a strong hold upon many. And indeed even the most impartial of students cannot but be struck by some of the as yet unexplained occurrences which have taken place.

Within recent years benevolent white witches have plied their profitable trade in more than one of our county towns, to whom the faithful of the district were wont to resort and pay their money and obtain, as they fancied, the relief which could not otherwise be procured. In a little country parish dwelt a respectable farmer, who suffered losses amongst his stock. Witchcraft no doubt was the cause, and an old woman of singular appearance and of strange retiring habits, whose keen penetrating eyes made her neighbours shiver as she looked at them, was suspected as having worked the mischief. Some twenty miles had to be traversed before a white witch could be found, but when found he confirmed the farmer in his sagacious suspicion. There was only one cure—to draw the witch's blood. Hurrying home he laid wait for the poor old creature and scratched her savagely with a large nail till the blood flowed.

In that district it was a favourite remedy for scald head in a baby to hang cotton wool on a "thornen hedge" by moonlight.

As was at one time the almost universal belief, clergymen were supposed to be well acquainted with the black arts. An old farmer described to the clergyman of his parish the mysterious doings which had taken place at the death of Parson A. in that district. Parson A. had been decently buried in his parish church yard; but on the return of the mourners after the ceremony, they found the old man sitting stern and still, in his armchair in his study. No prayer or argument could move the silent figure that took its place evening after evening, as the last ray of light died out behind the dusky moor, and the white mist came creeping further and further up the valley. But at last, the teller of the tale used to say, Parson B. was sent for, a mighty man whom no ghost or other evil thing could withstand, and at his coming the mysterious thing rose sadly from its seat and followed him out across the meadows in the dim light, till at last it disappeared with a flash as of lightning, on the brink of a deep dark pool, overhung by old gnarled trees. Or the old man would tell in hesitating fashion, the story of the last hours of a squire of the district notorious for his evil ways. As the squire lay dying, a great thunderstorm, though it was mid-winter, came up and shook the ancient house, and roared amongst the trees, levelling the great oaks of centuries' growth; and amidst the shrieking of the storm, strange wild voices and unearthly laughter resounded about the place, as, struggling as though with a deadly foe, with wild curses upon his lips, the squire passed away. What caused the storm? "Something you parsons know about," was always the answer. Near the same village there dwelt one versed in the black art. He was known to be so, for had not many "seen his book?" who wrought strange pranks amongst his humble neighbours. If anyone offended him, punishment fell at once, either upon the offender's family or his stock.

A farmer in the same district had great losses amongst his cattle. He felt he had been bewitched, and he set off to seek the nearest white witch, some thirty miles away. The visit confirmed his suspicions. It was as he suspected. He was under the influence of the evil eye, and his tormentor was named to him.

On a waste piece of land on the side of the moor above his house, a cottage, scarcely more than a rough shelter of walls built without mortar and roughly thatched, had long been inhabited by an aged woman. She was the evil doer. "She must die," shouted the angry farmer, as he poured the reward of divination into the white witch's hand, "nothing less than that will content me." He hurried home and up to the cottage with several friends. There, tossing in a strange fever, lay the witch already nigh her end; and when she had thus expiated her evil deeds, the neighbours came and burnt the house and pulled down the walls.

In the same neighbourhood was one whose wife lay month after month sick of an illness which no doctor could cure. "I wonder," said a neighbour, "you let your wife stay like that." "Like that; what else can I do?" replied the disconsolate husband. "Go to Exeter and see Mr. ——: he will help you." Now the farmer had never been to Exeter before, and knew no one there. As he entered one of the main streets he asked the first person he met where Mr. —— lived. "I am he," replied the stranger, addressing the countryman, to his astonishment, by his name, "and I know that you have come to consult me about your wife's sickness. Come back with me." It was the same story. His wife lay under the spell of an evil-minded neighbour, but, said the white witch "she lies (the evil-minded one) under the sentence of death for her evil deeds, and when she is buried I will give you a sign to show who the offender was." The countryman went home. Under the power of the wise man's spells his wife regained her usual health, and soon a neighbour, little suspected of witchcraft, sickened and died. It was a beautiful afternoon, still and clear, as she was being borne to the churchyard ; but as the procession drew near the house of the woman that had been sick, suddenly a great storm of wind arose and lifted off the bier-cloth from the bier and laid it against the woman's door. And so the woman knew that this was the promised sign of the identity of the worker of her trouble.

One hears how mothers with sick infants would rise in the dark early morning and saddle a horse and ride away, concealing the nature of their errand and speaking to no one by the way ; and how, hurrying back, after long hours of travelling, with the medicines given by the white witch, they found their children under his beneficent protection, happy and sleeping. Sometimes it was some invocation to be said, some strange rite to be performed, or some mysterious powder, which, sprinkled around the premises, prohibited the witch's approach.

One curious feature in the doings of witches is their desire to look on the mischief that they work. Some years ago there was great distress in a farm house near the north coast of West Somerset. Great losses had taken place amongst the cattle. Several members of the family were ill.

> "There was no luck about the place,
> There was no luck at all."

Of course it was evident what the matter was. The whole place was under some evil influence. The assistance of the nearest white witch was sought, and he gave the applicants a powder to strew round the place, which would prevent any evil thing approaching to hurt them; and he told them that before long they would see the worker of all the mischief endeavouring to approach the house. Scarcely had the son who had been to consult this beneficent ally returned, when the family beheld an old woman who lived a solitary life in a cottage not far off, endeavouring to look through the paling which hedged in the little garden in front of the house. Here then was the evil fate of the family. "Let the dogs on her!" cried the master of the house, and he tried to rise from the armchair in which he was sitting; but some occult influence held him fast, and gradually chair and all rose to the ceiling. The rest hurried out just in time to see the old woman vanish as she approached a thick hedge, and the dogs returning cowed and dismayed. But the story goes on that to this day the master of the house, stricken down by some mysterious ailment, remains a helpless cripple and demented.

To refuse a gift to a person suspected of witchcraft is as dangerous as to receive one from her. "The place was full of 'em" said an ancient person to me, "fifty years ago." And here is a typical story; for all these stories have a strong resemblance one to the other. A strange-looking old woman called one day at a small farm house, and leaning over the half door asked for a drink of cider. Cider was scarce that year and the request was refused. The old woman hobbled off, denouncing vengeance on the churlish ways of the farmer and his wife. "You will wish soon you had given me the cider." From that day nothing went right with the household. The stock died, and one after another the farmer's daughters sickened and pined away!

More than one case lives in the memory of the district, of some poor creature, sick to death of some mysterious ailment which the doctor could not diagnose, suddenly being restored to health and strength on the passing away of some ill-conditioned person who was supposed to have willed him ill. And still in many a village whilst the doctors are innocently administering their medicines, the magic rites and incantations prescribed by the white witch are at the same time being secretly practised. At sunrise secretly the weakly child afflicted with rickets or a tendency to hernia, is taken to the cleft ash and passed through it and round it with muttered words of incantation; and the parents afterwards anxiously watch the tree, for they know that should the split sides join together again their child will grow strong, but should they remain apart, their child will always be weakly.

The rite "had to be performed on a Sunday morning, just before sunrise, and the opening must be in the direction of east and west, for the child must be passed through it towards the rising sun . . . These rites can be considered as nothing short of dramatic representations of that which it is desired to accomplish—a remedy of congenital . . . . imperfection by a new birth."[1] This orientation is no doubt a remnant of the sun-worship of an early period in our history.

And very remarkable are the cures supposed to have been wrought by the mysterious touch of the seventh

1. F. T. Elworthy's *The Evil Eye*, p. 70.

child of the seventh child. Obstinate cases of king's evil, which have stubbornly resisted the treatment of the medical man, have yielded apparently to the will of the person possessing this mysterious gift.

In the ancient chimneys of grey old farm houses and cottages, myrtle and rose covered, a dark leathery substance filled with pins is sometimes to be found. And those who are wise in such matters shake their heads as they think of the pains that evil thing cost some faithless lover or foe, long ago laid to rest. For there was no surer way in the olden time to punish the one and injure the other, than to stick a sheep's or calf's heart full of pins, and silently and secretly to hang it up in the wide old chimney. There it hung, unknown and unsuspected, and did its fell work ; while the perpetrator of the vengeful deed rejoiced, as the foe, smitten with some sore disease, wasted and pined away. A heart so used, and which was found in the Quantoxhead district, is to be seen in the Taunton Museum. And in an old manor house, unique in its beauty and interest, in our district, a shrivelled heart full of pins is still seen hanging in the very place where it was hung perhaps two hundred years ago, to work dire pains on probably some faithless lover. These hearts were an evidence of the "old, old belief that the heart was the seat of life and therefore a fit representative of a living person. It was believed that the heart of the hated person would suffer from the pricking, and that as the latter dried up and withered so would the heart and life of the victim against whom the act was designed."[1]

And can we say that the belief of witchcraft is dead

1. F. T. Elworthy's *The Evil Eye*, p. 54.

and gone when our daily papers are still able to record such horrors as the fully reported and attested tragedy which took place near Clonmel, in April, 1895?

"The trial of old Julian Cox for witchcraft, at Taunton Assizes in 1663, is curious. Julian—who, in spite of the name, was a woman—was accused of practising the black art upon a young maid, 'whereby her Body languished and was impaired of Health, by reason of the strange Fits upon account of the said Witchcraft.' A large part of the evidence went to prove her 'a Witch in general,' in itself an indictable offence, while the rest was devoted to showing the specific damage she did by sorcery to the maid. The witnesses who speak to the former count are the more interesting of the two sets, illustrating, incidentally, the chief habits of skilled witches. A huntsman came forward to say how once he started a hare; the dogs were just upon it, when it slipped under a bush. He ran round on the other side to save it from the hounds, when he discovered that it was Julian Cox, with 'her head grovelling on the Ground.' He was horror-stricken, yet questioned her: 'She was so far out of Breath'—from the chase, and, perhaps, the rapidity of the transformation—that she could not utter a word. 'And the Huntsman with his Dogs went Home presently sadly affrighted.' No wonder! Hardly less alarming was the experience of another witness: 'Julian set a monstrous great toad' to bother him as he sat 'taking a Pipe of Tobacco' at home. He cut it in pieces, and the 'paddock' pieced itself together again. Another had his cattle driven mad, so that they ran their heads against trees: to find out who did it he was advised to cut off the ears of the bewitched beasts and burn them. This was as good as burning the witch, 'who would be in misery, and could not rest till they were pluckt out of the Fire.' Sure enough, the haggish Julian came and took them out, and then all was well again. Next came the unshaken testimony of a woman, who swore that she had seen the accused 'fly into her own Chamber-window in her full proportion, and that she very well knew her, and was sure it was she.' Finally, there was the astounding admission of the poor old body herself. '[It] was to this purpose: that she had been often tempted by the Devil to be a witch, but never consented; that one evening she walkt out about a mile from her own house, and there came riding towards her 3 Persons upon 3 Broom-staves, borne up about a Yard and a Half from the ground; 2 of them she formerly knew, which was a Witch and a Wizard that were hang'd for Witchcraft several years before. The third Person she knew not; he came in the shape of a black Man, and tempted her to give him her soul, or to that effect, and to express it by pricking her Finger, and giving her name in her blood in token of it; and told her that she had Revenge against several Persons that had wronged her, but could not bring her purpose to pass without his help; and that upon the Terms aforesaid he would assist her to be revenged against them.' She said she did not consent to it; but there can be no doubt that she believed in the genuineness of these apparitions. There was little difficulty after this in finding her guilty of 'practising' upon the maid. It was shown that Julian was angry with her for refusing her alms, and had told her that she would repent it ere night; that the maid had convulsions and saw Julian, 'when they in the same Chamber did not see or hear anything.' The judge and jury had but one conclusion to come to, which was that she be hanged four days after her trial. But some of the less blind and besotted spoke harsh words of judge Archer for his zeal and precipitancy, and openly declared poor Julian's innocence when advocacy could do her strangled corpse no good.

"In May, 1893, the Yeovil magistrates had a case brought before them in which a man was charged with having threatened a woman whom he believed to have been a witch, and to have cast a spell upon his sister. Applicant stated that defendant came to her house and called her an old witch, and asked her to take the spell off his sister. He said she ought to be burnt, and accused her of burning stuff all night to bewitch people with. The defence was that defendant really believed the complainant had put a spell upon his sister, and threatened to 'do' for her in his anger.

"In June, 1892, the late coroner, Mr. W. Muller, held an inquest on a young woman at Lufton, in which the evidence revealed an extraordinary belief in witchcraft. After the medical man who had attended the girl for some time had stated that there was no hope of saving her life, the parents considered she was suffering from a spell or a 'bad wish,' or that she had been 'overlooked,' and they consulted a quack with the idea of getting the spell removed. After referring to an almanac, he informed them that no one could 'overlook' her, as she was a first-born child, but he went to their house and stayed from Thursday evening to Saturday morning; and on the Friday he made some herb tea in a black bottle, which was given the girl. The father had also consulted another 'wise man' as to the 'bad wish' supposed to have been cast upon his daughter. In the course of his summing up, the coroner remarked that one of the reasons why that enquiry was held was because it was reported to him that the parents thought that deceased was 'overlooked,' and they consulted the quack with a view to removing the spell that was upon her. In this nineteenth century, with all the educational advantages in the county of Somerset, the belief in witchcraft appeared more extensive than he could credit. There is no doubt whatever that such superstitions are very largely believed in by the country people in this county, but it is comparatively seldom that they get brought before the public as they were in the above cases."[1]

In a West Somerset village a villager suffered for a long time from the theft of small goods. Sometimes it was garden produce, sometimes a fowl, that was taken. At last his tools and more valuable possessions began to disappear. He suspected a neighbour, but could obtain no evidence against him, until he sought the help of a white witch. The white witch confirmed his suspicions. The person in his mind was the thief. "You will however never recover your property," the white witch said, "but take this bag and hang it in your chimney, and the thief will never pass your way again." The robbed man did as he was bid; and

1. *Somerset County Herald*, 27 February, 1897.

straightway the suspected man showed a most extraordinary dislike to passing his cottage. It was observed that he would resort to any experiment rather than approach it, and the thefts entirely ceased. At length, however, some repairs were needed to the chimney, and the workmen removed the bag ; and that very afternoon the suspected thief passed the door once more.

It is related that a very holy man dwelt at one time near the Doone Valley, spending his time in a hermit-like seclusion. He spoke to none and entered beneath no roof tree but his own. But one day a witch enticed him into a circle which he had drawn. The holy man made the sign of the Cross, but the fall was irremediable. He followed the witch into his hut, and was never seen again. It is a widely known superstition that if a witch draws a circle on the floor and can get any one to step in it, that person will be in his power. And it is in connection with this superstition, perhaps, that in farm houses of the better class and old manor houses, ovals are often to be seen moulded on the ceiling of the hall or principal dwelling room. Whatever is said underneath these ovals is held to be inviolate.

The further one gets into the hill country the more numerous become the superstitions, the more universal and strong the belief in them. In a hill country parish lying in a fold of the Brendon Hills many strange stories still hold firm sway. A cottage beside a large wood has been vacated by tenant after tenant, because of the strange sounds which are heard there and the strange sights which are seen. One tenant, coming down early in the morning, saw a figure of an unknown man sitting in the chimney corner, which vanished slowly away as he approached. His wife, coming home one night, unlocked her door, but found it impossible to open it, although she knew there was no one within. And every tenant bore witness that strange indescribable sounds made sleep often impossible. The story runs that many years ago, a Jew pedlar stopped at the inn of the distant village, and showed his wares to the assembled villagers. Rough characters then inhabited the cottage, and were at that time at the inn, but left it soon after the pedlar. The pedlar never returned again on his customary round. But the cottager and his wife became flush of money, and the discovery many years afterwards of a quantity of bones beneath the floor of the outhouse belonging to the cottage, gave foundation to the suspicion that the pedlar had been robbed and murdered, and his corpse thus disposed of, but that his unquiet spirit still finds no rest. A keeper watching some time ago in the adjoining wood on a dark night, saw a mysterious light suddenly appear, and from the light a figure, huge, white, and terrible of aspect, develop, from which the man fled shrieking and demented.

Sudden darknesses, shaping themselves into terrific indescribable figures, are another hill country superstition. A man going to an outhouse in bright moonlight, saw an indefinable black object in the clear light, which, as he looked, grew larger and larger, until it shut out the moonlight altogether. He struck into the darkness with a stick he held in his hand, and the darkness passed away. A farmer, driving his wife to a neighbouring town on a clear star-lit night, as he ascended the wide road which leads over the head of the at-one-time open down, saw an appearance of the same nature. It was small and undefinable at first, and then expanded into a huge black uncouth appearance which occupied the whole road. So palpable was it, that the quiet horse which he was driving jibbed and turned, and galloped down the hill By the time the horse could be stopped and turned, the road rose clear and open as before.

A pleasanter story is that of a lady driving home from dinner in that same district, in one of the old fashioned gigs in use some years ago. A bright moon made the bright, clear summer night still clearer; and as the carriage approached an open part of the road, proceeding at a rapid pace, the lady saw a group of little children, prettily dressed, dancing across the road. "Take care," she cried to her driver; and he, fearing he would drive into them, at once slackened his speed, saying, "All right, I see them." But the figures became indistinct, and disappeared as the gig drew near.

In that same hill country parish, a headless horseman, at midnight on moonlit nights, rides up and down a four crossway as though to guard it; nor durst anyone pass, who can otherwise avoid it, a dark quarry beneath a hanging wood, where strange uncouth things have been seen by many folk to lurk in the deep shadows of rocks and trees. Many of these superstitions may perhaps date back to the times of the Civil Wars, or more probably to the time of Monmouth's rebellion, when the hill country was largely royalist.

The ghastly name of Forges Cross, given to more than one cross-way in that district, reveals the spots where the bloodthirsty Jefferies set up his gallows, adorned with the quivering limbs of some unhappy villager well known to his neighbour; or where some luckless skeleton long dangled in chains that creaked in the fierce winds that sweep over that "stark" country.

Farmer R. was so bewitched, that he lost the use of his limbs, while "toads and other unclean things could not be kept away from his door." The white witch bade him nail three new horse-shoes on the door of his house, and place some seeds he gave him about it; then if the witch came in she would be imprisoned and unable to escape. A neighbour went to the same white witch with regard to some bees that had been stolen. The white witch consulted "his book." "Yes, your first cousin's bees have already been burnt and the honey taken, otherwise I could have made the thief replace them."

At D——combe, "there in the meadow," the pixies light fires and dress their children; and in the same meadow there is a post, which none can pass at night, because a shapeless thing with rattling chains springs out against the passer-by. The pixies were active in our district in days gone by. If some favoured houses were left ever so dirty, they were found cleaned up in the morning. Even the unfinished operations of brewing have been found completed. The little people came through the keyhole, and expected to be paid by a basin of bread and milk being set for them in a corner. In some houses it was the custom to put a pail of clean water, towels, and soap ready for the use of the pixies. A woman of Minehead who had a relation who had dealings with the pixies, saw this relation one day in Minehead market filching pieces of meat from the stalls. She went up to him and spoke to him. "Which eye," he asked, "did you see me with?" She told him. Straightway he blew upon it, and she became blind in that eye. One luckless person saw twenty-four pixies "down to Great Gate." They discovered her watching them, and in revenge they led her about all night over the moor and about the woods, till, with the break of day, they left her. This was the fate also of Farmer B. returning from Minehead market. He was led about the fields and moor until morning. But another man thus mischievously troubled, bethought him of the sure remedy in such cases; he took off his coat and turned it, and got home at once without difficulty.

Ghosts do not appear ever to have been plentiful in our district, although the "great house" at Allerford was at one time supposed to be "troublesome." Some years ago a man passing a lonely cottage at night, which had long been empty, saw a bright light within, and heard the rattle of glasses and the noise of loud laughter; a story which was corroborated by a neighbour next day. Another man had a lodger who was engaged in quarry work which took him away sometimes for a night or two from his lodgings. One night the landlord and his wife heard the lodger's heavy steps on the stairs. The woman got up and went out to the little landing, and called to the lodger by name, thinking he would want food; but a figure resembling the lodger's rushed silently past her, and entered his room. Next day the news reached Selworthy that the man had been killed the evening before, by a fall of stone. A sexton in past days used to hear, when a death was about to take place, loud calls at night; and it was believed that ghosts before a death were to be seen hovering about the bier cloth, as though to announce that it would soon be required for use. A woman busy putting straight the house of a dead friend who had passed to her rest, used to be waked night after night by the clasping of icy cold hands about her. A young man went to work in London. One night, a long time afterwards, his parents heard a loud and continued tapping at their door, and they soon heard that at the time of the tapping their son was passing away in his lodgings in the distant metropolis.

The number of instances in which relations of dying people have been apparently warned by the passing spirit, are certainly most curious, and some very well authenticated. In this district a lady came down to breakfast in a house in which she was staying, in great distress, saying that repeatedly and vividly during the night she had seen her favourite brother, a midshipman, floating on the sea with seaweed clinging about him. She could not get over the impression, and in a few weeks the news reached her that her brother had fallen overboard and been drowned, on that very night.

Perhaps the most striking, as it is certainly one of the best authenticated of modern dreams of this nature, is the well-known vision of a Mr. Williams, a land-owner and a magistrate, at that time living near Truro, of the approaching murder, in 1812, of the Right Hon. S. Perceval, then Prime Minister. Mr. Williams dreamt three times during the same night very vividly that he was standing in the lobby of the House of Commons, and that he saw a man enter whose dress he accurately noted; and then another man, whose appearance was just as clearly impressed upon his mind, step forward and shoot him. Unable to sleep, he rode into Truro, and told his tale. Some of his friends who knew Mr. Perceval by sight, at once identified the murdered man in the dream as being the Prime Minister. So strongly impressed was Mr. Williams with the vision, that he wished to ride at once to London and warn the Prime Minister of possible danger. He was, however, persuaded that he would only be looked upon as a madman for his pains. Shortly afterwards the terrible news of Mr. Perceval's unprovoked murder, by Bellingham, reached Cornwall. Mr. Williams hurried to London, and recognised in Bellingham, the murderer he had seen in his dreams, and found that every detail of the scene in his dream, even down to the particulars of the dress of the assassin and his victim, corresponded exactly with those of the actual occurrence.

A strange story of a dream of a different nature, but equally well authenticated, comes from Mold, in Flintshire. A woman, living near Mold, dreamt on three consecutive nights, that she saw a man attired in gold armour, standing at a particular spot near a hedge-row. No notice was taken of her statement, but sometime afterwards some labourers at work at the spot, turned up what appeared to be some pieces of rusty iron which they threw on one side. Soon, however, it was discovered that the fragments were of gold, and not of iron. Some portions of the find had been abstracted for making rings and amulets before the news of the find reached the authorities at the British Museum. They were, however, successful in securing, almost in its entirety, the beautiful golden corslet which had thus been brought to light, and which is now on view at the British Museum.

For the following interesting information on this subject of minor superstitions I am indebted to Mr. C. Kille of Minehead.

If you are asked to a christening, and wish to carry luck to the house, and give the child a propitious start in life, you would do well to go to your cupboard and reach down a piece of bread and some of the best cheese you have got to put on the top of it. When you get out of your house, give the bread and cheese to the first child you meet. Take care, however, if you are going to assist at the baptism of a boy, you give your bread and cheese to one of the opposite sex, and observe a similar care also if it should be a girl, or your offering may not be propitious after all.

It is said that cats born in May will bring vermin into the house, such as snakes and toads, etc.

Cock-crowing in the night presages a death in the family, and bad luck is sure to fall on the unfortunate possessor of a crowing hen.

When a cock walks up to the door and delivers himself of a crow, it is a friendly intimation that you may expect a stranger.

If you want to prosper throughout the month, turn over your money when first you see the new moon, but take care that you do not catch sight of the moon through glass, or you might reverse all the money you possessed, and nothing would come but bad luck. Neither ought you to presume to point at the moon with your finger, or nameless misfortunes may be in store for you.

It is bad luck to allow an odd person to walk after a funeral ; all should be in couples.

If a corpse is put out at a window another member of the family will die before the year is out.

It is unlucky to bring May blossoms (hawthorn) into a house, or to keep peacock's feathers within doors.

A bird tapping at a window is a sign of death in the house.

If fruit trees or broad beans blossom twice it is a sign of death in a family.

A howling dog at night is sign of death.

Fruit stains on linen, etc., will disappear as the season for the particular fruit passes away.

It is lucky to see a flock of sheep go by while you are changing houses.

" Tucking " a baby—

" If you tuck him in May
You will drive him away."

Run when you first hear the cuckoo, or you will be lazy all the year. It is lucky also to wish for what you want, when you hear him.

If you hear a cuckoo after Old Midsummer Day you will not live to hear another.

Shelling peas. If a pod has nine peas, hang the pod over the doorway, and the first man who enters will be the sheller's future husband.

It is bad luck to return to a house after starting on a journey. Ill luck may be averted by the person sitting down before starting again.

> "If you would live aud thrive,
> Let the spider run alive."

Mist as a sign of rain:

> "Come from sea and go to hill,
> Have enough to drive a mill.
> Come from hill and go to sea,
> Won't have enough to drown a flea."

At Selworthy, a mist rising as high as the church is said to mean rain, but one along the valley implies drought.

If bees pitch on dry wood during swarming there will be a death in the family.

A cross baby is likely to be better tempered after baptism.

Hedgers should make hedges when the moon is growing, not waning, or they will not grow.

Also, the cut stripes (in making a hedge) should be laid away from the sun, towards the north if possible, for the same reason.

Water rising from a spring or running northward is good for sore eyes. The water from two springs running northward in Old Cleeve parish is reputed as good for sore eyes for that reason.

People sing to the apple trees and fire off guns to get a good crop the following season, on 17th January (eve of Old Twelfth Day). In Hasted's *History of Kent*, Rogation Week is the time; in Bohn's *Antiquities*, New Year's Eve is given for Sussex and Devon;

in Herrick's *Hesperides*, mention is made of its being done on Christmas Eve. Libations, too, of hot drinks are poured out beneath them, just as still the "Congo natives place calabashes of water under certain trees, that the tree spirit may drink when thirsty."[1] This custom is the remnant of the old belief that spirits dwelt in trees. The wassail song runs as follows:

"Apple tree, apple tree I wassail thee,
To blow and to bear
Hats vull, caps vull, dree bushell bags vull,
And my pocket vull too!"

Village maidens, too, still love to hide a piece of wedding cake beneath their pillows, for they know that it will bring them visions of the fortunate man whose good luck it will be to lead them in their turn to the altar.

Birds hold their place in folklore. The raven is held to be a bird of ill omen, as it is seen swiftly passing, high over head, to its inaccessible eyrie in some precipitous cliff or lofty tree, croaking harshly as it goes. To a single magpie you must take off your hat, to avoid the ill luck that would follow if you did not. It is also considered to be a bird of portent. In this district we say:

"One for sorrow,
Two for mirth,
Three for a wedding,
Four for a birth."

It is considered a wrong thing to kill a robin. No doubt the respect paid to this pretty little bird arises

1. F. T. Elworthy's *The Evil Eye*, p. 102.

from the beautiful old legend that a robin toiled to extract the nails from the pierced and bleeding hands of the Saviour as He hung upon the Cross, and that the drops of the sacred Blood fell upon and stained its breast.

The writer is aware that these childlike beliefs of our forefathers will appear to many to be too puerile to be recorded, but he still sets down a few of those which have come to his ears, as a contribution towards that interesting science which is still in its infancy, but has assuredly a great future before it, the science of comparative folklore. Many of the simple superstitions and practices, still prevalent in country places, have their history back in dim and distant days of which as yet we know but little. Some are of later origin. Of this class, the following story is an example. An Oxford undergraduate was recently crossing a Cornish moor at night in company with a miner. The conversation turned on ghosts. "If you meet a ghost," said the miner, "there is only one thing to do; you must stand up square and say your 'Nummy Dummy.'" In which gibberish the miner, unknown to himself, was repeating a corrupted form of the priestly exorcism, "In nomine Domini."

CHAPTER X.

Flora of the Holnicote Valley.

AS no account of any country is complete without a notice of its Flora, a short description of the flowers of this beautiful vale will not be out of place.

In the winter, the Holly Trees (*Ilex Aquifolium*), with their shining leaves and scarlet berries, enliven the scene; and, as spring advances, the hedges are filled with Primroses, and in some places the sweet white Violet. In the meadows and orchards around Bossington grow in profusion the white Narcissus, which however is not an indigenous flower; the Daffodil—Lent Lily, or Lent Rose, as it is severally called—some with doubled flowers (*Pseudo-Narcissus*), and the Snowdrop (*Galanthus nivalis*). Later on in the year, we find the Wild Cornel or Dogwood (*Cornus sanguinea*); the blue Iris (*I. foetidissima*), whose opened capsules and bright scarlet seeds are so much prettier than the insignificant flower; Common Elder (*Sambucus nigra*), Common Celandine (*Chelidonium majus*), Lesser Celandine (*Ranunculus Ficaria*), Wood Sorrel (*Oxalis Acetosella*), the Honeysuckle (*Sonicera Periclymenum*), and the sweet wild rose :—

"Starring each bush in lanes and glades."

SOME RARE FLOWERS FOUND AT SELWORTHY

From a drawing by Miss Alice May

The ditches bordering the roads and fields are the habitats of the Yellow Iris, or Corn-flag (*I. Pseudacorus*) White and Purple Comfrey (*Symphytum officinale*), so often cultivated as fodder; and by the stream flowing down Selworthy Coombe grows very luxuriantly the Meadow Sweet, or Queen of the Meadows (*Spiraea Ulmaria*), the "Sweet Mace" of mediæval times.

The Geranium tribe is well represented in this district. Amongst commoner varieties may be found in the Selworthy lanes the shining Crane's Bill (*G. lucidum*), Mountain Crane's Bill (*G. pyrenaicum*), and on the North Hill, Sea Stork's Bill (*Erodium maritimum*), Here also, is the habitat of the Subterraneous Trefoil (*T. subterraneum*); and near Greenaleigh grows in profusion the Wood Vetch (*Vicia silvatica*). At Porlock the Tuberous Bitter Vetch (*O. tuberosus*) is found; and on the hills, Bird's-foot Trefoil (*Lotus corniculatus*), and the Common Bird's foot (*Ornithopus perpusillus*), the jointed legumes of which bear a singular resemblance to a bird's foot.

Brown and stern Hurlstone Point is clothed and softened with the bright pink flowers of Thrift (*Armeria maritima*); and in crevices of the rock near the sea may be gathered Danish Scurvy Grass (*Cochlearia danica*), and Sea Campion (*Silene maritima*). Going through the woods we find Common Moschatel (*Adoxa Moschatellina*), Wood Sanicle (*Sanicula europaea*), Great Leopard's Bane (*Doronicum Pardalianches*), the *yellow-flowered* White Mullein (*Verbascum Lychnitis*), "the only British station known for this form of the species,"[1] and Twiggy Mullein (*V. virgatum*).

1. *Journal of Botany*, January, 1894.

In a bog near Luccombe Hill grows the Pale Butterwort (*Pinguicula lusitanica*), Bog Asphodel (*Narthecium ossifragum*), Greater Skull-cap (*Scutellaria galericulata*), Lesser Skull-cap (*S. Minor*).

Walking down from Dunkerry, and following the Horner water, are seen growing all around tall Foxgloves, locally called "Poppies" (some of them from four to five feet high), Golden Gorse (*Ulex europaeus*), so characteristic of English scenery, Purple Heath (*Erica cinerea*), which in the autumn the parasite Dodder (*Cuscuta Epithymum*) will cover, together with its neighbour, the Gorse, with its red thread-like stems and pale blossoms; the pink bells of the cross-leaved Heath (*Erica Tetralix*), the Ling or Heather (*Calluna vulgaris*), the Whortleberry (*Vaccinium Myrtillus*), with red foliage and wax-like flesh-coloured flowers.

On the boggy sides of the stream we see the lovely pale blue flowers of the Water Forget-me-not (*Myosotis palustris*), mingling with the golden stars of the Yellow Pimpernel (*Lysimachia nemorum*), the fly-catching, flesh-loving Sundew (*Drosera rotundifolia*), Dwarf Red Rattle (*Pedicularis silvatica*), Greater Spearwort (*Ranunculus Lingua*), Lesser Spearwort (*R. Flammula*), Marsh Pennywort (*Hydrocotyle vulgaris*), Golden Saxifrage (*Chrysosplenium oppositifo lium*), and side by side the delicate bells of the Ivy-leaved Bell-flower (*Campanula hederaceæ*, or *Wahlenbergia*), with the rose-coloured blossoms of the Bog Pimpernel (*Anagallis tenella*), and in some places the aromatic mints.

The soft grassy turf of all the hills is strewn with bright Tormentilla (*T. officinalis*, or *Potentilla Silvestris*), the pretty blue and white Milkworts (*Polygala *vulgaris*), Common Filago or Cudweed (*Filago germanica*), and Mouse-ear Hawkweed (*Hieracium Pilosella*). Amongst the long grasses grow the sweet night-scented Butterfly Orchis (*Habenaria bifolia*), with the more common varieties of the Orchis family. Near Woodcombe grows Motherwort (*Leonurus Cardiaca*), in many places Wormwood or Absinthe (*Artemisia Absinthium*), and Puck would have no difficulty in finding Broom (*Sarothanus scoparius*), with which "to sweep the dust behind the door."

As autumn advances, the woods and hedges become brilliant with the orange and red trails of Black Bryony (*Tamus communis*), the scarlet berries of the Guelder Rose (*Vibernum Opulus*), the Wayfaring Tree (*V. Lantana*), the Mountain Ash or Rowan Tree (*Pyrus Aucuparia*), the beautiful rose-coloured berries of the Spindle Tree (*Euonymus europæus*), whose seed-vessels when ripe disclose the seeds wrapped in scarlet. The wood of this tree, like that of the Wild Cornel and Guelder Rose, was formerly used for making the spindles of the spinning-wheel, hence its name: now it is used for making butchers' skewers. Intermingled with these bright colours twines the Travellers' Joy (*Clematis Vitalba*), now changing its name to Old Man's Beard, from the grey silky tufts of its ripened seed-vessels.

Selworthy Lane was formerly noted for its rare ferns; now, alas! the hand of the spoiler in the shape of the "tourist" has robbed this pretty lane of all its treasures, but there still linger on walls, and in shady nooks, the Ceterach, Wall Rue, Male Fern, Lady Fern, Hart's Tongue, Hard Fern, Polypody, Adiantum, Black Spleenwort, and, near Bossington, Green Spleenwort.

CHAPTER XI.

The Holnicote Herd of Exmoor Ponies.

IT has been represented to the author that no history of Selworthy would be complete, which did not give some account of the famous herd of ponies, which is maintained on the Holnicote estate. But he feels that, like Dœdalus, he is attempting a subject too great for him. And he fears a failure as complete!

From the earliest days Exmoor has been a royal forest; and "when the Conqueror came," the three Saxon rangers of the forest, Dodo, Almar, and Godric, were "found at hame" at Withypole. Perhaps, even in those days, there were ponies on Exmoor. Certainly the compilers of Doomsday note carefully the existence of several horses in each of the parishes surrounding the moor. But, however this may be, from time immemorial the forest has been the home of a breed of tiny ponies almost as wild as, and second only in interest to, the lordly red deer themselves.

It is said, that when in 1818, the government of the day decided to sell such portions of the forest as belonged to the Crown, the ponies running practically wild on the moor, numbered five hundred. These

EXMOOR PONIES

(Showing Gateway to Steyning Manor House.)

ponies would have been principally the property of the Acland family, as the heads of that great west-country house had held at that time the lease of the forest since 1784.

The portion of the moor claimed by the Crown, amounting to about 10,300 acres, was purchased by the father of the present Sir Frederick Knight, who also purchased Sir T. D. Acland's share of the forest for 5,555 guineas; and the herd of ponies was sold by auction. About twenty only of the original breed were reserved, which were sent to Ashway, a farm of Sir T. D. Acland's in the parish of Dulverton, adjoining the wide tract of wild moorland, called Winsford Hill. Their descendants are the only pure Exmoor ponies now in existence, and each pony in the Ashway herd bears on the near quarter the "anchor" brand, the mark which has distinguished the Holnicote breed for a hundred years.

The present Sir Thomas Acland has made more than one attempt to improve the quality of his ponies, while strictly preserving the purity of the breed. But the introduction of fresh blood, Mr. C. Birmingham, the Holnicote agent, informs the writer, has hitherto always proved a failure. The first generation may be improved in size and shape, but in the second generation the ineradicable Exmoor type has always re-asserted itself. More success, however, has attended the removal, for a few months, of the best of the mares and foals to the rich pastures about Killerton, Sir T. Acland's beautiful home in Devonshire. The more genial climate and the better keep of that district are found to have a distinctly beneficial effect on the growing colts, and the standard has been considerably raised and the shape improved by the experiment. Every year some twenty of the Holnicote ponies are drafted out for sale at the well-known horse-fair at Bampton, North Devon. There is generally a considerable competition for these ponies, which fetch good prices; £5 to £10 a-piece, perhaps. They average about eleven hands in height.

The jumping powers of these ponies are extraordinary, and they are wonderfully sure-footed. Marvellous stories, too, are told of their pluck and "staying" powers. It is narrated that on one occasion a great hunting man came down very spic and span, from Leicestershire to hunt for a day or two with the Devon and Somerset hounds. He asked a local sportsman to show him some one who knew the country, and whom he could follow. His friend pointed out, to the great disgust of the Leicestershire "swell," a farmer riding a pony so small that his feet almost touched the ground; but before the day was over, the visitor discovered that it was all his smartly accoutred two-hundred-guinea hunter could do to keep that tiny pony in sight, although its bit *was* rusty and its bridle mended with whip-cord!

The late Lady Acland used to tell a story illustrative of the hardy nature of these animals. A hill-country pony had been purchased for use at Holnicote, and, although it had been warranted quiet, it soon became unmanageable. The wife of the farmer who had sold the pony was interviewed on the matter. "We found it quite quiet," she said: "of course, with us, it lay out and had nothing but grass, and my son rode it over the farm in the morning, and my daughter and I generally drove it somewhere of an afternoon. Oh, yes, it was quite quiet. But you say (in a rapid *crescendo*), you kept it in stable, and fed it on hay, and gave it oats—*of course* it kicked!"

An amusing story is told of a pony belonging to the Ashway herd, which was bought some years ago by the present Duchess of Hamilton. It is recorded that the natural politeness of this little animal was so great, that when at home in the little enclosed fields about Ashway, he would rise on his hind feet and pull back the gates with his front feet for the ladies of his family to pass through.

Miss E. March-Phillips, in a brightly written article on "Exmoor Ponies," in the *Pall Mall Magazine* for October, 1896, tells us that the points most looked for in Exmoor ponies are these:—"First, good quarters, (as in this they are apt to fail) sloping shoulders, wide foreheads and nostrils, mealy nose and sharp pricked ears, short legs and good bone. 'A long horse with a short back, or a tall horse with short legs,' is the Exmoor saying; meaning that the bodies should be thick through—in build like a miniature cart-horse. The colour is also imperative; the most usual is a brown mouse colour, or brown inclining to bay, more rarely black or grey; chestnuts and roans are inadmissible. The coat is extremely long and thick—over a finger's length in winter; full shaggy mane, and tail long and sweeping, serving to flick the flies from chest and shoulder."

No notice of the Holnicote ponies would be complete without some mention of their keepers, the family of

Rawle. John Rawle, who took charge of the ponies reserved from the sale in 1818, was quite a character. He was a man of great strength, and could go into a herd of ponies and bring out unassisted in his arms any one of the little whinnying creatures, a feat which required skill, as well as strength, for the ponies fight very fiercely with their tiny forefeet. Rawle entertained for the head of the Acland family of the day the sentiment of a feudal retainer for his chief. It is said that when he accompanied Sir Thomas on any expedition, and his master entered a house for refreshment, Rawle stood at the door like a sentry, watchful and immovable, however long the delay, until "his honour" reappeared. Sir Thomas's wish was law to him. One day the last baronet said to Rawle, "I want to send two ponies to the Duke of Baden ; will you take them?" Rawle's travels had probably been before confined to Minehead on the one side, and Barnstaple on the other, and he could neither read nor write well, if at all, but he replied without hesitation, "If it please your honour." His troubles on the journey to Baden were manifold ; and they were increased by the arrival of a foal *en route*. He had only a pass for two ponies, but he succeeded in hiding the tiny baby pony under the straw of its bed when the Custom House officer came on board. He reached Baden at length in safety, and delivered his charges to the Grand Duke's servants. And the very next morning, before light, he started for home ; "his honour began black game shooting on September the first, and he must be present." He made his way straight back to Sir Thomas's shooting quarters, without stopping to see his wife on the way, and reported the safe delivery of the ponies; but, "Please your honour," he added, "the folk out there be the stupidest set of fools I ever did see. They couldn't understand a single word an honest man said to 'em."

The ponies are now under the charge of his son; a worthy chip of the old block.

In connection with the more sporting side of our parish history, we ought to make mention of the interesting collection of stags' heads preserved in the stables at Holnicote. They number thirty, and were obtained between the years 1785-93, when the ninth Acland baronet, who was always spoken of as "his honour," held rule at Holnicote. He was the son of the seventh baronet, and succeeded his nephew, Sir John. The seventh baronet had married the heiress of the Dyke family, who had inherited the estate of Tetton from her father, and the Pixton property from her uncle, Edward Dyke. Her husband took over the staghounds from Mr. Edward Dyke, and her son, Sir Thomas, hunted them after him in a truly princely fashion. It is said of this Sir Thomas, that his property was so extensive, that he could ride from Holnicote to Killerton, more than thirty miles, without going off his own land. The stories that have come down of his hunting parties, sound more like extracts from the pages of a mediæval chronicler, than records of ordinary west-country hunting expeditions.

It is said that when, bent on hunting, "his honour" set off for his hunting lodge at Higher Coombe in the parish of Dulverton, he was always accompanied by a cavalcade of his tenants from the Holnicote estate. By this party he was solemnly escorted next day to the wood which was to be drawn. It is further related that some members of the cavalcade were always prepared to act as a band, and that when the stag got away, this band struck up a hunting piece, the duration of which formed the extent of the "law" given to the deer.

A great punch bowl is preserved at Higher Coombe, which, in those days, was made expressly in China, and presented, together with twelve glasses, to Sir Thomas by the participators in his open-handed hospitality. The bowl has a stag-hunt represented upon it; and each glass bears the figure of a stag, and the inscription, "Prosperity to stag-hunting." A very interesting account of these merry, roystering days is to be found in the Hon. John Fortescue's book on stag hunting.

The two most notable heads preserved at Holnicote are that of a deer killed at Badgworthy in 1788, which weighed 14 score, 14lbs.; and that of one found at Deane Cleave, and killed at Raleigh Mill, in 1792. The head of this latter deer shows the extraordinary number of eighteen points.

"His honour's" hunting days came somewhat speedily to an end. He was taken ill on his way to London, in May, 1794, and died there on the 17th of that month. And good Mr. Brice, rector of Selworthy, wrote a copy of Latin verses to his memory (*vide* p. 98), which are a greater credit to the warmness of the good parson's heart than to the elegance of his scholarship.

APPENDIX A.

Will of Charles Staynings 1693.

In the name of God Amen. I Charles Staynings of Holnycote in the County of Somersett Esqre being of perfect mind and memory (I bless my God for the same) and not knowing the certaine time of my departure I doe make and appoint this my last Will and Testament revoking and annulling all former Wills and Testaments by me heretofore made. Impr's. I committ my body to the dust to be decently buried by my Executor hereafter named in my Great Grandfather's Grave next my wife as my Trustees and Executor shall direct and my Soul I give to the Great God that gave him. Item. I give and bequeath unto Robert Siderfin of Croydon in the County of Somersett Esqre and Richard Troyte of Stream in the same County Clerke and to the survivor of them and to the Executor and Administrator of such survivor All my messuages lands tenem^{ts} mills and hereditam^{ts} with the appurten'nces lyeing within the severall p'ishes villages or tythings of Nether Stowey and Over Stowey in the aforesaid County of Som'sett. To have and to hold the aforesaid messuages lands tenements mills and hereditaments whatsoever with the appurten'nces unto the aforesaid Robert Siderfin and Richard Troyte their executors and assigns and to the Executor and Admin^{r} of the survivor of them for and during the whole terme and time of ninety nine years fully to be complete and ended. If Lewis Staynings my brother and Grace Oram of Sellworthy in the County of Somersett Widdow they or either of them shall soe long happen to live nevertheless to be only lyable to the trusts and for the uses hereafter mens'oned (that is to say) to lease out the said pr'mises att an yearly rent and to pay the sume of Eighty Pounds in manner and forme following (that is to say) forty pounds p'te of the said Eighty Pounds, I doe appointe the said Robert Siderfin and Richard Troyte and the survivor of them of the Executor and Adminr of such survivor to pay annually unto my brother Lewis Staynings by quarterly paymts during his natural life and twenty pounds other p'te of the said Eighty Pounds, I doe appointe the said Robert Siderfin and Richard Troyte and the survivor of them and the Executor of such survivor to pay annually to Mrs Grace Oram before named during her naturall life and twenty pounds residue of the said Eighty Pounds I doe appoint the said Robert Siderfin and Richard Troyte and the survivor of them and the Executor of such survivor to pay annually unto my nephew Joseph Braford of the City of London during the naturall lives of my brother Lewis Staynings and Grace Oram and the survivor of them and llkewise to pay all rates taxes and other outgoings as shall become justly due and payable out of the aforesaid pr'm'sses during the said trust. And it is my Will and pleasure that the said Robert Siderfin and Richard Troyte and the survivor of them and the Executor and Adminr of such survivor doe annually account to my Executor hereafter named for all such sume and sumes of money as they shall receive and take out of the aforesaid messuages land tenements mills hereditam[ts] over and above the said sume of Eighty Pounds or the annuityes paid which said overplus I doe give and bequeath until my said Executor. Item. I doe give and bequeath unto my brother Lewis Staynings the house he now lives in called the West House being part of my Mansion House in the p'ish of Sellworthy aforesaid for the terme of his naturall life and after his decease I give and devise the said house unto my nephew William Martin of the City and County of Exeter Esq[r] his heirs and assigns for ever. Item. I give and devise unto my said nephew William Martin and his heirs All that my Mansion House Messuages Lands Tenem[ts] Barton Farme Mill and hereditam[ts] whatsoever with their and every of their appurten'nces lyeing and being within the severall p'ishes tythings hamletts and villages of Sellworthy and Luccombe in the County of Somersett. To have and to hold the said Mansion House and all and singular the said messuages lands tenements barton farme mill and hereditam[ts] whatsoever with their and every of their appurten'nces unto the said William Martin his heirs and assigns for ever. Item, I give and devise unto my said nephew William Martin and his heirs my Mannor of Hollincote with all the Royaltys and priveledges belonging to the same and all and singular my messuages lands tenements and hereditaments whatsoever with their and every of their appurten'nces lyeing and being in the severall p'shes tythings hamletts and villages of Sellworthy, Luccombe, Winsford, Exford, Porlocke and Dulverton in the aforesaid County of Somersett. To have and to hold the aforesaid mannor messuages lands tenements and hereditam^ts^ whatsoever with their and every of their appurten'nces unto the said William Martin his heirs and assignes for ever. Item, I give and devise unto the aforenamed Robert Siderfin and Richard Troyte and their heires and to the heir Executor and Admin^r^ of the survivor of them All my Mannor Messuages Mills Lands Temen^ts^ and Hereditaments whatsoever with their and every of their appurten'nces lyeing and being in the severall p'ishes villages tythings and hamletts of Nether Stowey and Over Stowey in the said County of Somersett upon this further trust (that is to say) after the death of my brother Lewis Staynings and Grace Oram and the survivor of them to and for the use of my nephew Joseph Braford for the terme of ninety nine years if he shall soe long happen to live. And after his decease or expiration of the said terme then in trust for such child and children as shall lawfully be gotten by the body of the said Joseph Braford such child or children liveing to the age of one and twenty yeares then to such child or children and the heirs of their body lawfully begotten and for default of issue lawfully begotten by the said Joseph Braford or for default of issue liveing to the age of one and twenty yeares or for default of issue by such child or children as shall be lawfully begotten by the said Joseph Braford then I give and demise unto my said nephew William Martin and his heires All my said Mannor Mills Messuages Lands Tenem^ts^ and hereditam^ts^ whatsoever with their and every of their appurten'nces lyeing and being in the aforesaid p'ishes tythings hamletts and villages of Nether Stowey and

Over Stowey. To have and to hold all the said Mannor Mills Messuages Lands tenements and hereditam[ts] whatsoever with their and every of their appurten'nces unto the said William Martin his heirs and assigns for ever. And I hereby will and authorize the said Robert Siderfin and Richard Troyte and the survivor of them and the Executor and Admin[r] of such survivor to allow and pay them and himself for such care cost and trouble as they or either of them shall reasonably deserve or be at in manageing the said trusts. Item. I give and bequeath unto the aforenamed Grace Oram now living with me the sume of One hundred pounds to be paid within one yeare after my decease. Item. I give and bequeath unto my trustees Robert Siderfin and Richard Troyte the sum of Tenn Pounds each to be paid within three months after my decease. Item. I give unto my servant Edward Stoate the sum of Twenty Pounds. Item. I give unto Joane Mitchell, Widdow, one other of my servants the sume of Five Pounds. Item. I give unto every other of my servants as shall be liveing with me at the time of my death the sum of forty shillings each. Item. I give to the poore of Sellworthy Twenty Pounds to be put in Stocke and the use thereof to be distributed yearly and to the poore of Luccombe Five Pounds to be put into Stocke and the use thereof to be distributed yearly, and to the poore of Dulverton five pounds to be put into stocke and the interest yearly to be distributed and fifty shillings to the poore of Winsford and fifty shillings more to the poore of Exford to be distributed at my death. Item. I give and devise unto my nephew William Martin and his heirs All my

Mannors Messuages Lands Tenan^{ts} and Hereditam^{ts} whatsoever (not by me already devised within the County of Som'sett and elsewhere). To have and to hold the said Mannors Messuages Lands Tenan^{ts} and hereditam^{ts} with their appurten'nces unto the said William Martin his heirs and assigns for ever. Item. After my legacies paid and funerall expenses borne I give and bequeath all the rest of my goods and chattles whatsoever unto my aforenamed nephew William Martin whom I doe constitute appoint and make my whole and sole Executor of this my last Will and Testament. In Witness whereof I the said Charles Staynings have published and declared this my last Will and Testament this fourteenth day of February Annoq. D'ni 1693 and in the sixth yeare of the Raigne of King William and Queen Mary.

CHA. STAYNINGS.

Signed sealed published and declared by Charles Staynings Esqre to be his last Will and Testament in the presence of us—John Galard Rect^{r} de Sellworthy—Elias Falvey Rect^{r} de Oare– Edward Stoate—Will Siderfin.

[Proved at Taunton the 4th day of February 1700 on the Oath of William Martyn the Executor.]

NOTES.

Extract from the Will of "William Martyn of Netherex in ye County of Devon, Esquire," date 28 Dec. 1661.

"Item. I give unto my daughter Susanna Martyn, ye summe of five hundred pounds to be payd unto her by my executor hereafter mentioned, when she attains to the age of twenty and one, and shall further leave her to be better provided for at ye good pleasure of her dear Aunt, my sister Stennings."

APPENDIX B.

Some Papers from the Church Chest.

This Indenture maide the second daie of January in the fyve and Twenteth yeare of ye Raigne of o^{r} Soṽaigne Ladie Elizabeth by ye grace of God Queen of England France and Ireland defendor of the faith tc̃, Betweene Peter Horne ats Sporrier of Westlynche wthin the Countie of Soñset yeoman, John Stodden of Allerford the elder wthin ye saide Countie husbandman & John Kitner of Tyvington wthin ye said Countie Clothier of thone ꝑtie And Edward Pyle of Browning strete wthin ye said Countie vitler Richard Phelpes of Selworthye wthin the said Countie Tanner Henry Horne ats Sporrier Walter Horne ats Sporrier Thomas Horne ats Sporrier three of the sons of the said Peter Horne ats Sporrier John Tayler the sonne of William Tayler deceased Edward Kitner the sonne of the said John Kitner Edward Tirrell of Tyvington aforesaid John Stodden ye sonne of ye said John Stodden thelder and William Stodden ye younger of Allerford aforesaid of thother partie. Witnesseth, that the said Peter Horne ats Sporrier John Stodden thelder & John Kitner for & on dyvers consideracons them therunto moving have geven grannted enfeoffed ⁊ assured and by these p̃ntꝭ doe geve grannte enfeoffee ⁊ assure unto ye said Edward Pile Rychard Phelpes Henry Horne ats Sporrier Walter Horne ats Sporrier Thomas Horne ats Sporrier John Tayler Edward Kitner John Stodden & William Stodden all y^{t} one Teñte garden & half acre of land with their appurteñnce in Allerford w^th^in ye parish of Selw̃thye aforesaid called or in anye sorte knowen by the name of Shelve late in the tenure of Walter Baker deceased be it more or lesse, and lying against the landes of John Arundell esquier of the Northe pte and the landes of theires of George Harrison of the South pte and abutteth on the Comon high waye on bothe thother ptes ⁊ is w^th^in the Tithinge of Allerford aforesaid, To habe ⁊ to holde the said Tent⁊ garden lande & all other ye pmisses wth all ⁊ singuler their appurtennces to the foresaid Edward Pyle Rychard Phelpes Henry Horne als Sporrier Walter Horne als Sporrier Thomas Horne als Sporrier John Tayler Edward Kitner Edward Tirrell John Stodden & William Stodden their heires ⁊ assignes for ever to be holden of the Chiefe Lorde or lordes of the fee thereof by the rents & services thereof due and of right accustomed to be paide upon this condicon that the foresaid Edward Pyle Rychard Phelpes Henry Horne Walter Horne Thomas Horne John Tayler Edward Kitner Edward Tirrell John Stodden ⁊ Willm Stodden & the survivor or survivors of them their heirs and assignes & theires & assignes of ye survivor of them shall yearlie for ever at the feast of Easter content satisfie & paye to ye Churchwardens of Selw̃they then for ye tyme ther beinge ⁊ to the fower side men of the saide pishe of Selw̃they aforesaid then also for the tyme ther being fyve shillings of lawful Englishe money, And also all fynes issues profittes & Comodities that they ye said Edward Pyle Rychard Phelpes Henry Horne Walter Horne Thomas Horne John Tayler Edward Kitner Edward Tirrell John Stodden ⁊ Willm Stodden or the survivor or survivors of them or theirs or assignes of the survivor of them shall or may without fraude or Covin thereof make to this intent ꝑ purpose that they the said Church wardens ꝑ fower sidemen shall yearelie for ever imploye the saide rentꝑ issues fynes ꝑ profittes thereof coming ꝑ growing for & on the reparacõn of the parish churche of Selw̃they aforesaid or els on the setting fourth of soldiers to serve the Queenes Matie in her warres of Irelande or els where or els for mayntennance of the poore ther or for the defraying of anie other chardge wherw[the] the inhabitants or pisheñs of Selw̃they aforesaid are or ought in anie sorte to be chardged with by the lawes of this Realme. And the said Edward Pyle Rychard Phelpes Henry Horne ats Sporrier Walter Horne ats Sporrier Thomas Horne ats Sporier John Tayler Edward Kitner Edward Tirrel John Stodden ꝑ William Stodden doe for themselves their and everie of their heires and assignes and the survivor and survivors of them their heires assignes covenante and grannte to ꝑ with y[e] saide Peter Horne John Stodden and John Kitner their heires & assignes by these ꝑntꝑ that they the said Edward Pyle Richard Phelpes Henry Horne Walter Horne Thomas Horne John Tayler Edward Kitner Edward Tirrell John Stodden & William Stodden and and the survivor or survivors of them their heires or assignes shall and will at all tyme and tymes when & as often as they or anie of them or y[e] survivor or survivors of them their heires or assignes or the survivors or survivor of them shalbe thereunto required by y[e] said Church Wardens and side men of y[e] said pishe for y[e] time then being & then at y[e] time of the said request if ther be in full life of ye feoffees before herein mentioned but onlie fower persons or under reassure convey and infeoffe to tenn other psons being honest inhabitants at the time of the said request of ye saide pishe of Selw̃they and be thereunto noĩated by ye Church Wardens & side men of ye saide pishe of Selw̃they to have and to hold ye said Teñte garden and lande before mentioned unto the said tenn persons or their heires so to be noĩated as aforesaid And ye same assurance or feoffem^t^ to be made as aforesaid to contayne all and everie suche coveñnte Article & condic̄on and the rente reservac̄on power & auctoritie & none other then herein are contayned expressed declared and sett forthe **And further** y^t^ ye said feoffees pties to these p̃nte or anie of them shall not at any time hereafter alyen assuer or convaye away his or their right titell estate or interest that he hath hereby in the said teñte garden & lande, nor shall make any lease or leases thereof other than joyntlie wth all the feoffees then at the tyme of the said leas or leases being in full lyfe & y^t^ for one twoe or three lyves joyntlie or by waye of remaynder or for one & Twentie yeares reserving therupon the yearelie rente of fyve shillinges to contynewe during the said leas or leases, And at noe tyme hereafter or by anie of their actes to determyne or extinguishe the same.

Provided allwayes anie thing herein contayned to the contrarie not w^th^standinge y^t^ if the said feoffees pties to theise p̃nte & everie of them & the survivor & survivors of them & his or their heires doe not at all tymes hereafter well and truely observe pforme fulfill and keepe all and everie ye Coveñnts Condic̄ons

Articles & Agreem^ts herein conteyned according to the trewe meaninge hereof That then & from thenceforth it shalbe lawful to & for the said Peter Horne John Stodden & John Kitner into the said tēnte garden & lande and into everie pte thereof to reenter & the same to have againe as in their former estate fynally the said Peter Horne John Stodden & John Kitner have constituted & appointed and by theise presents doe constitute and appoint John Reede of Selw̃they William Stodden thelder of Allerforde to be theire trewe and lawfull Attorneys joyntlie or severallie to enter into the p̃misses or into some parte thereof for them & in their names, and possession & seison thereof or of some pte thereof in the name of the whole for them & in their names to take & have, And after such possession & seyson thereof so taken and had the same to delyver unto the said Edward Pyle Rychard Phelpes Henry Horne Walter Horne Thomas Horne John Tayler Edward Kitner Edward Tirrell John Stodden & William Stodden or to some or one of them in the name of them all to have the the same according to the effect and trewe meaninge hereof, ratyfyinge confirminge & alowing all & what soever their said Attornies or anie of them shall doe in or about the premisses. In witness whereof the parties above said have hereunto interchangablie putt and sett their handes & seales the daie & yeare abovesaide.

Peter Horne Johannis Kitner Johannis Stodden

Endorsed:—Seled and delivered in ye p̃sence of thos whos names are under written the xvij^th daie of Marche anno dñi 1582.

T.me Willm Fleete, rectorem de Selworthie.
John Elstone
Edward Youd
William Don
Gregorii Darche

possession & seson was taken had and delivered over by the attornes within named according to the tener of theise pnte the xvij[th] of Marche in the yere w[th]in wrytene anno dñi 1582. Gregory Taylor and Passka his wyfe did attourne tenants to this deade the xvij[th] daie of Marche in the yere w[th]in wryten. In the presence of us whos names are subscribed

Willm Fleete pson of Selworthie
Edward Rawle
Geoffrie Brudge
Andrewe Horne
John Ewd

There is another Indenture of this date, precisely the same, with exception of Endorsement. This little estate was regularly granted out by the feoffees on lives up to the end of the last century. On the expiration of the last lease the estate was not reclaimed, and in course of time the existing tenants obtained a title to it. The old house at Allerford Bridge is, no doubt, practically the same now as it was when the above deed was executed.

This Indenture made the thirtieth daie of Aprill in the fyve and Twentyeth yeare of the raigne of our Sovaigne Ladie Elizabeth [1583] by the grace of God,

Queene of England France and Ireland, Defendor of the Faithe **Betwene** Willm Harte of Westlinch wthin the Countie of Somerset, husbandman, Lewes Tayler of Selw̃they wthin ye saide Countie husbandman George Phelpes of Selw̃they aforesaid husbandman of thone ptie **And** George Ewde of Tyvington wthin ye said Countie husbandman, George Sporrier ats Horne of Allerford wthin ye said Countie Dyer, Edward Rawle ats Yowd of Allerford aforesaid husbandman, Willm Tayler ats Hensley of Honicote aforesaid Carpenter, Rychard Dennise of Selw̃they aforesaid, Tanner Robte Phelpes of Selw̃they aforesaid husbandman George Elson ats Hooper of Tyvington aforesaid husbandman John Tayler ye younger of Honicote aforesaid Clothier & Michaell Tayler ats Hewes of Honicote aforesaid husbandman of the other ptie **Witnesseth** whereas Robert Crosse of Nettylcombe wthin ye said Countie Yeoman was lawfully & rightfully seized in his demesne as of fee of and in all that messuage or mansion howse called the Church howse scituate and beinge wthin ye parish of Selw̃they aforesaid and of all and all manner of houses gardens, rentes reṽsions pfitts comodities advantages & hereditamts whatsoever to the said messuage belonging or apptayning, **And** so being thereof seised did by his deede sufficient in ye Lawe and bearing date ye eight daie of Aprill in ye fowerth yeare of ye Raigne of our soṽaigne Lord kinge Edward the sixth [1550] geve grannte bargaine, sell assuer and convaye all that ye said messuage, gardens, howses, edifices rentes reṽtions and all other hereditamts whatsoever to ye saide messuage then belonging or apptayninge until one Michaell Laughwell,

Henry Sporier Wiłłm Pyers and John Stodden & to their heires and assignes to their owne ꝑper use and behoofe for ever as in and by the said dede doth and maye appeare. And also wheras the said Michaell Lawghwell Henry Sporrier Wiłłm Pyers and John Stodden being by force of the said assurance feoffm^t^ and conveyance seised of the said messuage and other the premisses & of everie ꝑte thereof in their demesne as of fee did for dyvers considerc̃ons them therunto movinge by their dede also sufficient in ye Lawe bearinge date ye tenth day of Aprill in the said fowerth yeare of the raigne of our said Soṽaigne Lorde kinge Edward ye sixthe geve grannte enfeoffe convaye and assuer all that the said messuage called ye Chureh howse & other the ꝑmisses wth his appteñces seituate and beinge w^th^in ye said parishe of Selw̃they aforesaid and all and singuler howses gardens ꝑfittes Comodities hereditam^ts^ and all other the ꝑmisses therunto belonging unto one Richard Ewde Edward Westcott, John Sporrier Rychard Sporrier George Kent John Boyse Wiłłm Hare Lewes Tayler George Phelpes Geoffrey Frase and to their heires and assignes to their owne ꝑper use and behoofe for ever as also in & by ye saide last recited ded dothe and maye fullie & playnlie at large appeare That nowe ye said Wiłłam Harte Lewes Tayler & George Phelpes being the survivinge feoffees named in ye last recited dede and having ye whole estate of ye premises and also being nowe lawfully and rightfully seised of the said messuage & other ye premises in their demesne as of fee the reste of the said feoffees named in the said last recited dede being all dedd, have for divers and sundrie good causes and considerc̄ons them therunto specially moving geven grannted enfeoffed and assured and by these presents doe give grannte infeoffe and assuer unto the said George Ewde George Sporrier ats Horne Edward Yewd Wiłłm Tayler ats Hensley Henry Stodden Rychard Dennise Robert Phelpes George Elson ats Hooper John Tayler Michaell Tayler ats Lewes, all that the said messuage called the Church howse gardens orchard landes howses profittes comodities advantages rents rev̓tions and hereditamts whatsoever wth all and singuler their apptenñces scituate & being within the said parish of Selw̃they wthin the said Countie of Somerset and in anie sorte mentioned or contayned in anie of the said recited dedes. **To have and to hold** the messuage &c, to the said George Ewde &c, &c, at the yearly rent of two shillings, &c, &c.

[Same conditions as former Indenture].

Signed, Georgii Ewde, Georgii Spurrier, Edwardi Ewde, Wiłłm Tailer, Henrici Stodden, Richardi Dennis, Roberti Philpes, Georgii Elston, Joħna Tailer, junr. Michaelis Tailer.

Endorsed :—Sealed and delivered in the p̉sence of us Wiłłm Fleete clarke, pson of Selworthie Wiłłm Stodden the elder John Henslie the elder Gregorie Darche and George Phelpes the xvthe daie of Aprill anno domini 1583.

Spurrier and Stodden use a seal with the design of a "rose bush" on it. The other seals are unintelligible.

This Indenture made the xxv^th^ day of Marche in the xxxij yeare of the Raigne of o^r^ Sovaigne Ladie Elizabeth &c, &c, **Between** John Elston ats Hooper, John Kitner ats Chebett John Tailer ats Hensley Edward Pile, Lewes Tailer, and Edward Rawle ats Yewde the fower men & Churchwardens of the parishe of Selworthie in the Countie of Somersett of the one ptie & George Sporier ats Horne, Alice his wife and Richarde the sonne of the said George & Alice of thother ptie. **Wytnessceth** that the said John Elston John Kitner, John Tailer, Edward Pile, Lewes Tailer & Edward Rawle the said fower men and Churchwardens of the parish aforesaid in the names & behalfe of the whole parish aforesaide for and in consideraco̅n of the so̅m̅e of Thirtie shillinges of lawfull money of England to us the said fower men and Churchwardens in the behalfe and to the use of the said parishe before the ensealing hereof fullie satisfied contented & paide **have demysed** grannted and to ferme letten and by these presentes do demise and to ferme Lett unto the said George Sporrier Alice his wife and Richard theire sonne all this one peace of grownde called and knowne by the name of the hoppe yarde apptayninge and belonginge to the said pishe wth all and singuler the Apptenn̅ces to the same grownde belonginge or appteyninge late in the tenure of Alice Peers widowe, deceased and nowe in the occupaco̅n of the said George scituate lyeinge and beinge in Allerford w^th^in the parish aforesaid conteininge by estimaco̅n one yarde of grownde more or lesse lyeinge betwene the tenn̅te late in the tenure of the said Alice Peers widowe deceased on the sowthe parte and the quenes highway on the weste parte and one comon water course called Allerford water on the north parte. **To have & to hold** the said peace of grownde with all and singuler the Apptenñces to the said George Sporier, Alice his wife and Richard their sonne and every of them and their assignes and to the assignes of every of them for & during the terme of their naturall Lyves and the longest Lyver of them successively one after another, **Yeldinge** and payeinge therefore yerely rente unto the fower men or Churchwardens of the parishe aforesaid or to any of them to the use and behoofe of the said parishe twelve pence of good and lawfull money of England at fower termes in the yeare, that is to say the feast of St John Baptiste St Michell Tharkangell the birth of our Lord God and Thanūcac̄on of our Ladie Marye the Virgin by even porc̄ons **Yeldinge** also after the deceases of the said George Alice and Richard and every of them dieinge tennants six pence of lawfull money of England in the name of a heriott And if it happen the said yerely rent of xij[d] to be behind and unpaid in pte or in all on or after anie of the said feast daies in w[ch] it ought to be paide and ten daies after being lawfullie demanded of the said George Alice or Richard or either of them being tennants and no sufficient distresse to be had in or upon the fore letten premisses **That** then it shall be lawfull for the said John Elston, John Kytner, John Tailer, Edward Pile, Lewis Tailer or Edward Rawle their successors or assignes into the fore letten premises and every parte and parcell thereof to enter and the same to have agayne retayne & repossess as in their former estates and the said George Alice and Richard and all other person and persons from thence utterly to expell amove and putt out this present Indenture or anything herein conteyned to the contrary in any wise notwithstandinge **And** the said George Sporier aīs Horne Alice his wife and Richard their sonne do coveññte for them and their assignes to and with the said fower men and churchwardens their successors and assignes that they the said George, Alice & Richard and their assignes at all tyme and tymes when and as often as need shall require at his and their own proper costes and charges shall well and sufficiently repaire and meyntaine the said peace of grownde in hedginge and ditchinge and all other reparaēons as shalbe needful or may appertayne unto the same during the said terme **And** the said John Elston John Kytner John Tailer Edward Pile Lewes Tailer and Edward Rawle do coveññte for them and every of them their successors and assignes to and with the said George Alice and Richard and with every of them by these presentes that they the said John Elston John Kitner John Tailer Edward Pile Lewes Tailer and Edward Rawle and their successors the said peace of grownde wth all and singuler thappurteññces unto the said George Alice and Richard and to every of them in manner and form aforesaid against all people shall warrant acquitt and defend by these presentes **In Wytness** whereof the said parties to these Indentures interchangeably have putte theire handes & seals, geven the day and yere first above written.

Be hit knowen unto all men by these presents that we the said John Elston John Kitner John Tailer

Edward Pile Lewes Tailer and Edward Rawle have constituted ordeyned and in o[r] places putt o[r] trewe and wellbelovid in Christe, Andrewe Sporrier ats Horne and William Tappescott o[r] trewe and lawfull Attorneyes jointly and severallie for us and in o[r] names and in the names of every of us to enter into the free letten ꝑmisses with the appurtenñces and possession and seison thereof to take and after such possession and seison of all and singuler the ꝑmises so had & taken for us and in our names and in the names of every of us to deliver to the said George Alice & Richard and to every of them accordinge to the strengthe forme effect and purport of these ꝑsentes and whatsoever o[r] said Attorney or Attorneys shall do in the ꝑmisses we ratifie confirme and allowe as fullie holely and suerly as if we and every of us were ꝑsonallie ꝑsent In witness wherof to these ꝑsents interchangeablie have putt o[r] handes & seales geven &c.

Endorsed :—

Signed sealed and deliv̾ed in the presence of Edward Horne, George Hensley, John Pile, John Tailer, Lewis Hensley, John Smith, and others.

Possession & seison taken and delivered accordinge to the tenore of this Indenture in the ꝑsence of John Sporier John Bond.

Another Indenture of same date, to same effect.

This Indenture made the fifteenth daye of October the Two and Twentieth yeare of our sovaigne Lord James [1623] by the grace of God Kinge of Englande Frannce and Ireland, Defender of the Faith, and of Scotland the lviij[th] Between Walter Horne als Spurrier thelder of Selworthy in the County of Somerset yeoman, Edward Terril of Dunster in the County aforesaid, yeoman and William Stodden the younger of Selworthy aforesaid, Tanner (the survivinge feoffees in trust to the use of the parish of Selworthy aforesaid of the lands and tenements hereafter in these presents mencõned of thone ptie and Walter Horne als Spurrier the younger Henry Hensley als Tailer, John Phelpes soñe of John Phelpes of Allerford, George Blackford als Stodden, Henry Horne als Spurrier, George Hensley soñe of George Hensley, Edward Pile the younger George Howe, Robert Coffin and Robert Pile all of Selworthye aforesaid of thother partie, Witnesseth that the said Walter Horne Edward Turril and William Stodden for and in performance and accomplishment of the trust in them reposed and at the speciall request of the Churchwardens and sidemen of the parish of Selworthy aforesaid have given grannted enfeoffed and confirmed and by these presents doe give grannt enfeoffe and confirm unto the said Walter Horne the younger, Henry Hensley, John Phelpes, George Blackford. Henry Horne, George Hensley, Edward Pile, George Howe, Robert Coffin and Robert Pile and their heires, All that messuage, tenement, garden, and half-acre of land be it more or less wth thappurteñces sett lying and being in Allerford within the parish of Selworthy aforesaid commonly called or knowne by the name of Shelve now or late in the tenure use or occupation of one Gregory Taylor or his assignes and all deeds writings or evidences concerning the same, **To have and to hold** the said premises unto the said Walter Horne &c, &c, and for the yearly rent of five shillings to be paid to the said Churchwardens, &c, &c.

Endorsed :—

Possession and seisin was taken had and and delivered over by the Attourneyes w^th^in named accordinge to the tenor of these p̃sents the last day of November in the yeare w^th^in written, viz: 1624, Gregory Taylor and Pasche his wife did attourne Teñnts to this deed the same day in the p̃sence of us whose names are subscribed.

Henry Byam Rector of Selworthye
John Youd, Jasper Howe.
The marke of Robert Huish
John Phelpes, James Reade.
The marke of John Kittnor
The marke of John Edbrake.

Sealed & delivered in the presence of us whose names are underwritten the last day of November 1624.

Henry Byam, Rector of Sellworthie
Jasper Howe, John Youd.
The marke of Robert Huish
James Reade, John Philpes.
The marke John Kittnor
The marke of John Edbrooke.

Wm. Stodden's seal is (apparently) a stag's head

coupéd. Edward Turril's is a heart, divided and surmounted by a cross. On the heart are the letters E. T. This is surely the ancient and well-known amulet against the "Evil Eye." The belief that certain people had power to injure their neighbours by "overlooking" them, a belief which has by no means entirely died out from amongst us, was as firmly held by our ancestors in the sixteenth century as it is held by the Neapolitans of to-day, or as it was held by the bishops assembled at the Council of Chalcedon, who cried as the emperor Marcian, "the new Constantine, the new Paul, the new David," entered the hall of meeting, "may the evil eye be averted from your empire."

Vicesimo Octavo die Octobr̃ Anno R.R. Car̃ Secd̃ nunc Anglie dc̃ decimo sexto Anno Dñi 1644.

Know all men by these p̃sents that I John Farthinge of Dulverton wthin the County of Somerset yeoman for divers good causes and considerac̃ons me the saide John Farthinge hereunto especially movinge have remised released exonerated quite claymed acquitted and discharged and by these p̃sents for me my heirs and executors and admin^{ors} doe remise release exonerate quite clayme acquitt & for ever discharge John White of Withypoole ye County aforesaid husbandman his exec^{rs} adminis^{rs} and assignes and every of them of and from all bills bonds judgements execuc̃ons debts tresposses accõns covents assumptions and demands whatsoever wch I the s^{d} John Farthinge now have heretofore had or at any tyme hereafter for any matter or cause whatsoever shall or may have wth him the s^d^ John White his execo^rs^ adm^rs^ or Ass^s^ or any of them from the beginninge of the world to the day of the date hereof. In testimony whereinof I ye s^d^ John Farthinge have here unto sett my hand and seale on the day and year first above written

Sealed and delivered
in the presence of — John Farthinge
Ric. Blackford
Henry Pleise.

Endorsed :—John Farthinge release to John White

The deed is sealed with the arms of John Farthinge, a talbot, on a chief three coins: crest, a man's head and shoulders. Tinctures undecipherable.

The following inventory gives us an interesting account of the personal property of a well to do yeoman in our parish in the seventeenth century.

A true and pfect Inventory of all the goods and Chattles of John White of the pish of Selworthy deceased taken and prized by Robert Spurrier and Robert Beage of the said parish as followeth (viz.)

	li.	*s.*	*d.*
Imprimis his wearing apparel and the money in his pocket	02	00	00
Item for one table board and all the timber stuff in the house	00	06	08
Item for pewter and brasse	00	05	02

Item for his dust beds and the furniture belonging	00	13	04
Item for ruffe meate and Iron stuffe	00	02	02
Item for money uppon specialtye	15	00	00
Item for things forgotten and out of mind, we doe value	00	02	02
The sume total			

The marke of Robert Spurrier
Robert Beage.

Exhibitum fuit huiōi. Inventarium p vero etc. sub ptestačone tamen de addend. quodsi etc. apud Taunton vicesimo nono die mensis Martii Anno Dni (stilo Anglie) 1675° Coram Discreto viro Mgr̃o Jacobo Douch[1] clerico in Artibus Baccl̃io Surrõ Veñlis viri Guilielmi Peirs sacre Theologie Doctoris Archiñi Archiñatus Taunton ltim̃e constitut. In vim juramenti Honore White Relicte dicti defuncti Cui concessa est ad° bonorũ. etc. dicti defuncti de bene etc. Deq Com̃pto etc. per Comiss^{um} jurat etc. salvo iure etc.

Tho. Bennett, Regr^{Eius}

Administration was granted by the archdeacon of Taunton, William Peirs, to the widow, Honor White, March 9, 1675.

APPENDIX C.

THOMAS LUTTRELL. In the days of Elizabeth many who were apparently members of the reformed

1. See *Somerset Incumbents*, 358, 404.

church were still in their hearts secretly attached to the old faith and its teachings; and the severity of the Roman Catholic bishop of Bath and Wells towards them in their youth, seems to have thrown somewhat of a shadow over the otherwise prosperous career of Thomas and Margaret Luttrell. No doubt these early difficulties were the cause of the otherwise unintelligible reference to the legality of their union, in the inscription on the splendid tomb to their memory in Dunster Church. The inscription at this present moment runs thus:—

". . . beth Queene of England and being then High Sheriff of the Countie of Somerset and one of the yongest sones of Andrew Luttrell knight, The sayd Thomas being lawfully married unto Margaret Hadley daughter and sole Heire of Christopher Hadley of Withycombe in the said Countie Esquire, by whom he had issue," etc.

APPENDIX D.

RECTORY OF SELWORTHY.[1]

Selwurthy.

Ric̃ Denyse Rc̃or ib'm.

Rectoria ib̃m valet p̧ annū viz in terr' d̃nical' xxvj*s* viij*d* x^ma^ lanę & agnoꝝ lxiij*s* iiij*d* x^mis^ predial' viij*li* x^mis^ p̧sonal' cū al' casual' lxxv*s* . . . . xvj*li.* v*s.*

Richard Denyse, Rector.

Rectory there is worth per annum, namely: in

1. Valor Ecclesiasticus.

dominical lands 26*s.* 8*d.*; tithes of wool and lambs 63*s.* 4*d.*; from predial tithes £8; from personal tithes with other casualties 75*s.* xvj*li.* v*s.*

41. SELWORTHY.[1]

Lights and obitt*e* foundyd w^t^in the paryshe churche ther.

Are yerely worthe in

Landes teñt*e* and other hereditament*e* in the tenure of sondery psones as maye appere pticulerly more at large by the rentall of the same . . . . . xiiij*s.*

Wherof in

Rent*e* resolute pd yerely . . . . ij*d.*

And so

Remaynethe clere . . . . xiij*s.* x*d.*

Memord.

Alexaunder Popham and William Halley esquiers alleage that the Annuall rent of iij*s.* iiij*d.* pcell of the saide some of xiij*s.* x*d.* cum̃yng out of certeyne landes and teñt*e* pcell of the possessions of the late Dissolued Hospitall or com̃aundrie of saincte Johans of Buckelande prioris in the saide countie of Somerss was discharged by reason that the saide late Hospitall or com̃aundrie w^t^ all the possessions thervnto belonging came unto the handes of oure late sou̾aigne lorde of famouse memorie Kinge Henry the viijth, by the dissolucõn of the late priory of saincte Johans Jerlm in Ingland, wch com̃aundrye of Buckelande prioris afore-

1. *Somerset Chantries*, vol. ii, pp. 40, 41.

saide, and all the landes and hereditamentę thereto belonging amongst other thingę the saide Alexaunder and William did purchace of the saide late Kinge to them and to their heires for eu͠l, and have shewed before the com̄issionors their lres patentę in that behalf, beringe date the xvjth daye of ffebruary in the xxxvjth yere of the saide late kinge his reigne, and thervppon prayen to be discharged of the saide Rent.

APPENDIX E.

WILL OF WILLIAM AYSHE OF SELWORTHY, dated 21 April, 1537. (From Rev. F. W. Weaver's unpublished MS. collection of Wells Wills.)

To the Ch. of S. my best gowne—my dau. Alsyn, £6—my dau. Agnes £5—my son Edward my londs in Watchett & my scherys [shears].

Res.—my wyf Thomasine.

Witn.—Sir Ric Denys, parson.
Rob. Terell, Mich. Layghwell.

Dettes that the above owed.

Selworthy Church	20*s.*
Johan Hensle	18*s.*
Michaell Gelys	20*s.*
St. Leonard of Tuvynton	10*s.* 2*d.*
his dau. Alson Yase	6*l.*
his dau. Agnes Yase	5*l.*

The debts that be owed unto the s[d] William

Thomas Tegge oweth	20*s.*

Nicholas Powle	43*s.* 4*d.*
Raymonde Roche	15*s.*
Symon ffestyn	3*l.* 6*s.* 8*d.*
Rychard Layghwell	20*s.*
Thomas Tomas in Corrynton[1] for ij peces of blak chamlett, iij ballyts[2] of canvas	5*l.*
Peter Boys	25*s.*
Thomas Capuar	16*s.*
John Stokeham	11*s.*
Alsyn Rowe	20*s.*
John Badcok	34*s.*
Hugh Wyte	49*s.*
John Genar	13*s.*

APPENDIX F.

SIR OLIVER BROMLEY

First comes before our notice as "curat" of Exton in the year 1532 (*Wells Wills*, p. 86).

The writer is not quite sure whether this means *Rector*: the word *curatus* is sometimes equivalent to Incumbent (see *Wells Wills*, p. 91, etc.)

On 15th August, 1535, Tho. Clerk and Will. Vowell write to Cromwell thus:

"On the 14th the Vicar-general of Wells sent for us to the Cathedral and showed us that Sir Oliver Bromley curate of Exton, spontaneously admitted that he had not fulfilled the Bp's command in declaring the usurped power of the bishop of Rome, nor put out the name of the Pope from the service

1 Perhaps Torrington.

2 Ballette O.F. Balete, Ballete a smale bale. *New English Dictionary.*

book. He said that his conscience would not allow him, because he heard that the bp. of Rochester and the father of Sion had suffered death for it. He confessed that he prayed every Sunday in the pulpit for the King as supreme head of the Ch. of England, for queen Anne and the princess Elizabeth, and in the afternoon he confessed to us that he repented his lewdness, and was willing to declare the usurped power of the Bp. of Rome.

We have committed him to ward. Wells, 15 Aug.

Letters and Papers Henry VIII, Vol. ix, No. 100.

17 Aug. John, Bishop of Bath, to Cromwell.

On Sat. last my Vicar general sent word from Wells that a certain parish priest of Exton, Sir Oliver Bromley, had not spoken to his parish against the Bp. of Rome's usurped authority nor done anything in execution of the commandment given for that purpose. My V.G. had him examined before two justices of the peace, Wm. Vowell and my servant Tho. Clerke, and on his confession he was committed to prison. The bearer can tell you more of Sir Oliver, who must be either very simple or very lewd, otherwise the King's commandments would have been obeyed throughout the diocese.

Banwell, 17 Aug.

Letters and Papers Henry VIII, Vol. ix, No. 109.

On June 8, 1551, Mr. Bromley witnesses a Selworthy will and is styled Sir Oliver Bromley " curat."

APPENDIX G.

ALLERFORD SCHOOL. This is a commodious building, with about 112 scholars on the books. The school is conducted by a board of nine managers, elected by the subscribers and the parents: a plan that is found to work very well. Selworthy has for long been to the fore in educational matters. That able woman, the Hon. Mrs. M. Fortescue, grandmother of the present baronet, was a great educationist, and very kind to the poor. And since those days, the advance of education and the well-being of their poorer neighbours have been objects which her descendants have kept steadily before them. The poor and distressed have always known where to look for help, and the schools have been carefully maintained. It is to the cause of education and the bettering of the people that the present baronet has persistently devoted, through a long life, the powers of a singularly vigorous mind; and it is to such men as Sir Thomas Acland that we owe the great change that has passed over our country within the last fifty years. Fifty years ago, six or seven shillings a week, out of which house rent had to be paid, was the starvation pittance on which a man had to support and clothe himself and his family. In those days in many parishes there were no schools, and to eke out the narrow means at home, the children, both boys and girls, were driven out at five or six years of age to "keep birds" through the long winter days, hungry and half naked, in wind and rain, and snow. "Often," said a woman to the writer in speaking of those evil days, "I had nothing to give my children for their breakfast, save some bran from the pig's tub fried with a little lard. And when they came home tired and wet, and cold, it went to my heart to have to send them crying with hunger to bed. It was a rare treat indeed when some kind farmer would give me a few turnips out of his field to boil for our supper." The same woman told how that once when her husband was ill, and she had a houseful of young hungry children at home, she went out to try and get a little work herself, so that she might buy some bread for her starving little ones. But she was unsuccessful; and at last, in despair, she sat down by the roadside and wept, not daring to go home to the wretchednesss she could not relieve. The sequel is striking. In her trouble she prayed to Him who turneth him unto the poor destitute, and despiseth not their desire, and as she prayed, a stranger appeared beside her, enquired into the cause of her distress, and gave her the assistance she so sorely needed. Such days, thank God, are gone, and now the peasantry are well housed, well fed, well paid, and their children receive a good education free of cost.

By what title can any man desire better to be remembered, than that he has assisted in promoting changes rife with such happy consequences? Sir Thomas' passion for educational advancement has been handed down to both his sons; and Selworthy is proud to remember that she has an interest in the late Minister of Education, and the author of that great act of popular enlightenment—the firstfruits of the future abundant harvest of which we are but just beginning to reap—The Technical Instruction Act.

APPENDIX H.

SELWORTHY GREEN. One of the most attractive and best known features of Selworthy has almost escaped without notice. Year by year an increasing number of tourists seek Selworthy Green, with a just admiration of this charming spot. The picturesque cottages around the romantically situated Green were formed by the late Sir Thomas Acland, out of the houses and buildings of two or three small farms, which stood about what was, perhaps, the ancient village green. Some of the existing cottages are evidently of great antiquity, but they were much beautified and altered by Sir Thomas. The Green itself was also laid out and planted by him at the same time as he planted the then bare hill side above it. The cottages are held rent free by such old and deserving people as the owner for the time being chooses to put into them.

APPENDIX I.

JOHN HATCH or HACCHE, rector of Selworthy. His brother, or a near relation of his, Robert Hacche, was, in 1363, abbot of Athelney. The abbot of Athelney was accused at a forest court held at Somerton, of stealing one of the king's deer. "They say," *i.e.* the king's officers, the Roll runs (Ralph Perceval was then deputy keeper of the forest of Exmoor), "that Robert Hacche, abbot of Athelneye, and Henry his brother, made a stable (*i.e.* a shelter or resting place) in the wood called Lefhangre without the forest, on Monday next after the feast of Saint Michael year aforesaid (1363), and in the same place caught one calf stag."[1]

Lefhangre, or Hanger Wood as it is now called, is

1. *Annals of Exmoor*, E. J. Rawle, pp. 73, 74.

situate not far above Blackford Farm. It formed part of the large tract of land which king John attached wrongfully to the forest of Exmoor, and it was disafforested after the boundary of the forest was re-fixed by the perambulation of 26 Edw. I. It must have been in those days a quiet secluded covert, well suited to the nefarious designs of the venison-loving abbot, whose property the wood itself may have been. The incident gives us a curious glimpse into mediæval life. It seems strange to us nowadays to hear of this theft of the king's deer being carried out by the brother of a great ecclesiastic like the abbot of Athelney, and apparently with his consent and connivance. Was the rector of Selworthy implicated with his relations we wonder, in this piece of poaching? If he was, he at all events erred in good company! And if he was not directly implicated, no doubt some part of the stag thus unlawfully slain, found its way up the hill to the rectory larder. Henry Hacche may have been his brother the abbot's steward, and have lived where the quaint old house, by tradition called the Priest's House, still stands beside Lynch Chapel.

APPENDIX K.

ACLAND FAMILY. In Mr. E. J. Rawle's *Annals of Exmoor*, p. 75, we find the following entry concerning a member of this family. Pleas of the Forest, no. 16 (A.D. 1366): "Inquisition held at Wells, on Thursday next after the feast of the Apostles Peter and Paul in the 40th year of the reign of king Edward the third after the conquest, before Peter Attewode, etc. . . . . . they (the king's officers) say that Roger Acklelane and Walter Trommere caught and killed one calf stag w thin the hundred of Wytherugge (Witheridge) within the regard of the aforesaid forest of Exmoor . . . . . on Monday next after the feast of All Saints in the 38th year of the aforesaid Lord King (1364)." One does not wonder that the neighbouring land-owners found it difficult sometimes to keep their hands off the lordly deer, which came down from the moor and carried off their crops from before their faces!

APPENDIX L.

FREEHOLDERS IN SELWORTHY. Although our parish has been for some period now very largely in the hands of one owner, this has by no means always been the case. Besides the families mentioned in the body of this book, the Worths of Luccombe and of Worth, near Tiverton, an ancient family who have lived at Worth from a very early period; the Gould, and perhaps the Coffin and Tayler families, held at one time estates in the parish.

Now, besides the rector in right of his glebe, the only freeholders left in the parish other than the owner of the three manors, are the Clarke and Stoate families. The Clarkes, as already stated have for a long period lived on their property at West Lynch (while a branch of their family have also occupied East Lynch), and have for many generations taken a leading and honourable part in the affairs of the valley. The Stoates, too, have been connected with the parish for a great number of years. The last of the Selworthy branch of the family, old "Counsellor Stoate," as he was always called, lived at Allerford, and must have been somewhat of a character. He was also a man of considerable substance.

Another old family connected with the parish is that of Siderfin. This family is probably an offshoot of the family of Siderfin of Croydon, in the parish of Timberscombe, a family of some importance in our district in the seventeenth century.

APPENDIX M.

THE following song by a former resident in Luccombe, gives some idea of the varying aspects of Dunkery Beacon :—

DUNKERY BEACON.

A Song.

STERN and black, stern and black,
Low lies the storm on the mountain track :
Black and stern, black and stern,
Hardly may we thy face discern
By the light westward—lurid and red—
And the thunder voices are overhead !
Where the lightning is never still,
Who'll now come with me over the hill ?

Grey and sad, grey and sad,
With a rain-wrought veil are thy shoulders clad :
Sad and grey, sad and grey,
Weird is the mist creeping up to-day,

Ghostlike and white from the stream where it lay,
Hanging a shroud o'er the lone wild way.
Hidden and still, hidden and still,
Who'll now come with me over the hill ?

Fair and bright, fair and bright,
Purple and gold in the autumn light,
Bright and fair, bright and fair,
The butterflies float in the warm soft air,
Float and suck midst the heather bells,
And green are the ferns in the deer-loved dells.
Now who will, now who will
Come with me, come with me, over the hill ?

Molly Heard
Born 1713
Died 1797
married John Brown
of Leigh

Ghostlike and white from the stream where it lay,
Hanging a shroud o'er the lone wild way.
Hidden and still, hidden and still,
Who'll now come with me over the hill?

Fair and bright, fair and bright,
[illegible] in the autumn light

INDEX.

LUCCOMBE PEDIGREE.

Hugh de Luccombe.=Elizabeth

By the 1st inq. p.m. taken at Luccombe, Somerset, on 6 June, 16 Edw. II (1323, no. 45, it was found that he was seised in fee of the manor of Luccombe, held in capite of the king by the service of two knight's fees; and by a second inq. p.m. taken at Donestor, 10 July, 19 Edw. II (1325) no. 61, the various tenements in the manor were set out. And it is also found that he holds the advowsons of Luccombe and Selworthy. It was also found on the 22 Aug., 19 Edw. II, 1325, that the manor of Luccombe was held of the honour of Pinhanage.

Elizabeth received from Edward II the manor of Stockley Luccombe, Devon, for the maintenance of her son, John, a minor. (See writ of 29 July, 19 Edw. II, 1325.)

John de Luccombe.=Sibilla

In his father's 1st inq. said to be eight years old at its date and so born A.D. 1317. He died 1325. There were several inquis. p.m. concerning him which are not intelligible, but he seems to have left a son, Hugh, who died in infancy, on whose death the manors in Somerset and Devon descended to his aunt, Elizabeth.

Sibilla: Held Stockleigh Luccombe, in Devon.

Hugh de Luccombe, died an infant.

Oliver St. John.=Elizabeth de Luccombe, born at Stockleigh Luccombe, 20 May, 13 Edw. II, 1320, and baptised the 21st at Cheriton Fitzpaine, in which parish the manor of Luccombe is situate. Probatio ætatis taken at Cheriton Fitzpaine on Monday before 24 June, 9 Edw. III, 1335, no. 71, first number; and it was found by it that she was sister and heir of John de Luccombe, and that she was then the wife of Oliver St. John.

The arms of De Luccombe are: Arg. a chevron between three lions heads erased gules. This is no doubt the coat to be seen on the wall plate of the chancel of the church.

y, died 1406.=Isabella.

hn, born March, 1394-5.=Joan.
: in Hilary Term, 27
1448-9; providing for
d Joan his two younger
inq. p.m.

See Pla
Ric. II, nc
and 8 Ric.

rice,=Joan St. John, heir to her brother, William. By indenture 6 April, 17 Edw. II, 1477, she settled the manors of Luccombe and Selworthy on Alicia, widow of her brother William, for her life. She died 5 June, 1482. Inq. dated as follows: Somerset, 26 July, 22 Edw. IV, no. 48. Devon, 29 and 31 July, same year; ad. 1482.

Died s.p. 2463;
p.m. takented
before I438,
(Tuesdayohn
13 Edwtate
and Sorvall,
inq. p.m and
Oct., san

otes on Arundell Family, p. 188.

PEDIGREE OF ST. JOHN.

Alexander St. John = **Elizabeth**

Alexander St. John: Tenant for life of the manor of East Luccombe, and the advowsons of Luccombe and Selworthy, under deed of 13 Oct., 13 Edw. III, 1339. Inq. p.m. 13 Edw. III, no. 25, and 2nd inq. p.m. of 21 Oct., 13 Edw. III, as to the manor of Stokeleigh Luccombe in Devon.

Elizabeth: Inq. p.m. taken 24 Sept., 19 Edw. III, 1345, no. 26. Tenant for life of the Somerset manor and advowson mentioned under her husband's name, and seised of the manor of Pyehanage.

Children:

- **Sir Oliver St. John** = **Elizabeth de Luccombe**. Sir Oliver: Tenant in tail after death of his father and mother; died Aug., 43 Edw. III, 1373. Inq. p.m. taken 22 June, 3 Richard II, 1380, no. 37.
- **John.**
- **Theobald.**
- **Henry**, died 1406 = Isabella.

Son of Sir Oliver St. John and Elizabeth de Luccombe:

John St. John = **Elizabeth**, who claimed dower, but her right was denied on the ground that her husband was never seised.

John St. John: Died abroad in his father's lifetime or his uncle Henry asserted, but when and where uncertain.

Son of John St. John and Elizabeth:

John St. John, a boy under age, who was brought forward as claimant of the estates by Elizabeth St. John, but was said to be supposititious or illegitimate.

See Placita in Chancery, Ric. II, no. 18, and 7 Ric. II, and 8 Ric. II.

Son of Henry St. John and Isabella:

Edward St. John, born March, 1394-5 = Joan. Edward St. John: Living Hilary Term, 27 Hen. VI, 1448-9, providing for Thomas and Joan his two younger children in inq. p.m.

Children of Edward St. John and Joan:

- **William St. John** = **Alicia**, who survived Joan Arundell, her husband's sister. William St. John: Died s.p. 20 Sept., 1473. Inq. p.m. taken at Exeter Tuesday before Feast of All Saints (Tuesday before 1 Nov.), 13 Edw. IV, 1473, no. 31, and Somerset and Dorset inq. p.m. taken 29 and 30 Oct., same year.
- **Thomas**, died s.p.
- **Joan St. John** = **Nicholas Arundell** of Trerice. Joan St. John: Heir to her brother, William. By indenture 6 April, 17 Edw. IV, 1477, she settled the manors of Luccombe and Selworthy on Alicia, widow of her brother William, for her life. She died 5 June, 1482. Inq. dated as follows: Somerset, 26 July, 22 Edw. IV, no. 48; Devon, 29 and 30 July, same year, all 1482.

  Nicholas Arundell of Trerice: Died April, 3 Edw. IV, 1463; marriage settlement dated 26 Sept., 27 Hen. VI, 1448, by which his father Sir John Arundell settled the estate of Gwilly in Cornwall on Nicholas Arundell and Joan his intended wife.

For descendants see notes on Arundell Family, p. 128

)LNIC

Trevely

ohn Woo
r, Marga

eiress of !

te, esq.=

se

of Wm. I

daughte
ıard Will

J
married I

o.s.
c Earl

Argent, a
chevron c

STAYNINGE OF HOLNICOTE

William,
or, and a strong Lan-
his brother, fled into
he Lancastrian cause
t Barnet. From him
the Lucars of Water-
471 he may have lived

, da. of Thomas Trumbull
don, 15 May, 1541.

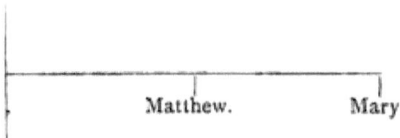

Matthew. Mary.

ly Charles Steynings of Holnicote.
r;

bridled or.

LUCAR OF SOMERSET.

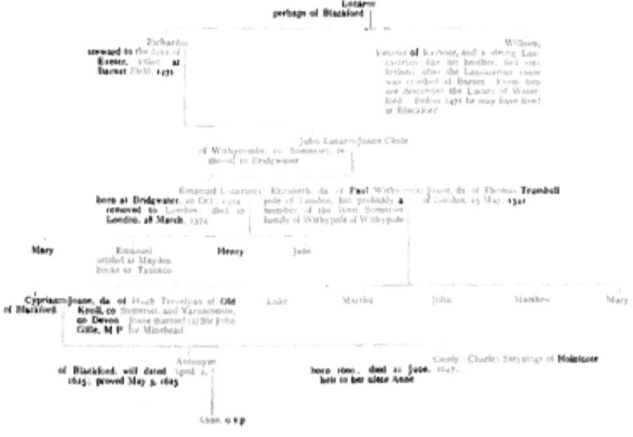

Lucar
perhaps of Blackford

Richardus,
steward to the duke of Exeter, killed at Barnet Field, 1471

William,
forester of Exmoor, and a strong Lancastrian like his brother, fled into Ireland after the Lancastrian cause was crushed at Barnet. From him are descended the Lucars of Waterford. Before 1471 he may have lived at Blackford

John Lucar = Joane Clode
of Withycombe, co. Somerset, removed to Bridgwater

Emanuel Lucar = (1) Elizabeth, da. of Paul Withypoll of London, but probably a member of the West Somerset family of Withypole of Withypole = (2) Joane, da. of Thomas Trumbull of London, 13 May, 1541
born at Bridgwater, 20 Oct. 1494, removed to London; died in London, 28 March, 1574

Mary

Emanuel
settled at Maydenbrooke nr. Taunton

Henry

Jane

Cyprian = Joane, da. of Hugh Trevelyan of Old Knoll, co. Somerset, and Yarnscombe, co. Devon. Joane married (2) Sir John Gille, M.P. for Minehead
of Blackford

Luke

Martha

John

Matthew

Mary

Antonius
of Blackford, will dated April 2, 1625; proved May 3, 1625

Cicely = Charles Steyninge of Holnicote
born 1600, died 21 June, 1647, heir to her niece Anne

Anne, o.s.p.

Arms.—Arg. a chevron sable between three horses heads erased gules, bridled or.

PEDIGREE OF THE FAMILY OF FRANK OF EAST LYNCH.

Godfrey Frank=Edith

Roger Frank=

William Frank=

PEDIGREE OF THE FAMILY OF FRANK OF EAST LYNCH.

Godfrey Frank = Edith

Roger Frank =

William Frank =

John Frank =

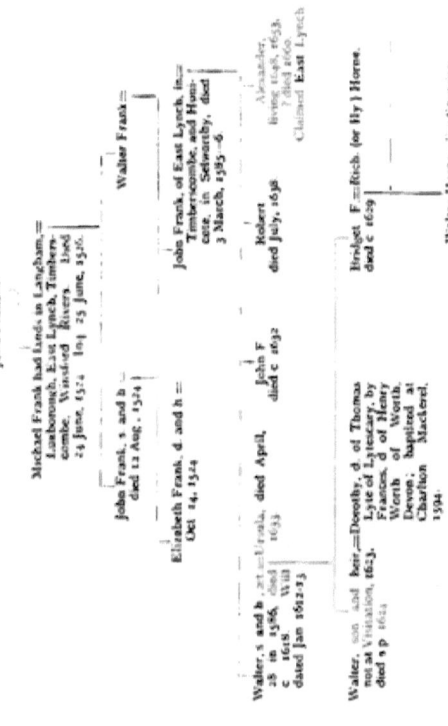

Michael Frank had lands in Langham, Luxborough, East Lynch, Timberscombe, Winsford Rivers. Died 24 June, 1524 Inq 25 June, 1526. =

John Frank, s. and h. = died 12 Aug., 1524 | Walter Frank =

Elizabeth Frank, d. and h. = Oct 14, 1524 | John Frank, of East Lynch, in Timberscombe, and Honicote, in Selworthy, died 3 March, 1585–6. =

Walter, s. and h., æt. 28 in 1586, died c. 1618. Will dated Jan 1612-13 = Ursula, died April, 1633 | John F. died c. 1632 | Robert died July, 1638 | Alexander, living 1648, 1653, ? died 1660. Claimed East Lynch | Philip, George, Grace, Agnes, Mary

Walter, son and heir, not at Visitation, 1623, died s.p. 1624 = Dorothy, d. of Thomas Lyte of Lytescary, by Frances, d. of Henry Worth of Worth, Devon; baptized at Charlton Mackerel, 1594. | Bridget F. died c. 1629 = Rich. (or Hy.) Horne.

Walter Horne alias Spurrier | Philip

ł, mentioned
:hard's will,
thy 5 Sept.,

Hawkins.=— Blackford, mentioned in Richard Blackford's will.

One son.

Thomas Dyke of Tetton.=Sidwell Blackford.

Thomas Dyke of Tetton.=Mary Dyke, daughter of Edward Dyke of Pixton.

Elizabeth, heiress to her father and uncles, Edward and John.=Sir Thomas Acland.

See p. 182.

Mary.

John, described "of Holnicote Court," o.s.p. 1732.

Margaret.

James Smith of St. Audries.

BLACKFORD OF SELWORTHY

— Blackford of Selworthy

Son and two daughters

One son

Thomas Dyke ... = Mary Dyke, daughter of Edward Dyke of Pixton.

Elizabeth = Sir Thomas Acland
heiress to her father and uncles, Edward and John

See p. ...

Thomas Dyke ... Tetton.

... o.s.p. 1759

Margaret

James Smith ... of St. Audries

Joh
e
I
g
C

and
sq. S
her hus

mas D
other's
Deane
his fa
June,
ct., 17
obate
eane.

John
Fe

rton=
her's
d in

abeth

mention

Edw
es Smy
es
17
21
pr
bu
be
7th
as
wa
2 N
bu

myth.

Sir T
ma
inc
pr
Ac
an
W
Pr
6 A

www.ingramcontent.com/pod-product-compliance
Lightning Source LLC
Chambersburg PA
CBHW020235240426
43672CB00006B/539